Photoshop Studio with Bert Monroy:
Digital Painting

New Riders | VOICES THAT MATTER™

Photoshop Studio with Bert Monroy: Digital Painting
Bert Monroy

New Riders
1249 Eighth Street
Berkeley, CA 94710
510/524-2178
510/524-2221 (fax)

Find us on the Web at: www.newriders.com
To report errors, please send a note to errata@peachpit.com
New Riders is an imprint of Peachpit, a division of Pearson Education

Acquisitions Editor: Pam Pfiffner
Project Editor: Susan Rimerman
Developmental Editor: Anne Marie Walker
Production Editor: Hilal Sala
Art Direction: Charlene Charles-Will
Design & Composition: Zosia Rostomian
Indexer: Karin Arrigoni

ISBN-13: 978-0-321-51587-2
ISBN-10: 0-321-51587-0

9 8 7 6 5 4 3 2 1
Printed and bound in the United States of America

Acknowledgments

This is my favorite part of writing a book, not only because it means the book is done, but it is here that I get the chance to thank all those folks who helped me along the way.

The first thank you has to go to my loving wife Zosia. She puts up with the long hours I keep, and when I decided to write another book, she worked on it with me. She was my first-line editor. She made sense of the words that flowed from my head onto the screen. Zosia also designed and produced this book. It was the first time I saw the entire production process unfold. She worked long and hard. She has been my life partner for 20 years, and our love continues to grow with each and every day.

A hug has to go out to my good, long-time friend Pam Pfiffner. She made sure I got this thing started. Pam sketched ideas, wrote outlines, and kept me motivated.

The incredible gang at Peachpit Press who I consider friends deserves a round of applause: Nancy Ruenzel who has been my friend for decades and always makes me feel as such; Hilal Sala who kept everything flowing smoothly; Susan Rimerman and Charlene Will for their professional supervision of the overall project; and Anne Marie Walker, the wonderful editor who dotted my i's and crossed my t's, which helped make the words glide over the pages. Special thanks to Becky Morgan and Victor Gavenda who stepped into a meeting, gave their opinions, and completely changed the book from what it was to what it is today.

I want to thank Scott Kelby for writing such a glowing Foreword. He has become a good friend in the past few years, and I look forward to many more years of friendship and collaboration.

I would like to show my appreciation to Dan Margulis, a man whose friendship I truly cherish. His expertise as my technical editor has been invaluable for this and all my books.

Special thanks go to my son Sean for providing me with images for the book. He has provided me with his work for so many books and TV shows. He gets better and better.

I want to thank the incredibly talented Stephen Johnson and George Lepp for letting me publish their fabulous work in the book. My heartfelt thanks go to Jeff Schewe for another wonderful portrait. I am thankful for his talent with a camera and Photoshop! A special thank you goes to Vincent Versace for making the trip from LA up to my studio to take a picture of my hand holding a stylus. I am forever grateful for friends like these.

A big thank you goes to Drew Hendrix of Red River Paper for providing me with all the paper I needed to proof the pages along the way. On that same note I want to thank Dano Steinhardt from Epson for filling my studio with printers and ink to use on that paper.

How could a Photoshop book be written and not acknowledge the two individuals that started it all—Tom and John Knoll. These two brothers changed the world of graphics forever. With them I must mention the incredible cast of characters, past and present, from Adobe Systems—a company that has always had vision and direction.

Talking about vision and direction, I must add a thank you to Apple, Inc. It was the Mac 128 that put me on the digital path and has kept me there hungering for more.

I can't forget the folks at Wacom for their incredible screens and tablets that I use every day.

I want to say thank you to my daughter Erika, my nephews Mark and Chris, and all my friends for being patient and not complaining that Zosia and I had no time for them because we were working on the book.

Finally, I would like to give my warmest and sincerest thank you to all the wonderful people who I have taught over the years. It is a great reward to know that sometimes I have touched your lives and helped your creativity soar. It is for all of you that I continue to do my podcasts, books, and seminars. Thank you for the opportunity to share! I love you all!

—Bert Monroy

Table of Contents

Foreword

Each year it's my job to put together the team of instructors that will teach at the Photoshop World Conference & Expo, which is the largest Adobe Photoshop event in the world. Twice a year it brings together thousands of Photoshop users from all over the globe, and if you've ever been to Photoshop World, you know that our instructors are absolutely the cream of the crop.

It's a "dream team" of the very best and brightest instructors on the planet and includes many bestselling Photoshop book authors, celebrated academics, and teachers who make their living passing on what they've learned through years of experience in the field. As you might expect, these instructors are at the top of their game, and if they make "the team," they're the best that our industry has to offer.

So why am I telling you all this? It's because although this elite group of more than 50 or so instructors are in the top half of 1 percent of Photoshop knowledge in the known universe, each and every one is still humbled and amazed by Bert (who is a key part of this "instructor dream team").

He is, in a sense, a hero in our industry because quite frankly, nobody does what Bert can do, and what really torques us is that he does it all so effortlessly. He has a mastery, understanding, and control of Photoshop beyond anyone I've ever met. But aside from Bert's enviable skills as a world-renowned Photoshop artist, he's a passionate, engaging, and brilliant teacher who is able to take the miracles he creates in Photoshop and share them with us in a way that lets us do things in Photoshop that we never thought we could.

I'll never forget the first time I sat in one of Bert's sessions. Since I'd written more than 40 books on Photoshop, I felt like I had a pretty good feel for what Photoshop could do—but I have to tell you, my jaw was on the floor. He showed me things and took the class places I've simply never been. I was in the back of the class, right along with everyone else, scribbling down notes as fast as I could write. He kept it up the entire hour, showing things in a light I'd never considered and using tools, brushes, and parts of

Photoshop I'd never explored. He was doing it all right before our eyes while teaching us step by step how to do it ourselves. I was just blown away. We all were.

And now you're holding something very special— a book through which you'll embark on a journey that will open a way of working, thinking, painting, and creating that will change the way you use Photoshop forever.

I wish I could be there to see the look on your face as you uncover some the wonders Bert shares in this book. Knowing Bert, I know he wishes he was there beside you, too, because for him this is what it's all about. He loves this stuff. He lives this stuff. In fact, he's dedicated his entire life to creating the uncreatable. Not only does he show you how it's done, he shows you how to turn around and do it yourself. It's why Bert is so beloved in his industry; it's why Bert was one of the first individuals inducted into the Photoshop Hall of Fame; and it's why he has legions of fans all around the world that anxiously await his articles, podcasts, and live sessions, and who have been dying for Bert to write the book you now hold in your hands.

I couldn't be more excited or honored to introduce you to this book and to my friend, colleague, an absolute gentlemen in every sense of the word, and a true living legend—Bert Monroy.

—Scott Kelby
President, National Association
of Photoshop Professionals (NAPP)

Introduction

Hello!

My purpose for writing this book is not only to teach you the features of the latest version of Photoshop, but also to pass on techniques that I have developed through my years of working with digital media. My main goal in producing this book is to inspire you to look at Photoshop and the digital medium from a different perspective—to approach the tools in ways other than the obvious usually outlined in the manual.

My hope for this book is to motivate you to experiment and explore new ways of doing things—basically, to encourage you think outside the box.

This is not a book on Photoshop basics. I do not explain how the Lasso Tool works. Instead, I deal with complex issues such as Calculations and Layer Styles and how they pertain to your creative process. At one point this book did get into a lot of detail on the basics. However, the direction of the book changed along the way. Allow me to give you a little background on the writing of this book.

After I had written seven chapters, the book took a dramatic turn. Each chapter originally dealt with a specific Photoshop feature. For example, Chapter 2 was an in-depth look at layers. Chapter 8 was going to be about putting it all together in the creation of my paintings. Upon completing the first seven chapters I took a day off and accompanied my wife down to the Peachpit offices for a production meeting. My wife, who designed and produced the book, had been saying all along that the book did not concentrate enough on how I specifically use Photoshop. That day at Peachpit, an editor popped into the meeting and said there needed to be more of Bert in the book. She called in another editor who agreed with her opinion. Maybe it was meant to be because upon arriving home I received the first round of tech edits from my good friend Dan Margulis, and his comment was, "Where is Bert in all this?"

So I had to start over from scratch. New deadlines were set, plans were rescheduled, and somehow the book you hold in your hands came to be.

All was not lost! Two of the original chapters remained in the book. I convinced everyone to keep the remaining five chapters I had written and offer them as free Web downloads for those who purchased the book. They are excellent primers on Channels, Brushes, Filters, and Pen Tool/Patterns and I will refer to them often. I'll give you the details on these later.

The Content

In the first chapter I discuss the thought process and preparation that goes into a piece. I explain the workflow from the procurement of reference material to the planning of the composition. The basics of perspective are outlined to facilitate the placement of elements within a three-dimensional plane. I also talk about organizing and controlling your workflow.

The second chapter introduces you to the concepts of lights and shadows. These are the components that give an image its character.

Each chapter thereafter focuses on a specific painting. The paintings are presented in the order in which they were created. I go into the "hows" and "whys" of what I do. This book is about my personal journeys into my work. My paintings are very personal. They capture a moment in time—a feeling, a particular emotion, an experience that has touched me and begs to be shared with others. Viewers take away their own interpretations. I offer no personal opinion. I simply present the place for the experience to be felt.

I am often asked why there are no people in my paintings. Did you ever stand and study a work of art in a museum and then suddenly realize that someone else is standing next to you? You start to think you might have been standing there too long. Should you move on? As a result, your concentration is broken! In my paintings there is no one else there to disrupt your solitude. Stand there and breathe. Take it all in. Meditate. My paintings are like being there—everywhere you look, the elements and details come into focus.

The moment of inspiration is a wonderful feeling! The painting presents itself to me. I usually have a camera with me and immediately start taking reference shots of what I felt. The camera never captures what my eye sees. The camera only gives me a reference to take what my mind has captured and bring it to life on the computer screen. The painting is in my mind's eye. From there my hands transpose the image to the screen using Adobe Illustrator and Photoshop as my tools.

My sense of color goes beyond what the camera can capture. I was influenced early in life by the work of Maxfield Parrish. The richness of the colors he created has always been my inspiration. My subject matter is influenced by artists like Richard Estes, one of the greatest photorealist painters of our time. Another influence was my surroundings. I was born and raised in the heart of New York City. Depicting the urban landscape has always intrigued me. Though moving to California resulted in a lot more greenery appearing in my work.

The Studio

As I did in my other two books that concentrated on my personal art, I want to invite you into my studio where it all happens. If you own those books and compare the pictures of my studio in them, you will notice a big change. No, I did not move. I am still in the same place, but I rebuilt the studio in 2007.

My main workstation is a dual 3.2 GHz Quad-Core Intel based Mac. It has 16 GB of RAM and over three terabytes of online storage. I work on two Wacom Cintiqs with an Apple 30-inch HD display for viewing my work and reference materials. On a recent visit my good friend, internationally renowned photographer, Vincent Versace shot the picture of my workstation and where you see me sitting at the helm ready to cast off on a new journey. The wireless keyboard is usually not in front of me. I have programmed the most often-used keyboard commands into the buttons and sliders available on the two Cintiqs as well as the Wacom tablet that I use to navigate around the Apple monitor. This way I only need the keyboard to type.

Enough of all this! Let's take off! Let's take a journey together and see what you can discover.

The east side of the studio where I sit and work.

The three monitor setup at my main machine.

Photo: Vincent Versace

Me at the helm.

Photo: Vincent Versace

How to Use This Book

Each chapter covers many techniques. Some chapters cover the same technique with slight modifications to achieve a different result. I want to stress this now as I will throughout the book—it is not the end result that is important, it is how I got there. The techniques outlined can provide solutions to many situations. Sometimes a slight change in color or mode will give you an entirely different result.

Chapter 10 provides you with a series of tutorials that allow you to put into practice what you have read throughout the balance of the book. Several images can be downloaded to accompany the tutorials.

These images can be found on the Peachpit Web site at www.peachpit.com/digitalpainting. It is on this site that you will also find the original five chapters. The chapters are in PDF format and are named for their content.

I recommend that you take the time to download these files. In fact, I beg you to. I spent so much time preparing them I hate to see them go unread.

When you access the site for the first time, you will be asked to enter the book's 10 or 13-digit ISBN number found on the back cover. You'll then be asked a security question and given access to download the files. To access them again go to your account and find the registered content page.

The Workflow

Inspiration

I'll start this book by giving you an idea of the workflow process in the creation of my work—how it all begins, the many stages that go into the various aspects of development of an image, and how I stay organized.

When people ask me why I chose a particular street or specific rusty sign, I usually reply that the subject chose me. I don't go looking for a subject to paint. I could be just walking down the street on my way to run an errand when suddenly I see a painting. The mood, the light, or something about what I am seeing catches my imagination. I actually see the painting!

As you will learn throughout this book, the inspiration for each painting comes from totally unrelated situations. The "Oakland" painting came to me as I was researching a commercial illustration that I was commissioned to create. When I envisioned the painting "red truck," I was out for a stroll in the neighborhood. For me, at least, the inspiration for a painting is purely spontaneous and unsolicited.

Figure 1.1 "2005-12-3_4_pre" by Stephen Johnson

Figure 1.2 "SunflowerHorizontal" by George Lepp

But for the "Damen" panorama featured on the cover of the book, other influences were at work when I created it. Panoramas were on my mind. It started when I was visiting a good friend, Stephen Johnson. A few days later, while teaching a week's course at the Lepp Institute (the Institute at the time was run by another old friend, George Lepp), I began looking at all the images that Stephen and George were outputting on their Epson printers. A thought occurred to me that hadn't crossed my mind since going digital—create a painting with the print in mind.

Both Stephen and George are well-known photographers, educators, and authors who have stitched together many of their images to form spectacular

panoramas. They have been gracious enough to allow me to reproduce their work in this book. Their art is shown in **Figure 1.1** and **Figure 1.2**.

Viewing my art on a monitor was always the preferred way of displaying my art. Painting the light that I see makes painting with light on a computer a perfect match. Still, the print never drove my creative process. But based on the colors that George and Stephen were getting from the printers that matched the richness of the RGB image and, more important, the length of the rolls of paper, I suddenly started thinking panoramically!

A short time later while in Chicago doing a seminar, I had lunch with another dear friend and well-known photographer, Jeff Schewe. We spent our time talking photography, art, and whatever else came to mind (which with Jeff could be anything). After our visit Jeff drove me to the train stop close to his home so I could return to my hotel. That train stop was called Damen.

As I waited on the platform on that beautiful day, the sun shone strong, casting sharp shadows that cut deeply into every angle. I stood looking down the track toward downtown when suddenly the painting just presented itself to me. I looked across and felt the expanse of what lay before me—not just a corner, not a rusty, old sign but an entire panorama of urban life. So much detail! So many angles! I was excited at the prospect of creating a piece that could stretch out forever!

With my trusty point-and-shoot that is always with me, I took a series of shots, two of which are shown in **Figures 1.3** and **1.4**. These shots became the basis from which the painting would take shape. Of course, I would need additional detail shots, but I'll discuss those later in this chapter.

Figure 1.3 Shot of the Damen station platform.

Figure 1.4 Second shot of the platform from which I started to form the panorama.

The Sketch

For me it all starts with a blank canvas. As stated in the introduction, the image already exists in my head. I am then faced with the task of transferring that image onto the screen. As when I worked with traditional media, I start with a sketch.

For the initial "Damen" sketch, I first established the perspective. I decided where my horizon line would be and plotted a vanishing point on it. From this vanishing point I extended a series of vanishing lines that would set the edges for various elements—the platforms and structures on the platform in place within the scene. **Figure 1.5** shows all the vanishing lines in place.

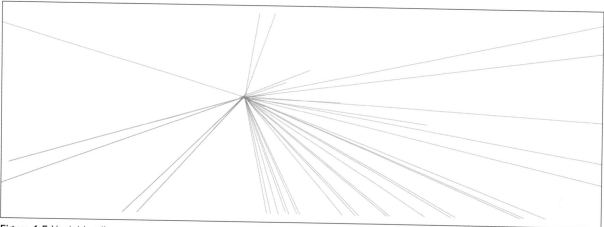

Figure 1.5 Vanishing lines were created to serve as guides for the perspective of the image.

Definitions of Perspective Terms

Let's take a moment and briefly review the concept of horizon lines, vanishing points, and vanishing lines.

How do you determine how perspective works? **Figure 1.6** illustrates how perspective works. All the different aspects of perspective are outlined. Notice how the relationship between the two boxes and their environment creates the illusion of spatial reality.

A few terminology definitions will help you to better understand perspective.

Horizon. The eye level of the person viewing the scene. This is always depicted as a straight line. It is usually placed at eye level, but you can alter the position of the horizon line. Place the horizon above eye level for a worm's eye view of the perspective. Place it below eye level for a bird's eye view of the perspective or the feeling of flying above the scene. Place it near the ground line for a normal view.

Ground line. The bottommost edge of all the objects being rendered. This is also known as the ground plane. Place it below the horizon for a bird's eye view. Place the ground line above the horizon for a worm's eye view. Place it near the horizon line for a normal view.

Vertical measuring line. The part of the object closest to the person viewing the object. It also determines the height of an object. Place it on the left to see more of the right side of the object. Place it on the right to see more of the left side of the object.

Vanishing points. The points on the horizon where parallel horizontal lines converge.

Vanishing lines. Horizontal lines of the object that converge on the vanishing points.

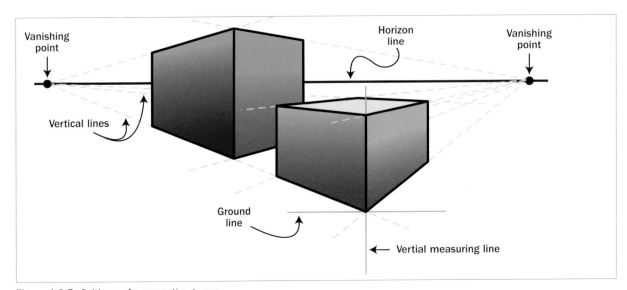

Figure 1.6 Definitions of perspective terms.

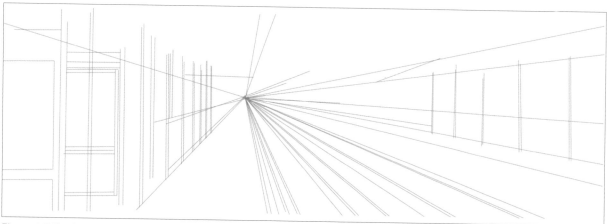

Figure 1.7 Vertical guides were added to represent the elements within the image.

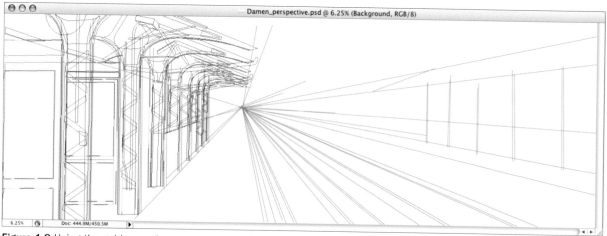

Figure 1.8 Using the guides, paths were created with the Pen Tool to start forming the shapes for the elements.

Completing the Sketch

Within the vanishing lines of the painting I then created a series of vertical guides. These guides established the vertical positions for the various elements on the platform. **Figure 1.7** shows the guides that I created in a layer to serve as the guidelines for the elements within the image. Using these guides,

I started to construct the shapes for those elements with the Pen Tool. The subsequent paths generated by the Pen Tool were later used to select the shapes and fill them with gradients and such, thus giving the elements their substance. **Figure 1.8** shows the paths for the girders on the platform on the left.

Reference Material

To achieve accuracy in what you are trying to portray in your image, you must have reference material. Never guess how a shadow will travel along a wall or the ground. Instead, study reality to depict it accurately. If you try to guess, you run the risk of getting it wrong. When others look at your painting, they will most likely notice that it doesn't look right or looks phony, but they might not know why.

To avoid this problem, study the world around you to ensure the exact realism you are trying to achieve. In the painting "Lunch in Tiburon," discussed in Chapter 8, there is a glass on the upper right that is shown in the close-up in **Figure 1.9**. Note the reflection of the tablecloth in the base of the glass. I didn't guess how that reflection might look: I studied reality to get it right.

I made a small, flattened file of the tablecloth and printed it out on my laser printer. I then placed a mirror over it and studied how the reflection worked by looking at it at an angle that matched the angle in the scene. **Figure 1.10** shows the improvised model that I used for the study.

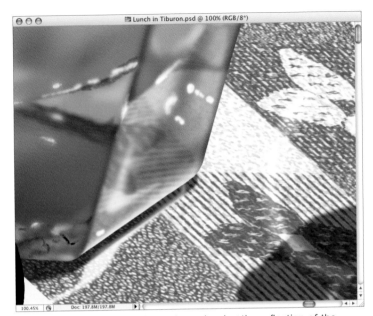

Figure 1.9 Close-up of the beer glass showing the reflection of the tablecloth on the glass.

Figure 1.10 A small model was set up to study how the tablecloth would reflect on the glass.

Steps to Accuracy

When you approach a painting, you should always follow a few crucial steps. These steps will provide you with enough reference material to tackle the job accurately. First, take as many shots of the scene as you think you might need. Be sure to take close-up shots of signs and small details. Second, sketch the scene on paper. This step helps to get the angles right. The camera lens tends to distort angles. Sketching the scene gives you a better representation of angles based on how the eye sees them rather than how the camera captures them. Third, make written notes. These notes can contain important information not captured by the camera; for example, what an object is made of. Fourth, work up the sketch. As mentioned earlier, the physical sketch helps you commit to paper what your eye is seeing. Notice that in the sketch in **Figure 1.11** the angles are more in line with the finished painting.

To better understand these concepts, let's look at the progression for a particular piece. **Figure 1.12** shows the painting "Spenger's."

Figure 1.11 The sketch of the scene.

Figure 1.12 "Spenger's"

On the day I saw the painting, there was one of those beautiful autumn sunsets in California where the world is bathed in a bright orange glow. Unfortunately, I was in my car at the time, and the camera I used then, unlike the one I use today, did not fit on my belt, so I was unable to capture the scene. The painting, however, became etched in my mind.

When I returned a few days later to take some reference shots, the light was different. **Figure 1.13** shows a reference shot. The colors and the emotion of the original scene had to come from my memory of the experience. The reference shot is perfect. All the information I needed to re-create the elements in the scene is there.

Reference Shots for Fine Details

For your paintings to be precise, you will always need additional reference shots. **Figure 1.14** shows one of the detail shots taken for "Spenger's." There will always be some details that are impossible to make out from the original reference shots, so these supplementary reference shots become very important when you have to re-create some minute detail like what a particular sign says.

Figure **1.13** The original reference shot for "Spenger's."

Figure **1.14** A close-up shot for a detail for the painting

To further illustrate the need for detail reference shots, let's look at another example. **Figure 1.15** shows the end of the platform in the original reference shot for "Damen." A warning sign, or at least what looks like a warning sign, is posted on the railing. But since I couldn't make out what the sign said, I needed additional reference shots.

Fortunately, the Damen train stop was close to Jeff Schewe's home. Recall that I was having lunch with Jeff the day I actually saw the painting. Jeff was gracious enough to lug his equipment over to the station and photograph the sign and about a dozen other elements for which I needed reference shots. It's good to have friends!

Figure 1.16 shows the shot of the sign that Jeff sent me. **Figure 1.17** shows the various signs in the Illustrator file where they were created. **Figure 1.18** shows the sign in position in the painting.

Figure 1.15 At the end of the platform is what seems to be a warning sign.

Figure 1.16 The shot Jeff Schewe took confirming the warning sign.

Figure 1.17 The sign in the Illustrator file.

Figure 1.18 The sign in position in the final painting.

The Need for Taking Notes

With all the details that are contained in a scene, your notes will be of utmost importance. For example, **Figure 1.19** depicts a close-up of part of the sign in the original reference photograph I took for "Spenger's." The black diagonal line going up the center looks like nothing more than a black line. But my notes describe the line as a metal cable encased in a transparent plastic tube. **Figure 1.20** is a close-up of the same area in the painting where you can easily see the cable encased in the plastic tube. Without that fact being outlined in my notes, the final painting would have had only a black line to indicate the cables that support the sign.

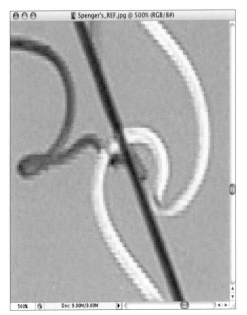

Figure 1.19 Close-up of the cable in the reference photograph.

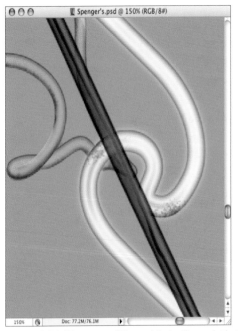

Figure 1.20 Close-up of the cable in the painting.

Researching References

In the "Damen" painting, some very important details were necessary to produce accurately—the buildings in downtown Chicago. I wanted the experience of the viewers to be as if they were standing on the platform looking toward the city. I knew that if an element was faulty, someone would write and tell me that such-and-such a building was incorrect.

When you look at the close-up of the city in my original photograph, you see that there is no detail from which to work (**Figure 1.21**). But when you look at the same area in the painting, you see that the details are crystal clear (**Figure 1.22**).

Let's look at a specific example. **Figure 1.23** is a close-up of the Civic Opera House. You can't tell that there are windows on the facade of the building or how many rows of windows there are. If I didn't paint the windows correctly, that would have been a perfect reason for someone to complain that the painting was flawed. **Figure 1.24** shows the Civic Opera house in the painting with all the necessary details in place. How did I get this information? Did I go back to Chicago and shoot all the buildings up close? Nope! I used the Internet!

Figure 1.21 Close-up of the city in the reference photograph.

Figure 1.22 Close-up of the city in the painting.

Figure 1.23 Close-up of the Civic Opera House in the photograph.

Figure 1.24 Close-up of the Civic Opera House in the painting.

The World Wide Web has greatly simplified the procurement of reference materials. Back in the day, I would spend hours
at the main branch of the New York
Public Library's Picture Collection, scour-
ing through hundreds of folders trying to
find detailed photographs of what something looked like. Today, it's simply a matter of clicking a few buttons and entering
a URL: The world is at your fingertips.

The Web provided me with references
for all the buildings. Using Google Earth,
I entered the Sears Tower as my point
of reference and set up an angle that
matched the view from the train platform (**Figure 1.25**). By turning on the
street name view I was able to identify
buildings that surround the Sears Tower
(**Figure 1.26**). I then had visual identi-
fication and addresses. Armed with this
information I went to the Emporis.com
Web site.

Emporis.com lists all the buildings in the
United States. I clicked on the Chicago
section (**Figure 1.27**), chose the link for
High-rise Buildings, and was provided
with additional links. I chose a link called
Completed, which provided page after page
of buildings and important information. I
easily found what I was looking for—the
Civic Opera House (**Figure 1.28**).

In the section devoted to that particular
building, a vast collection of photos were
taken from various angles (**Figure 1.29**),
giving me all the reference I could ever
want to accurately depict the building in
my painting.

Figure **1.25** Window in Google Earth showing 3D views.

Figure **1.26** Street index view in Google Earth.

Figure 1.27 Main window for Chicago in Emporis.com.

Figure 1.28 Window with the Civic Opera House.

Figure 1.29 Main page for the Civic Opera House.

The Photoshop Workflow

Once I have my perspective lines in place and I have my reference materials, I can start making the image come to life!

Working in Sections

Working on an image of such immense proportions is next to impossible in Photoshop. The width of the painting is ten feet and there are upwards of 15,000 layers. So, to get around the limitations of the hardware and software, I work in sections.

Over 50 individual files went into the creation of "Damen." Chapter 9 starts out explaining the need for these separate files. In addition to those files were hundreds of subfiles that contained smaller bits. To give you an idea of a subfile, **Figure 1.30** shows a close-up of the tracks where you can see some bolts. The bolts were created in a subfile in Illustrator.

Figure 1.30 Close-up showing the bolts that run along the tracks.

Figure 1.31 shows the basic bolt in the Illustrator file. By making slight alterations to the shapes and colors of the bolt, I could create many different bolts based on the original. **Figure 1.32** shows the two sets of bolts at different perspectives. The two large sets on the upper left were the working bolts. Once I had a good variety to choose from, the sets were reduced in size to match the size I needed for the painting.

NOTE: Illustrator, because it is an object-based program, allows you to work at any size and then resize the elements without loss of detail.

When the finished bolts were imported into Photoshop, dirt and additional details were added to ensure that no two bolts looked exactly alike. Hundreds of bolts were on the tracks, and they all looked different. A more detailed description of this process is found in Chapter 9.

The main elements were also created in this fashion. But there is an added consideration with the main elements: They must fall within a specific area of the overall image. The bolts were easy to incorporate into the painting. I just placed them along the tracks, reducing them in size as they extended farther back. Main elements, like the city, had to be precisely placed.

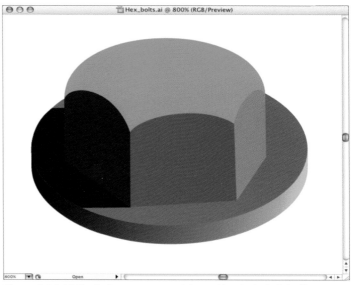

Figure 1.31 All the bolts were created from this single bolt in Illustrator.

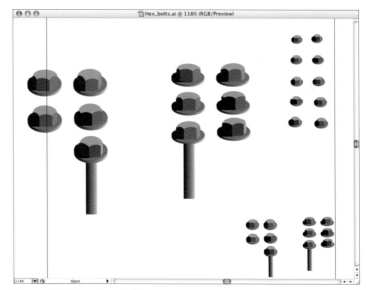

Figure 1.32 A variety of bolts created from the first bolt.

The Composite File

In the main file that contained the vanishing lines, I created guides for where the shapes of the buildings in the city would be. These guides were of a different color to distinguish them from the vanishing lines. **Figure 1.33** shows the small green lines that eventually became the city. This file is what I call the composite file. It is the file in which all the various elements are brought together to form the final image. The composite file is the overall size and resolution of the final image. In "Damen," the working file was five feet wide. Creating all the elements for the image in one file far exceeded the limitations of Photoshop, so creating the various individual elements in separate files allowed me to put in as much detail as I wanted.

> **NOTE:** Use as many layers as you need in a separate file so as not to tax the hardware to the point of slowing down the process.

When the individual elements were finished, the layers were merged into a single layer that was then imported into the composite file and placed in position.

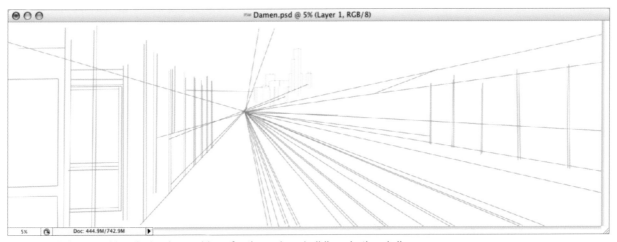

Figure 1.33 Green guides depict the positions for the various buildings in the skyline.

Creating Separate Files

Creating the individual, separate files is quite easy. The layer with the vanishing lines was hidden, and the area of the city was selected with the Rectangular Marquee Tool (**Figure 1.34**). The selection was saved to an Alpha channel (Select > Save Selection), and the channel was named in the dialog box that pops up when a selection is saved (**Figure 1.35**). The Alpha channel (**Figure 1.36**) was then set to serve the purpose of placing the city precisely where it should be. You will see this later on.

The selected area for the city was copied and placed into a new file, as shown in **Figure 1.37**. This file contains the exact same dimensions as the selected area.

> **NOTE:** When something is copied to the clipboard from any program and you create a new file in Photoshop, the parameters of the new file will be set to match the dimensions and resolution of the contents in the clipboard.

The buildings were further segregated into separate files for each building. The shape for the Civic Opera House was given some additional details, and the vectors created with the Pen Tool were copied and pasted into Illustrator.

Figure 1.34 The area for the city is selected with the Rectangular Marquee Tool.

Figure 1.35 Save Selection dialog box.

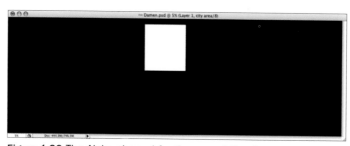

Figure 1.36 The Alpha channel for the area of the city.

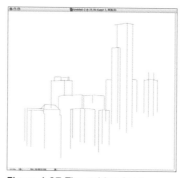

Figure 1.37 The guides for the buildings in their own file.

Figure 1.38 shows the vectors in the Illustrator file. Notice that there is a small version just off to the left of the shape. That is the actual size that I needed for the painting. I wanted as much detail as I could get, so I worked much larger. The green lines are the guides that I used to create the building. Once completed, all the shapes were reduced to the size needed for the Photoshop file. At that point, those resized vectors were copied and pasted back into the Photoshop file. **Figure 1.39** shows the completed building.

After all the buildings were completed, they were assembled in position in the file created for the city (**Figure 1.40**). The layers were merged into a single layer and selected and copied to the clipboard. Back in the main composite file the Alpha channel was made into a selection (**Figure 1.41**). This can be done by choosing Load Selection from the Select menu or, as I prefer, Command-clicking (Ctrl-clicking on a PC) it in the Channels panel. Paste then places the city exactly where it belongs, as shown in **Figure 1.42**.

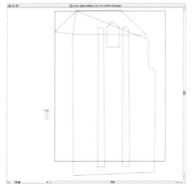

Figure 1.38 The guides for the Civic Opera House in their own file.

Figure 1.39 The completed Civic Opera House.

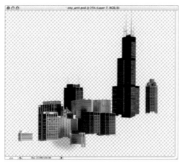

Figure 1.40 All the buildings for the city are merged into a single layer.

Figure 1.41 The Alpha channel is made into a selection in the main composite file.

Figure 1.42 The city is pasted into position.

Staying Organized

One last, very important factor to consider in your workflow when working digitally is organization. Good work habits make life easier no matter what you're doing. This applies to all aspects of computer use, not just Photoshop. Digital photography makes it easy to take many more photos than its costly and limited film counterpart. You'll find yourself taking many more shots than you normally would have when you were limited to 36 shots per roll and the cost of processing the film. The shots that make it to an album are easy to monitor, but many might be relegated to an endless stack of shoeboxes. Keeping track of what is where is a task for the strong at heart. With digital photography you are basically dealing with a warehouse full of shoeboxes without the physical clutter.

Where are last week's emails? Where is that list of what the client wanted changed? Where is that recipe for Polish cheesecake? All aspects of your daily lives can be connected in some fashion to the computer. Keeping track of all that stuff so that you can get to it easily and quickly requires organization. Otherwise, you'll end up with lots of digital clutter.

Your best bet to stay organized is to label your computer folders to indicate their contents. If you are on the phone with a client who is asking questions, you need to be able to access certain information immediately. But you'll only be able to do that by being organized. Why do I stress this so much? Because I am the type of person who easily gets lost in paperwork. I put things down and then forget where I put them. Sound a little familiar? To alleviate this stress, try to at least organize folders and files on your computer.

Figure 1.43 shows the breakdown of how I store information. Note that I use a folder called "Work." The folder contains individual folders for each client. Inside each client folder are folders for each job. The job folders are further broken down into various folders. "Reference" contains any images that are used as examples. "Emails" contains all correspondence between me and the client. "Comps" contains the layouts provided by the client and the concept art sent to the client. "Art" contains the work.

The Art folder is further broken down into "Revisions," which contains various iterations of a project, and "Pieces," which contains two additional folders that house vector elements and raster elements.

Keywords are assigned to files to make it easy to find them with Bridge. There is nothing more embarrassing than fumbling through a maze of folders trying to find a file while your clients are looking over your shoulder, especially if they're working on their fourth cup of coffee.

As you can see, there's a lot that goes into the creation of my work. The rest of the book gives you a deeper sense of the process and techniques that I employ.

I hope this book will serve as a guideline for you to work, not only creatively, but efficiently as well. May it inspire you to unfold your creative wings and soar to places you only dreamed about before.

Figure 1.43 The organizational structure of my hard drives.

Figure 2.1 "Bodega shadows"

Lights and Shadows

2

The World Around You

Before getting into the actual creation of the art, one of the most important aspects of a painting to consider is that lighting sets the mood for an image. The composition and subject matter are central, but it is how they are lit that tells the story. The time of day, the light source, and the subsequent shadows are the elements that create the ambiance for the scene. Watch "Citizen Kane," any old Hitchcock movie, or any other great black-and-white movie and you will see a strong play of lights and shadows that add drama. Good lighting techniques made up for the lack of color in old movies and brought the audience into the scene.

Shadows also add dimension to an image. Without them an object appears flat. Shading a scene properly gives it the illusion of a third dimension. Both Illustrator and Photoshop are two-dimensional programs. The third dimension is mimicked through the use of shading and perspective.

Composition-wise, lights and shadows determine the relationship of one object to another and their place within the total scene.

Paintings That Focus on Lights and Shadows

Some of my paintings have been devoted purely to the light sources and shadows. "Bodega shadows" (**Figure 2.1**) and "shadowplay" (**Figure 2.2**) are examples of paintings in which the shadows are the main focus. The objects casting the shadows are off to the side. It is the shadows they cast that become the main focus of the image.

In "blue door" it is the complexity of shadows and reflections of light (**Figure 2.3**) that make the image. Without this dramatic interaction between the lights and shadows, the image would bear little interest.

Again, it is the intensity of the light source and the contrast of the shadows working together that give "late afternoon," "red doors," and "street light" a place in time and space (**Figures 2.4, 2.5,** and **2.6**).

Figure 2.2 "shadowplay"

Figure 2.3 "blue door"

Figure 2.4 "late afternoon"

Figure 2.5 "red doors"

Figure 2.6 "street light"

Using Light Sources

If you use the sun as your light source, then how the shadows fall depict the time of day in a painting. It is the shadows in "Damen" that set its place in time.

When you're compositing multiple objects into one scene or adding an object to an existing scene, it is crucial that the lighting and shading for each object match correctly. Even an untrained eye will be able to spot a discrepancy. For instance, an object sitting under a lamp can't have a shadow on its top. The light intensity and color must correspond to each other. The direction from which the light is emanating must also match.

Figure 2.7 shows the way light travels and affects an object that blocks it. Light travels in a straight line. As it meets an object, it casts a shadow that falls within that straight line. If you add an object to an existing image, you first need to determine the light source and its direction. **Figure 2.8** shows the left platform of the "Damen" painting. If you placed an object on the platform, it would have to cast a shadow onto the platform that matches the shadows in the rest of the scene.

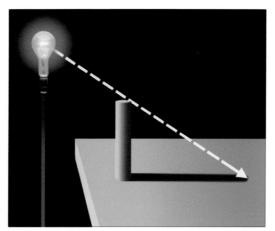

Figure 2.7 Light travels in a straight line.

Figure 2.8 A line is drawn to determine the direction of the light source.

Figure 2.9 An object is placed on the platform.

To determine the position of the sun in the painting, a line was drawn in a layer from the edge of the canopy top where the light starts to become visible to where the shadow first appears against the railing below. Following this line tells you precisely where the sun is in the sky. In **Figure 2.9** a cylinder has been placed on the platform. It looks out of place and doesn't belong there. Why? Because there are no shadows.

The line depicting the angle of the light source is moved to touch the top of the cylinder, as shown in **Figure 2.10**. The line shows where the shadow will fall against the platform. Using the Pen Tool, a path is created and filled with black, as shown in **Figure 2.11**. The opacity for the layer containing the shadow is lowered to match the intensity of the rest of the shadows in the scene. The result makes the cylinder appear as if it belongs there (**Figure 2.12**).

Figure 2.10 The line that indicates the direction that light is traveling in is moved to meet the top of the cylinder.

Figure 2.11 With the Pen Tool, a shape to represent the shadow is created and filled with black.

Figure 2.12 The layer with the new shadow is lowered in opacity to match the existing shadows in the scene.

Creating Lighting Effects

There are many factors to take into account when creating lighting effects for your scene. Among them are:

- The number of light sources
- The position of the light sources
- The strength of the lights
- The color of the lights
- Whether other objects block the light
- The material that the objects in the scene are made of and how reflective they are:

The position of the light source will affect the length of the shadow cast. The lower the light source, or closer to the horizon, the longer the shadow will appear. A tree in a meadow at sunset will cast a long shadow (**Figure 2.13**). The same tree at noon will cast a shadow directly below (**Figure 2.14**).

The surface that the shadow is cast onto will also affect the shape of the shadow. If the shadow travels along a surface that gets interrupted, there will be a change in the shape of the shadow.

Figure 2.13 At sunset the light is low on the horizon, casting long shadows in the scene.

Figure 2.14 At noon the light source is directly above, casting small shadows directly below.

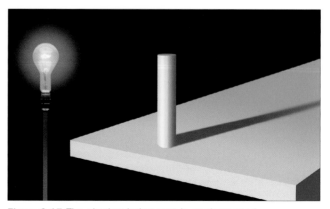

Figure 2.15 The shadow being cast is unobstructed.

Figure 2.15 shows an unobstructed shadow. It travels along the ground and gets softer and lighter as it extends farther away from the light source and the shape casting it. In Figure 2.16 a wall is placed in the background that creates a disruption in the shadow's path, causing it to travel along the ground and then up the wall.

In Figure 2.17 the wall has been angled, creating yet another transformation in the shape of the shadow. Since the angle of the wall is away from the shape, the thickness of the shadow increases. The diagram in Figure 2.18 illustrates this effect. Since light travels in straight lines, you can see why the shadow has the appearance of getting thicker as the wall becomes angled.

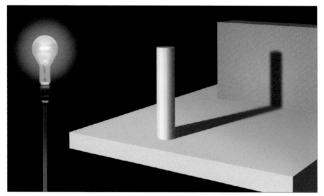

Figure 2.16 The wall creates a bend in the shadow.

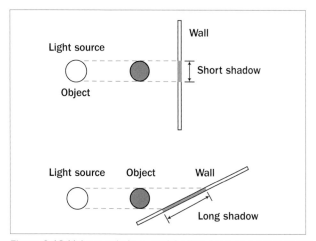

Figure 2.17 If the wall or object blocking the path of the shadow is angled, the shadow becomes thicker.

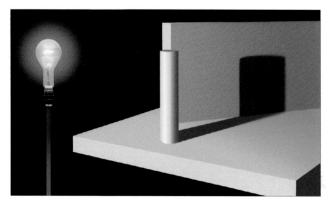

Figure 2.18 Light travels in a straight line. Here you see how the shapes of shadows are affected when they are cast onto different angles.

The Drop Shadow

All the shadows discussed to this point have been complex shadows. But there is a simple shadow that is cast by one object against another that has become a staple of computer graphics—the drop shadow (**Figure 2.19**).

Before the introduction of layers, the process of creating drop shadows was achieved through an elaborate assortment of calculation and Alpha channel techniques. Today the process for creating a drop shadow has been dramatically simplified; it has become a layer style. To get this effect, you simply choose the layer that will cast the shadow, go to the layer style for that layer, and choose Drop Shadow.

The Layer Style dialog box that pops up when you double-click a layer in the Layers panel gives you full control over the attributes of the particular style, in this case the Drop Shadow. It allows you to set the Color for the shadow. Color is crucial because different colored lights will affect the color of the shadow they cast. The Mode, Opacity, Angle, and Distance can also be set. Size controls the blur factor, allowing you to soften the edges of the shadow. A strong spotlight will create a sharp-edged shadow. Diffused light will produce a soft-edged shadow. Spread and distance are determined by the proximity of the object to the surface.

Figure 2.19 The drop shadow has become a staple in computer graphics. Here you see a logo casting a drop shadow on the background.

Figure 2.20 shows a logo with a flowing calligraphic style. To add some drama to the logo, you can add a drop shadow—not just any drop shadow, but a colored drop shadow.

In the logo example (**Figure 2.21**), a soft, red drop shadow has been added.

These attributes can be modified at any time. The resulting shadow becomes part of the layer that contains the object casting the shadow. In the Layers panel the layer is marked as containing an effect.

For a more detailed explanation of layer styles, refer to the Layers PDF file. Download it at www.peachpit.com/digitalpainting.

PDF

Figure 2.20 A logo

Figure 2.21 The Drop Shadow dialog box gives you full control over the attributes of the shadow.

The Layer Style Global Light

One feature in the Layer Style dialog box that makes lighting uniform is Global Light. You may have noticed that every layer style that has an angle control also has a selection box next to it titled Use Global Light. This feature guarantees that the light source will affect all elements in the same direction.

Suppose you have 40 layers, and they all have a Drop Shadow layer style applied. But the shape of one of the items hides the shadow. So you move the light source for that layer so the shadow will show. If the other 39 objects don't shift accordingly, the object will look awkward.

In **Figure 2.22** you see a rivet from the girders in "Damen." (How the rivet was created is outlined in Chapter 9, "Damen.") A Drop Shadow and Bevel and Emboss layer style has been applied to the rivet. In **Figure 2.23** a duplicate has been generated and repositioned below the original. They work well together as do all the rivets on the girders in the painting.

Figure 2.24 shows that a light source has been added that comes in centered between the two rivets. It is easy to see that the rivet at the bottom looks off. The highlight continues to come from below, casting shadows where now there is light.

If you access the layer style for that layer, you will see that the Angle for the Shading has been changed (**Figure 2.25**). And as you study Figure 2.25 you see that even though you are in the layer style for Layer 1 copy, Layer 1 is being affected as well. The feature Use Global Light automatically adjusts the Shading Angle for all the other layers whether they are targeted or not. Turning off Use Global Light, as shown in **Figure 2.26**, allows you to modify the current layer independently of the other layers. In **Figure 2.27** you see that the two rivets now have different angles for the highlights and shadows that conform to the light source between them.

Now that you have an understanding of the workflow and certain theories of lighting and shading, let's see how they apply to the creation of my work.

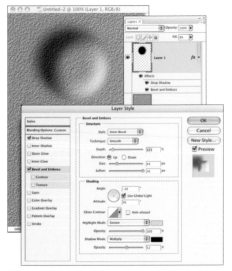

Figure 2.22 A rivet from the platform in "Damen."

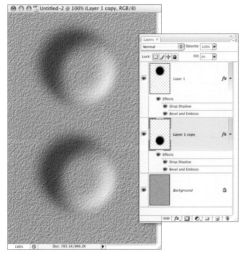

Figure 2.23 The rivet has been duplicated and placed below the original.

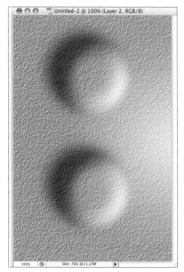

Figure 2.24 A light source has been added that comes in centered between the two rivets.

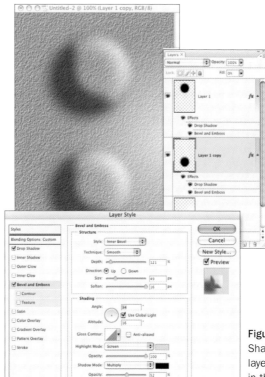

Figure 2.25 Altering the Shading Angle for one layer affects the other in the same fashion due to Global Light.

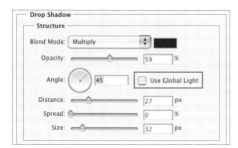

Figure 2.26 The feature Use Global Light is turned off.

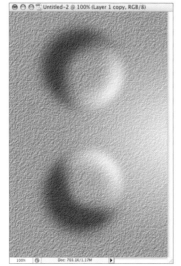

Figure 2.27 The two rivets now reflect the light the way they should.

Figure 3.1 "Oakland"

3

Oakland

A Turning Point

As the first journey into the process of creating my work, I'll use the painting "Oakland" (**Figure 3.1**). It is a great place to start because "Oakland" was a turning point in the way that I approach my work.

The Oakland Fox Theater is a beautifully ornate structure that sits as a testament to greater times. Long abandoned, it still proudly struts its colorful façade to entice passersby to stop and marvel at the craftsmanship that went into creating this relic of a bygone era. The wide palette of colors used to decorate the marquee dance in the brightness of the midday California sun, distracting onlookers from noticing the decay and neglect that permeate the once bustling entrance. The smell of popcorn laced with real butter still lingers amidst the litter that hides the stone of the entryway.

The theater has friends. There is a movement to restore her. So perhaps someday the ticket booth will again be filled with the sound of a sweet voice asking, "How many?" Though I doubt it will be followed by, "Two? That will be 50 cents."

Starting the Painting

The day I got close to the Fox I was doing research for a Broadway poster that I was commissioned to create. I chose the Oakland Fox as the model to serve as my reference. She possessed enough neon and lightbulbs to satisfy every need. While shooting all the reference shots for the poster, the painting you see presented in this chapter revealed itself to me.

As mentioned earlier, this painting was a turning point in how I work. It was the first painting created on my recently purchased Mac G4 Tower. At the time, it was the most powerful machine. Bigger files meant more detail—greater realism!

I started the file using the measurements of 20 inches wide by 15 inches deep. Why those specific numbers? I remembered that when I worked with traditional media, the Bainbridge boards that I worked on always measured 15 x 20. Another important reason was the fact that 15 x 20 is divisible by all the standard frame sizes, like 8 x 10, 9 x 12, 640 x 480, and so on.

I set the resolution to 480 pixels to an inch because I heard my friend Jeff Schewe say that 480 dpi got the best results from the Epson 2200, which was the printer that I was using for proofing. Although 300 to 350 dpi, or twice the halftone screen, is best for most traditional printing methods, ink jet printers are different. A 480 dpi value gave me more room to add details that would be difficult to achieve at lower resolutions. Needless to say, the file size was quite large at those settings—197.8 MB flattened, to be exact. Add a couple of hundred layers and the hardware starts to smoke.

As I outlined in Chapter 1, to make things easier, I relied on a trick I used when machines sported single-digit megahertz with 20 MB RAM capacities. Let's not even talk about 20 MB drives that cost in the thousands. I worked on the individual segments of the painting in separate files that made the hardware limitations less objectionable. I created a single file called Oakland_Composite.psd that I would use to combine the different elements after they were finished.

Using the Pen Tool, I sketched all the basic shapes for the marquee, the walls, and the rest of the composition. **Figure 3.2** can be considered my pencil sketch.

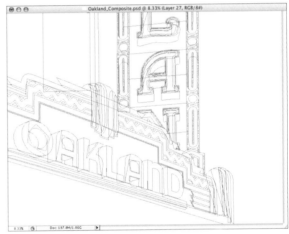

Figure 3.2 The basic shapes were created with the Pen Tool.

I provide greater detail about the "Oakland" sketch in the Pen Tool and Pattern PDF file, which you can download at www.peachpit.com/digitalpainting.

Building a Stone Wall

I'll begin with the stonework of the building visible on the upper left of the painting (**Figure 3.3**). The creation of the stone texture involved many tricks I have written about in some of my books. I did, however, come up with a few new techniques that enhanced the weathered look of the stone, thus greatly improving the realism that I try so hard to establish in my work.

It's important to note that the creation of textures, such as the one I am about to discuss, can be used in a variety of situations. By simply substituting different colors you can simulate different materials. The resulting textures can also be used as texture maps in 3D applications.

The first thing I needed to do was to establish the framework of brick shapes that made up the wall. The wall was not the traditional brick pattern but rather a collection of randomly sized blocks of sandstone. Using the Pen Tool, I created a grid that formed the individual shape for each brick. In a layer to serve as a guide, the paths were stroked. **Figure 3.4** shows the grid, which was created using red so that it would be easy to see once the wall started to take shape behind it.

Figure 3.3 The stone façade of the building.

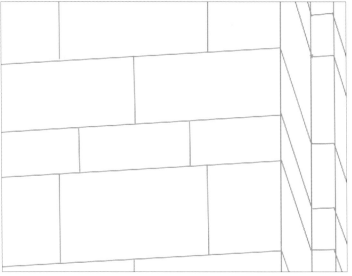

Figure 3.4 A grid was created to establish the shapes of the individual bricks in the wall.

In a new layer to contain the actual wall, I selected a shape with the Polygonal Lasso Tool and filled it with a soft gradient for the overall wall (**Figure 3.5**).

I then gave the layer a basic texture to simulate the material. The Texturizer filter (Filter > Texture > Texturizer) has a texture that matches perfectly— Sandstone (**Figure 3.6**). I set the Scaling and Relief to a low value so that the texture would be subtle. The Light source was set to Top to match the lighting of the rest of the scene.

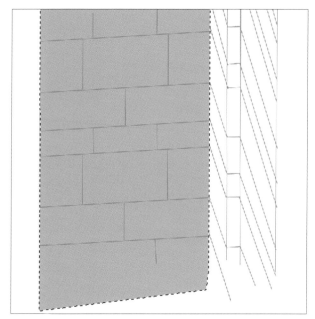

Figure 3.5 The overall shape of the wall was filled with a color to match the sandstone material of the actual wall.

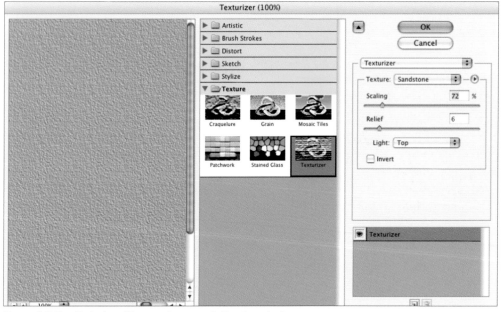

Figure 3.6 The Texturizer filter creates a realistic stone texture.

Aging the Stone

The steps in the preceding section will give you a decent looking solid wall, but age and the elements had left their mark on the wall I was trying to replicate. Stains created by rains coated with the soot and grime of the city littered the bricks. Rather than painting these elements onto the stone, I pulled them out of the existing colors and texture by using the Dodge and Burn Tools.

A special brush tip was needed to give the existing texture the random quality of grime settling into the texture grooves in an equally random fashion. I began by choosing one of the Spatter brush tips included with Photoshop. Normally, the brush tip will simply stroke across the canvas. A little modification was necessary to make it work the way I wanted. I started by increasing the Spacing in **Figure 3.7**.

I wanted the spatters to appear as random smudges of varying shapes and sizes. Changing the actual shape of the brush tip is limited to size, angle, and roundness. By applying these attributes in a random fashion, your eyes will not detect any repeat patterns in the brush stroke. In **Figure 3.8** you see the Shape Dynamics section in the Brushes panel after the modifications have been set. **Figure 3.9** shows the adjustments to the Scattering section of the Brushes panel. The resulting stroke looks believably random. The final brush shape was saved as a preset because I had further

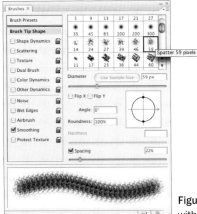

Figure 3.7 The Brushes panel with the Spacing increased.

Figure 3.8 The Shape Dynamics section was modified in the Brushes panel.

Figure 3.9 The Scattering was modified in the Brushes panel.

plans for that particular brush in a future application.

Using the Polygonal Lasso Tool and the grid layer as a guide, the shape for each of the bricks was selected and altered with the Burn Tool (**Figure 3.10**). Each brick was handled separately to give the wall the look of being a collection of individual bricks rather than one big slab of stone.

The Sponge Tool, in both Saturate and Desaturate modes, was used to colorize or to lessen some of the color that was intensified during the color burning process.

A few highlights were needed here and there to give the texture additional life. The Dodge Tool was used for these touches. The same brush tip created for the Burn Tool to create the stains was used with the Dodge Tool to create the highlights (**Figure 3.11**).

Using layer styles for effects

At this point the wall was starting to look real. It was time to add the effect the heavy hand of time had on the stone. Deep gouges needed to be dug into the surface of the stone, and there were places where the stone was chipping away from the surface. How to create these effects was an interesting challenge.

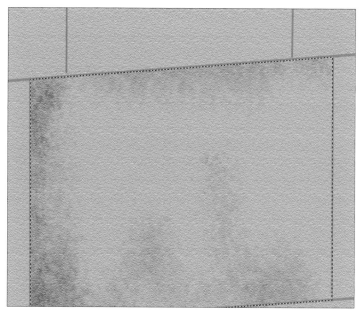

Figure 3.10 The shape of each brick was selected and altered.

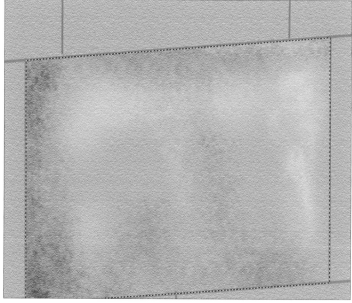

Figure 3.11 The highlights were added to the texture with the Dodge Tool.

The texture was already there. What makes these artifacts visible to observers is how they react to light. With this in mind the answer was clear to me—layer styles.

I created a new layer that would serve as the gouges in the stone. I named the layer "damages." I double-clicked the layer to bring up the layer style for it. I chose Bevel and Emboss and played with the settings to get the intensity of the highlights and shadows I wanted. One important step was to set the direction of the light source. Notice in **Figure 3.12** that the light source is from the bottom (small disc in the Shading section of the dialog box). This is the opposite of what I set for the texture and the lighting of the overall scene. The result is the illusion that the strokes I apply with the Paintbrush will appear to be cut into the stone. Also note that Use Global Light has been turned off, even though the default is to have it on. This opposing light source, as mentioned earlier, created the effect of depth.

Layer styles created the effect of the highlights and shadows on the stone in the layer below it. There was no need to add any color in this layer. In the Blending Options: Custom section of the Layer Style dialog box, the Fill Opacity was lowered to zero (**Figure 3.13**). Fill Opacity is the opacity that applies to the actual pixels that were created for the layer—the colored brush stroke. The pixel values that were generated for the effects in the layer style remained

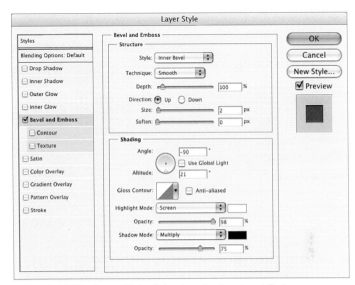

Figure 3.12 The Layer Style dialog box for Bevel and Emboss.

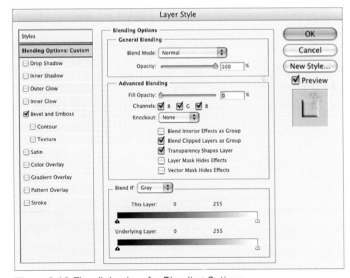

Figure 3.13 The dialog box for Blending Options.

at 100 percent transparency because the Opacity was still set at 100%. Only the original pixels became transparent.

> **NOTE:** Opacity affects the entire layer, thus reducing the pixel values of the layer styles as well. Fill Opacity affects only the original pixels in the layer.

> An in-depth explanation of Opacity and Fill Opacity can be found in the Layers PDF file at www.peachpit.com/digitalpainting.
>
> **PDF**

With the Paintbrush Tool and a small, round brush tip, I painted shapes that looked like cracks, as shown in **Figure 3.14**. Using the modified Spatter brush tip that I created for the stains in the styled layer, large indented areas were added to the stone (**Figure 3.15**).

Sandstone tends to peel and flake off over time. To create this effect, I needed to make the stone look as if bubbles were forming on the surface. Layer styles were the answer once again!

A new layer called "peeling paint" was created to contain the peeling stone fragments. The layer style for this layer was called up. The same Bevel and Emboss was used again, but notice in **Figure 3.16** that the direction of the light source is now from the top. This layer has the shapes protruding from the stone, as opposed to the previous

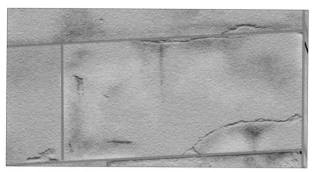

Figure 3.14 Small cracks were painted in the layer with the layer style with a small brush tip.

Figure 3.15 Large indentations were painted in the layer with the layer style with a Spatter brush tip.

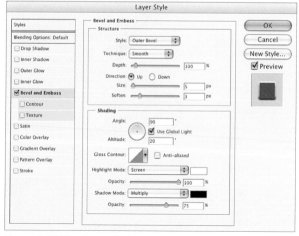

Figure 3.16 The Layer Style dialog box for Bevel and Emboss.

layer that has the shapes indented into the stone. The Style was set to Outer Bevel. Once again, Use Global Light was turned off and the Fill Opacity was reduced to zero.

By first painting with a soft-edged Paintbrush, large bumps were added to the stone wall (**Figure 3.17**). Then to make the stone look like parts were chipped off, a hard-edged Eraser was used to erase the bottom edge of the stroke (**Figure 3.18**). Keep in mind that the effect takes place in the layer with the layer style.

The layer with the stone texture is not touched during this process.

Finally, switching to the "peeling paint" layer, I used a hard-edged Paintbrush to add a small section under the bubbling stone where the stone had fallen away (**Figure 3.19**). Also visible in Figure 3.19 are a few extra cracks and shadows added for detail.

This process was repeated many times over the entire wall to complete the texture (**Figure 3.20**).

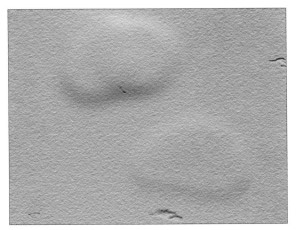

Figure 3.17 Large bumps were painted onto the stone wall.

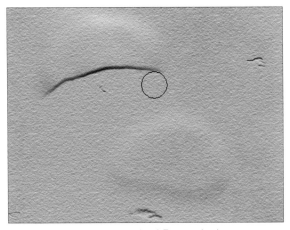

Figure 3.18 With a sharp-edged Eraser, the bumps were turned into cracked bubbles.

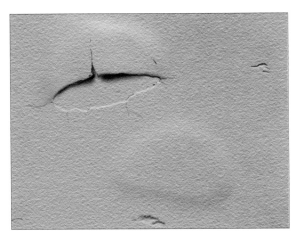

Figure 3.19 Below the cracked bubbles, indents were added to the texture plus a few additional cracks.

Figure 3.20 The completed texture.

The Building Blocks

Now to create the space between the bricks. A new layer called "bricks" was created for the spaces. I chose the Paintbrush Tool with a small, hard-edged brush tip. I made a minor alteration to the brush in the Brushes panel, as shown in **Figure 3.21**. I set the Size Jitter and Angle Jitter to 100%, and set the Roundness Jitter to 65%. This gave me an uneven line. I chose a dark brown color to simulate the indents between the bricks. With the Paintbrush Tool I stroked the paths that I originally created as guides for the brick shapes (**Figure 3.22**).

The corners where the bricks meet were thickened and rounded to add the effect of worn stone.

The Add Noise filter (Filter > Noise > Add Noise) was applied to the layer to give it some texture (**Figure 3.23**). To create the illusion of depth in the cracks, a layer style of Bevel and Emboss was applied to the layer (**Figure 3.24**).

Creating the additional sides of the walls was an easy task. All the layers that made up the wall were first merged into a single layer. Then the layer was duplicated and distorted with the Distort Tool (Edit > Transform > Distort) to conform to the angles of the side wall (**Figure 3.25**).

The small, indented wall, visible in **Figure 3.26**, was created with a thin, vertical selection from another duplicate of the original wall layer (**Figure 3.27**).

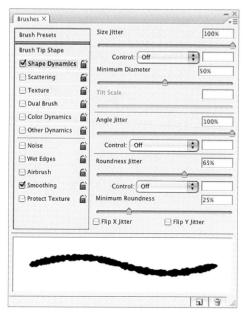

Figure 3.21 The Brushes panel with an uneven line brush.

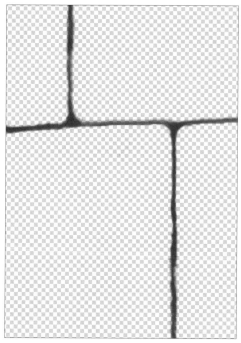

Figure 3.22 The paths for the bricks were stroked with the uneven brush tip.

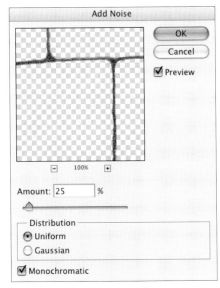

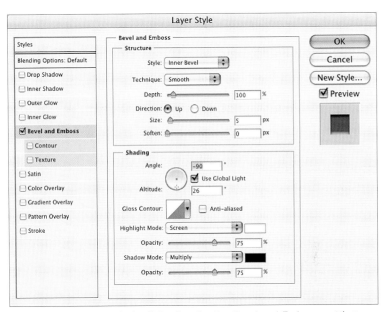

Figure 3.23 The Add Noise filter was applied to the lines for the brick divisions.

Figure 3.24 The Layer Style dialog box for the Bevel and Emboss settings for the brick lines.

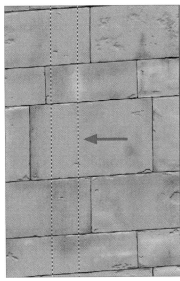

Figure 3.25 The layer of the wall was duplicated and distorted to form the wall on the side.

Figure 3.26 The wall indents as it flows forward.

Figure 3.27 The indent shape is made from a copy of the original wall layer.

Shadows

The shadows cast over the wall are black-filled shapes in a layer with the Opacity lowered (**Figure 3.28**).

The wall facing the vertical sign is completely in shadow. In this case, the ambient light from the sky casts a blue tone over the wall. To get this effect, a blue tone was added to the layer of the shadow (**Figure 3.29**).

The finished wall is shown in position in **Figure 3.30**.

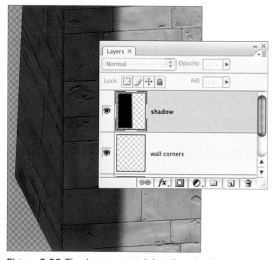

Figure 3.28 The layers containing the shadows.

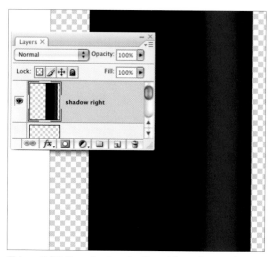

Figure 3.29 The shadow for the side wall contains blue reflections from the ambient light from the sky.

Figure 3.30 The finished wall.

Creating the Neon Tubes

Now I'll focus on the neon tubes that adorn the marquee with an entanglement of bright colors.

Even though the theater is no longer used, the lights are still turned on every evening. The otherwise darkened swath of Telegraph Avenue in Oakland, California, comes alive every night, turning the façade of the theater into a festival of lights. Eerily, the lights beckon the few passersby with the promise of a good time that it no longer can deliver.

Have I gotten a bit romantic? Perhaps. I simply want to share with you the feelings that this theater conveyed to me and what prompted the creation of the painting.

So without further ado, let's get into the details of how it was done.

Figure 3.31 zooms in on a corner of the marquee where you see a few different neon tubes. Some of the tubes are transparent or clear glass, others are colored. All of the neon tubes start out as paths created with the Pen Tool. **Figure 3.32** shows the paths for the long, straight tubes. **Figure 3.33** shows the paths for the zigzag tubes.

Due to the complexity of so many different tubes traveling all over the sign and in some cases overlapping each

Figure 3.31 A close-up of the sign showing the details of the neon tubes.

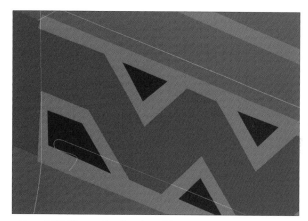

Figure 3.32 The paths for the white tubes.

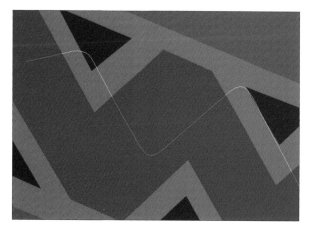

Figure 3.33 The paths for the zigzag tubes.

other, I decided to simplify the process by creating individual paths. Likewise, the stroking of the paths to complete the tube shapes was executed in individual layers for each tube.

To stroke the paths, I used the Paintbrush Tool. I chose a hard-edged brush tip. To get the effect I needed, it was necessary to make a slight alteration to the brush from its default state. I first changed the size to 30 pixels. This size was perfect for the girth of the neon tubes.

NOTE: Keep in mind that the sizes of the brushes depend on the resolution of the image you are working on.

I then changed the Spacing to 1% to ensure that a solid stroke would result.

Figure 3.34 shows the Brushes panel with the settings.

With the Paintbrush Tool selected and light gray as my Foreground color, I clicked the Stroke Path icon at the bottom of the Path panel. The result was the thick tube shape visible in **Figure 3.35**.

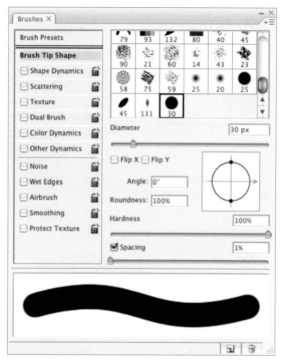

Figure 3.34 The brush tip was modified in the Brushes panel to stroke the paths for the tubes.

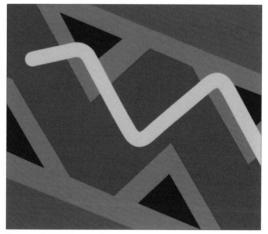

Figure 3.35 The path was stroked with the Paintbrush to create the neon tube.

Adding the Fine Details

To add a little dimension to the tubes, I gave the layer a layer style of Bevel and Emboss (**Figure 3.36**).

The parts of the tubes that connect them to the marquee are painted black. Since neon tubes are continuous glass rods, the sign maker paints areas of the tubes with black where one letter connects to another or, as in this case, where the tube connects to the electrical source. In a separate layer a dark gray was used to fill the connecting area of the tubes and clipped with the layer of the tubes as shown in **Figure 3.37**.

Some additional highlights were needed at key positions on the tubes to accentuate the reflective glass that they are made of (**Figure 3.38**). In a separate layer, a soft-edged brush tip was used with white as the color and stroked along certain edges. This layer was then clipped with the layer containing the tubes.

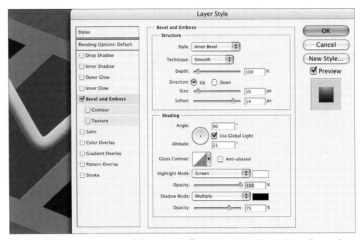

Figure 3.36 A layer style of Bevel and Emboss gives the tubes dimension.

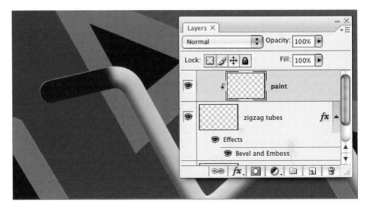

Figure 3.37 The part where the tube connects to the sign was filled with a dark gray.

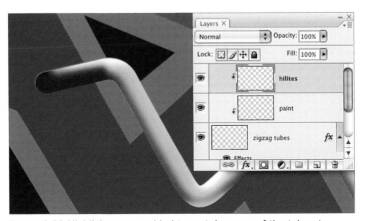

Figure 3.38 Highlights were added to certain areas of the tubes to simulate light reflections.

The marquee is outdoors and the theater is not in use, which means dirt accumulates on the tubes. **Figure 3.39** shows the layer with grime and additional shadows that were added to simulate this effect. The brush shape was identical to the Spatter brush I created to paint the damages on the stone wall outlined earlier in this chapter.

For some added dimension, a dark gray stroke was applied to the interior of the tubes (**Figure 3.40**).

Another touch that helps create that photographic look is adding the hotspots caused by the sun's reflection on the tubes. **Figure 3.41** shows one of these hotspots. In a separate layer, a large, soft-edged brush tip was used with the Paintbrush to give it the glow you see. The Opacity for the brush was lowered to soften the effect. Then, with the Opacity reset to 100%, a smaller brush size with a harder edge was used to add the hotspot of the sun reflected on the glass.

Finally, to make the tubes look like clear glass, the Opacity for the layer containing the originally stroked path was lowered to allow you to see the sign behind it (**Figure 3.42**).

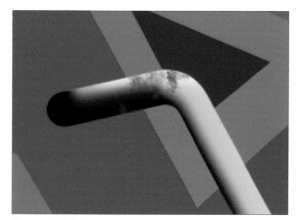

Figure 3.39 Grime was added to a layer.

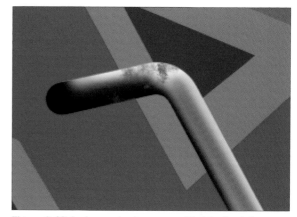

Figure 3.40 An inner shadow was added to the tubes.

Figure 3.41 Hotspots were added to simulate the sun being reflected on the glass of the tubes.

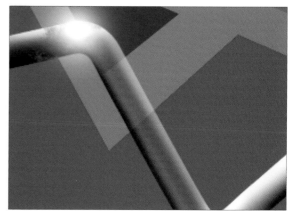

Figure 3.42 The Opacity for the layer containing the glass tubes was lowered to allow the sign behind it to show through.

Distortion Through Glass

Being the fanatic for detail that I am, there was one more thing to do to the tubes to make them look real. Actually, the effect was applied to the sign behind it, but you see it through the tubes. Glass, when it is rounded, as are the tubes, will refract light as it passes through. Anything being viewed through the glass will be distorted. To achieve this effect, I made the layer with the tubes into a selection by Command-clicking (Ctrl-clicking) on it in the Layers panel. I then hid them so I could see the layers underneath. I made the layer with the sign the target layer. Switching between the Paintbrush and the Smudge Tools, I then distorted the areas of the sign that fall directly behind the tubes to re-create that refraction. **Figure 3.43** shows a small portion of the sign that has been distorted through the selected area of the tubes.

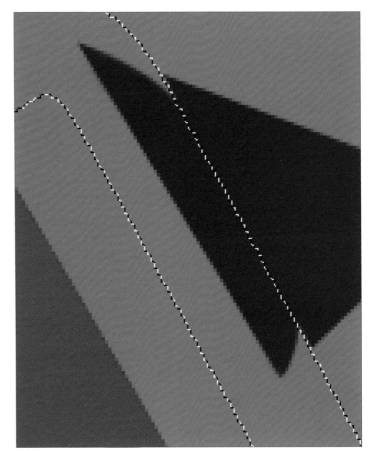

Figure 3.43 The layer with the sign was distorted through the selected area of the tubes.

The Alpha Channel

I'll briefly describe Alpha channels before I explain how I used them in the painting.

> The Channels PDF file that you can download from the Web site explains the concepts behind the Alpha channels in more detail. Download it at www.peachpit.com/digitalpainting.
>
> **PDF**

An RGB file has three channels, CMYK has four, and so on, but users can add additional channels. These additional channels can be used for different colors, such as spot colors. More commonly, they house masks needed for retouching, which are called Alpha channels. Though layer styles have simplified many of the processes that earlier required the use of Alpha channels, the channels still have very powerful functions.

With the exception of spot color channels, Alpha channels contain no color information. In fact they are purely grayscale channels. They are used as specialized, reusable selections or masks. Reusable because they reside within the file and will be there every time the file is opened, provided it is still a PSD file. Some formats will eliminate the Alpha channel. For example, saving a file as a JPEG will drop all the Alpha channels.

Making Selections

Selecting part of an image with any of the selection tools, such as the Lasso Tool, is a temporary state. Once you deselect it, the selection is gone. If that selection is saved to an Alpha channel, it can be recalled at any time.

When you have selected an area of an image, you have isolated that area for some action that will affect that area exclusively. Once the area is selected you can colorize it, filter it, scale it, or perhaps duplicate it. Anything you want to do will be done to that area while leaving the unselected areas of the image untouched.

Selecting can be done in many ways within Photoshop. Some selection tools, the Lasso Tool, Rectangular Marquee Tool, and the Magic Wand were designed specifically for making selections. Color Range, found under the Select menu, allows you to make selections based on sampled colors, specific colors, highlights, mid-tones, shadows, or colors that are out of gamut. As previously stated, these selections are temporary. Once the selection is made however, choosing Save Selection from the Select menu stores the selection to an Alpha channel.

So what is so important about an Alpha channel? Yes, you can save it; therefore, it is a reusable selection. But what is really cool about an Alpha channel is that it creates a controlled selection. You can control where something is going to happen and how much will happen.

The Alpha channel mask goes from black to white with 254 levels of gray in between—the level of gray equals the level of exposure. Where the Alpha channel is white, the image is exposed to an effect. Basically, white is the selected area; black protects the image.

The Alpha channel is a selection mask; therefore, anything that you can do in Photoshop can be done through the selection created by an Alpha channel.

Using an Alpha Channel

Figure 3.44 shows a close-up view of the neon tubes at the top of the marquee. Look closely at the different tones that give the neon tubes their three-dimensional appearance. Every one of the tones was added through an Alpha channel mask. Why not just use a layer style? A layer style will not work here because layer styles affect the entire shape evenly. I wanted to control where the tones would appear, thus enhancing the effect of lights and shadows on uneven surfaces.

Stroking paths in a layer created the basic tubes as described earlier in this chapter. The downloadable chapter on the Pen Tool explains this technique in more detail. The layer was turned into a selection by Command-clicking (Ctrl-clicking) on the preview icon for the layer in the Layers panel and was then saved to an Alpha channel (**Figure 3.45**). The channel is automatically named Alpha 1. Any subsequent channels are named in numerical sequence, but you have the option to rename them.

To create the soft edges, I duplicated the Alpha channel and blurred it with the Gaussian Blur filter (Filter > Blur > Gaussian Blur). The blurred Alpha channel, Alpha 2, is shown in **Figure 3.46**.

Figure 3.44 Close-up showing the details of the neon tubes.

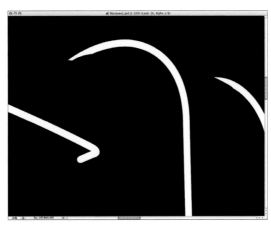

Figure 3.45 The Alpha channel for the neon tubes.

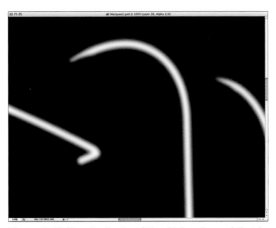

Figure 3.46 The duplicate of the Alpha channel that has been blurred.

I turned on the "eye" for both channels (**Figure 3.47**) to see their interaction. The default viewing color is red. I wanted to see where one channel was in relation to the other. To make this visualization easier, I double-clicked the channel in the Channels panel to bring up the Channel Options dialog box (**Figure 3.48**).

In the Channel Options dialog box I set the color to blue.

NOTE: This box has nothing to do with how a channel operates. The settings deal only with how you see the channel when other channels are visible.

The result was a mixing of the red for Alpha 1 and the blue of Alpha 2 that gave me a clearer depiction of the two channels, as shown in **Figure 3.49** and a closer view in **Figure 3.50**. Then I needed to create a single Alpha channel that was composed of where the two channels intersected. To do this, I relied on one of the most overlooked features of Photoshop—Calculations. I chose Calculations from the Image menu (**Figure 3.51**).

I placed the blurred Alpha 2 in Source 1 and the original Alpha 1 in Source 2. The position of the channels does make a difference. I set the Blending to Subtract and sent the Results to a New Channel (**Figure 3.52**).

The ensuing channel exposed the outer edges of the tubes (**Figure 3.53**). Making this Alpha channel a selection allowed me to introduce colors only where I wanted—limited to the outer edges of the tubes.

Moving the blurred channel up and down with the Move Tool, I followed the same procedure and created Alpha channels that exposed the top and bottom of the tubes independently (**Figures 3.54** and **3.55**).

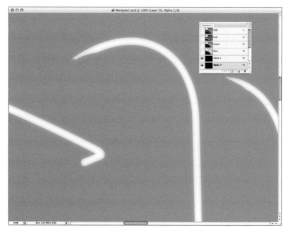

Figure 3.47 The two Alpha channels visible at the same time.

Figure 3.48 The Channel Options dialog box.

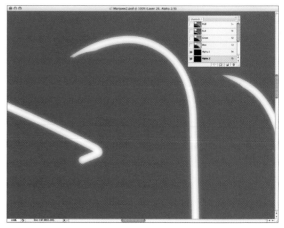

Figure 3.49 The changed color for the Alpha channel makes it easy to see it in contrast to the other visible Alpha channel.

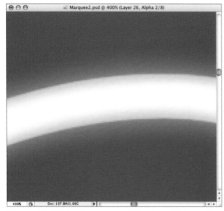

Figure 3.50 A close-up of the two Alpha channels.

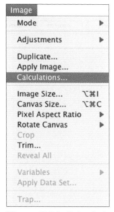

Figure 3.51 Calculations in the Image menu.

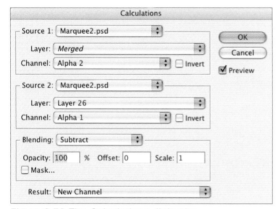

Figure 3.52 The Calculations dialog box.

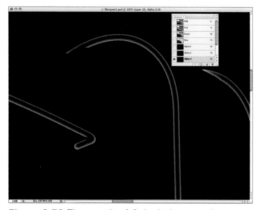

Figure 3.53 The result of Calculations on the two Alpha channels.

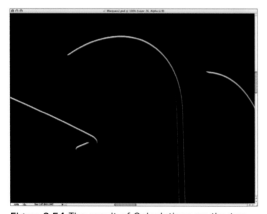

Figure 3.54 The result of Calculations on the two Alpha channels with the blurred channel repositioned, exposing the top of the tubes.

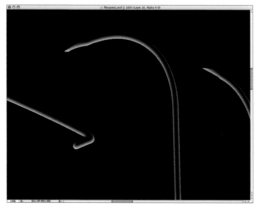

Figure 3.55 The result of Calculations on the two Alpha channels with the blurred channel repositioned in the other direction, exposing the bottom of the tubes.

Reflections

Satin is a very interesting layer style. It adds shapes to the contents of the layer. Satin played a key role in producing certain effects in the painting. Zooming into the neon tubes of the Oakland sign (**Figure 3.56**) you can see soft reflections on the surfaces of the tubes.

Figure 3.57 shows the neon tubes without the layer style. They are paths that were stroked with a light gray color.

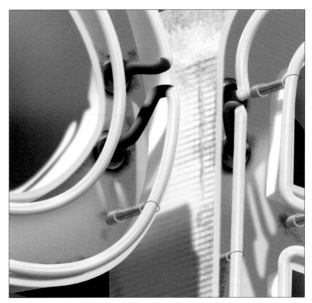

Figure 3.56 Zooming into the marquee, you can see a close-up of the neon tubes. Reflections are visible along the edges of the tubes.

Figure 3.57 The neon tubes before the layer styles were applied.

In **Figure 3.58** you can see that a Bevel and Emboss was applied to give the tubes a three-dimensional look. In **Figure 3.59** the Satin style has been applied. Note that a complex contour was chosen, and the Distance and Size were altered until I achieved the precise effect I was looking for.

The glass connectors where the neon tubes connect to the sign (**Figure 3.60**) also used the Satin layer style to add reflections.

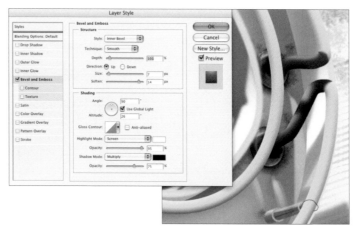

Figure 3.58 Bevel and Emboss was the first layer style.

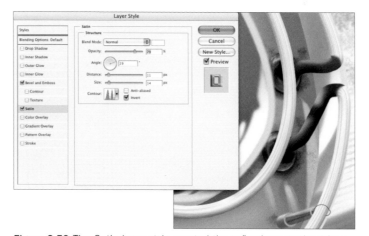

Figure 3.59 The Satin layer style created the reflections on the tubes.

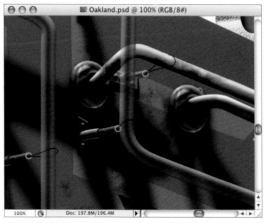

Figure 3.60 The glass connectors for the neon.

The connector started as an oval that was filled with gray (**Figure 3.61**). A second, smaller oval that was filled with black was placed at the center to represent the hole through which the neon is connected (**Figure 3.62**).

Using a soft-edged Paintbrush Tool, some highlights and dark reflections were added to the large oval (**Figure 3.63**).

Figure 3.61 The connectors started out as a gray filled oval in a layer.

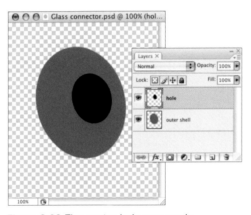

Figure 3.62 The center hole was made of a smaller oval filled with black.

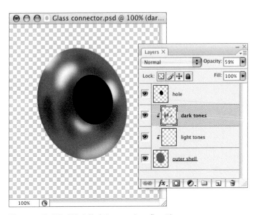

Figure 3.63 Highlights and reflections were added with the Paintbrush.

A Drop Shadow style was applied to make the glass connectors appear to be raised from the surface of the sign (**Figure 3.64**).

Bevel and Emboss gave it an edge (**Figure 3.65**).

And in **Figure 3.66** Satin was used to create the reflections. Once again the complex contour was applied. The settings were modified until I thought they were perfect, and the color was changed to a blue.

Variations on these techniques can be used to solve many types of situations you might be faced with.

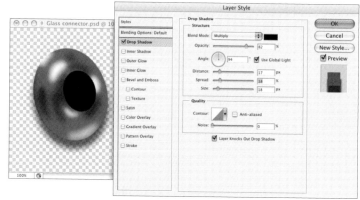

Figure 3.64 The first layer style, Drop Shadow was applied.

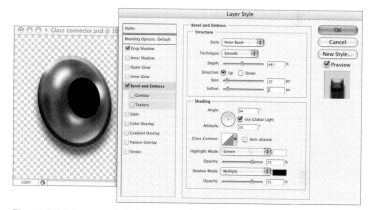

Figure 3.65 Bevel and Emboss gave the glass connector an edge.

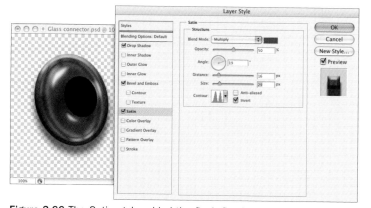

Figure 3.66 The Satin style added the final rflections.

Creating Tiny Lightbulbs with Layers

In this last section, I'll finish the journey into "Oakland" by tackling all those little lightbulbs you see in the upright sign.

I've covered many of the processes that I undertook in the creation of "Oakland." So now I'll focus on the important role that layers played in the preparation of the fine details that make the image so photorealistic.

The first time I saw layers used in Photoshop I was in a room filled with cameras facing a large one-way mirror at a testing site somewhere near Stanford University. Behind that mirror a bunch of Adobe folks were trying to measure the reaction of Alpha testers to this new feature as well as a few other features that were included in version 3. I was excited, to say the least. If you worked with Photoshop before layers, you know what I mean. The use of layers totally revolutionized the way I worked and paved the way for adding details to my work that bordered on obsession.

The slightest, tiniest detail can easily be made up of a myriad of layers, as you are about to see.

Figure 3.67 shows a close-up of a small portion of the marquee where four small lightbulbs are clearly visible.

Figure 3.67 This close-up detail shows the small lightbulbs that adorn the marquee sign.

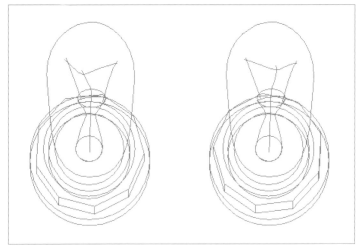

Figure 3.68 The paths created with the Pen Tool that make up the overall shape of the lightbulbs and sockets.

The Layers PDF file provides you with a more detailed description of how layers work. Download it at www.peachpit.com/digitalpainting.

PDF

The section is the small circular detail to the bottom right of the big letter "A" on the vertical portion of the signage.

As with everything I do in the creation of my work, I started by creating a series of paths with the Pen Tool to make up the overall shape of the bulb and the socket. These paths are shown in **Figure 3.68**.

Since there are many bulbs throughout the sign, I made two that were slightly different from each other in order to create the illusion that no two bulbs are alike. A slight modification to the finished bulbs with the Dodge and Burn Tools would later add to the randomness of the hundreds of bulbs that make up the sign.

Figure 3.69 shows the bottommost circle filled with a gray tone and a shadow streaked across the center.

The layer was duplicated and lowered slightly with the Move Tool. This duplicate was filled with a darker gray, and a highlight was added to the edge (**Figure 3.70**). It was then placed behind the original layer. When viewing the two layers together as in **Figure 3.71**, you get the impression that you are looking at a three-dimensional disc.

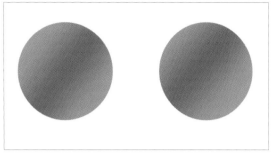

Figure 3.69 The paths for the bottom part of the sockets are filled with gray with a soft shadow cast through the center

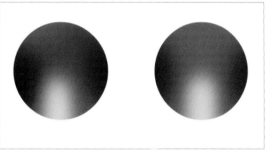

Figure 3.70 The duplicated layer with the discs is filled with a darker gray, and a highlight is added to the bottom portion.

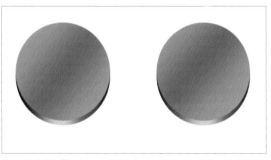

Figure 3.71 The two layers form a three-dimensional disc.

The next layer of the socket contained an octagonal shape that is used to detach the bulbs from the sign when they need to be changed. This shape required a little more work than the previous shape. In a new layer, using the Polygon Tool, a shape was rendered and filled with a medium gray tone. The number of sides was set to 8 (**Figure 3.72**).

As before, the layer was duplicated and repositioned. This layer was filled with black to make it easy to distinguish the two layers (**Figure 3.73**). Zooming in very close, using the Pen Tool, the four corners of each side were outlined, as shown in **Figure 3.74**. In a new layer, each shape was filled with a different gray (**Figure 3.75**). The particular shades of gray were determined by the way the shape was facing the light source. For the overall image, the light source is from above and slightly to the left. Additional reflections are from the marquee below.

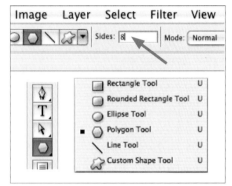

Figure 3.72 Using the Polygon Tool, a shape was created to make up the screw section of the socket.

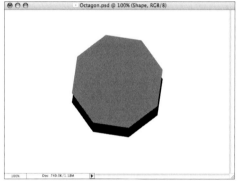

Figure 3.73 The layer was duplicated, moved downward, and filled with black.

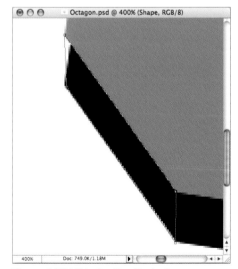

Figure 3.74 With the Pen Tool, shapes were created to form the sides of the screw edge.

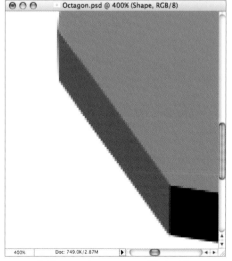

Figure 3.75 The shapes were filled with varying shades of gray.

Figure 3.76 shows the final octagonal shapes. **Figure 3.77** shows the octagonal shapes with the original circular shapes below.

Using similar techniques, a few other layers were added to the socket (**Figures 3.78** and **3.79**). **Figure 3.80** shows the addition of four layers that make up the basic shape of the bulbs. Notice that the bulbs layer has a layer style applied to give it a

three-dimensional look. The layer style is Inner Glow. The color I used is darker than the original yellow fill color in the layer. The Mode was changed from Screen (which is the default for a glow) to Multiply, thus adding a dark shade to the edges of the bulb. More layers that contained the wires and filaments were added to complete the bulbs (**Figure 3.81**).

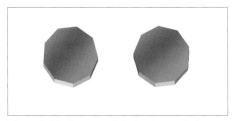

Figure 3.76 The completed octagonal shapes.

Figure 3.77 The octagonal shapes above the circular discs.

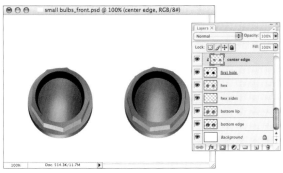

Figure 3.78 Additional layers make up more of the socket shape

Figure 3.79 Additional layers make up the socket where the lightbulb will be inserted.

Figure 3.80 The layers that make up the actual lightbulbs.

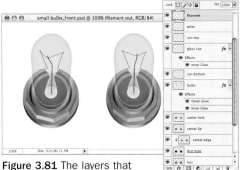

Figure 3.81 The layers that make up the wires and filament inside the lightbulbs.

Casting Shadows

With the overall lightbulbs completed, I needed to create a layer that contained the shadow cast by the bulbs onto the face of the marquee. A new layer called Shadow was created below all the other layers. All the layers that made up the bulbs were made visible. All the layers that made up the socket and the Background layer were turned off. With the Shadow layer active, I pressed the Option (Alt) key and chose Merge Visible from the drop-down menu of the Layers panel (**Figure 3.82**). Pressing the Option (Alt) key merges all the layers into the currently selected layer while leaving the original layers intact.

The Shadow layer was then flipped vertically (Edit > Transform > Flip Vertical). The layer was stretched to elongate the shapes to achieve the long shadows that I wanted (Edit > Transform > Scale) (**Figure 3.83**). The Transparency was locked for the shadow layer, and it was filled with black (**Figure 3.84**).

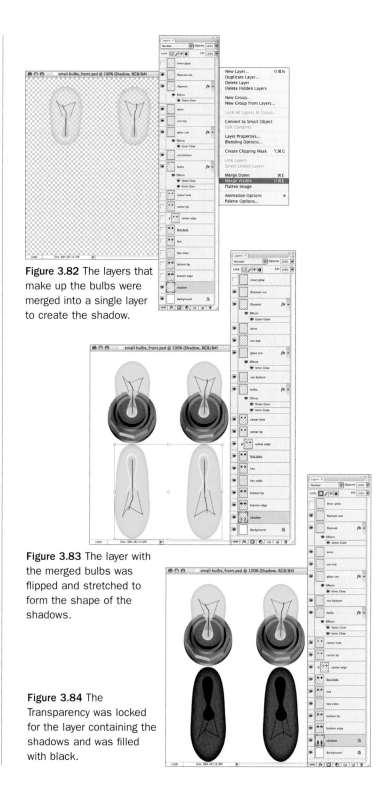

Figure 3.82 The layers that make up the bulbs were merged into a single layer to create the shadow.

Figure 3.83 The layer with the merged bulbs was flipped and stretched to form the shape of the shadows.

Figure 3.84 The Transparency was locked for the layer containing the shadows and was filled with black.

The Transparency was then unlocked for the shadow layer. A small shape was selected to represent the shadow cast by the socket assembly and filled with black (**Figure 3.85**). The Shadow layer was blurred using the Gaussian Blur filter (Filter > Blur > Gaussian Blur) and the Opacity was lowered (**Figure 3.86**). The completed layers with the bulbs and sockets were merged into a single layer with the shadow. The layer was then copied over to the main image file where the bulbs were placed in position all over the sign. In some cases where the bulbs are not hidden in the shadows, an additional layer was added to contain the reflection of the sun on the top of the bulb. This reflection is visible on three of the bulbs in Figure 3.67 at the beginning of this exercise.

The tiny shafts that connect the neon tubes to the marquee were also created using a series of layers. **Figure 3.87** shows the configuration of layers for the blue connectors. These connectors are shown in place earlier in this chapter in Figure 3.60.

When "Oakland" was complete, I rushed to print out this new higher-resolution image! Never had I attempted such detail before. Needless to say I was overjoyed at how photographic it looked! I was onto a new direction. It meant longer working hours, but the rewards were worth it.

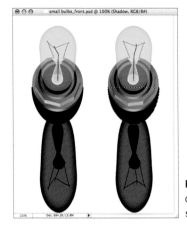

Figure 3.85 A shape was created to serve as the shadow of the socket.

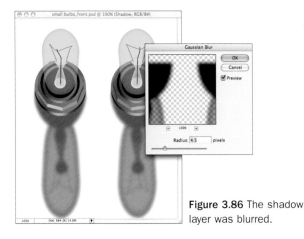

Figure 3.86 The shadow layer was blurred.

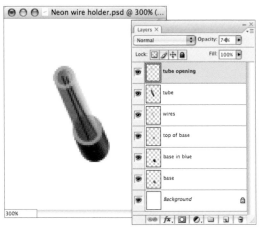

Figure 3.87 The small shafts that connect the neon tubes to the marquee were created using a series of layers very much like the lightbulbs.

Figure 4.1 "Shoe Repair"

4

Shoe Repair

Reflections and Shadows

Paul's Shoe Repair is one of those places that seems to defy the changes of time. As the surrounding landscape of Shattuck Avenue in Berkeley, California, has seen businesses come and go, this little shop continues to open its doors every day as it has for countless decades. The interior with its mountains of shoes yet to be done and the neat rows of shoes that have been repaired waiting for their owners to reclaim them give the shop the reputation of having served many generations of happy and loyal customers. Some of the displays of merchandise for sale are so old that they seem like props to accent the antiquity of the place.

Tucked away between other shops and restaurants, and partially hidden by trees that adorn the street, Paul's Shoe Repair sits there calmly and quietly as hundreds of shoppers and university students rush by it every day.

It was its outdated look and humble façade that attracted me to capture a moment of its lifetime. The worn canvas awning that protects the entrance, the stained neon sign, and the decoratively shaped tiles that cover the building, all gently bathed by the shadow of the tree in front begged me to commit them to the screen (**Figure 4.1**).

Many of the techniques that went into creating the painting were techniques that I had developed earlier, such as the damages on the concrete section above the awning (**Figure 4.2**). I employed the same technique that I used to create the damages on the wall in "Oakland" in the previous chapter.

In this chapter I discuss a few additional techniques and concepts behind this painting that will help you learn some very important practices when creating realistic imagery such as reflections and shadows.

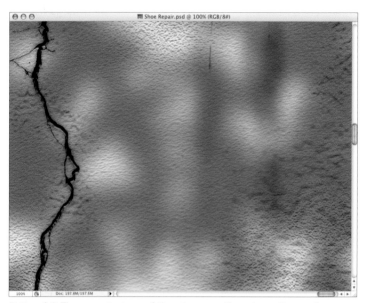

Figure 4.2 The worn texture of the stone section above the awning was created the same way the stone was aged in Chapter 3.

Reflections

Learning how reflections work is simply a matter of studying the real world. As I mentioned in Chapter 1, I never guess at what something should look like, I study models and real-world objects to determine how something should work.

Let's say you wanted to create an image of the straight-on view of an object being reflected into a mirror. You would only need to take the object and flip it horizontally (Edit > Transform > Flip Horizontal) to get a fairly decent reflection. If, however, the mirror was placed below or at an angle to the object, flipping the object vertically or rotating it would not be enough to produce a proper reflection. In this case, the reflection would show the bottom or unseen sides of the object, requiring you to alter the shape to produce the final effect.

Figure 4.3 The neon tubes can be seen reflected in the orange, plastic surface of the sign.

In the following example, note the reflections of the neon tubes on the orange, plastic letterforms of the sign (**Figure 4.3**). Creating the reflections was an easy task but making them look right required a little alteration.

The tubes were created exactly as the neon tubes in the previous chapter. The difference here is that the tubes are attached to a plastic surface that is reflective.

To create the actual reflection, I simply duplicated the layer that contained the tubes. Next, the layer was offset to the lower right to match the viewing angle (**Figure 4.4**). I renamed the layer "Paul's tubes refl" to differentiate it as the reflection layer. It was then turned into a clipping group with the layer that contained the orange letterforms (**Figure 4.5**).

An in-depth explanation of a clipping group can be found in the Layers PDF file at www.peachpit.com/digitalpainting. **PDF**

The one thing that needed to be altered was the area where the tubes bend inward toward the sign to connect to it (**Figure 4.6**). These tubes are bending away from the viewer toward the sign. But in the reflection they should appear to be bending the opposite way toward the viewer and away from the plastic sign. To accomplish this effect, I replaced the end of the tube with a new shape that would resemble a proper reflection, as shown in **Figure 4.7**. I also recolored the tubes to better simulate the soft reflection.

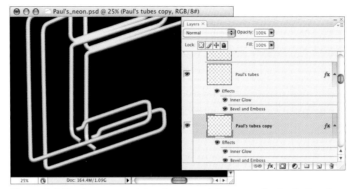

Figure 4.4 The layer containing the neon tubes was duplicated and offset to the lower right.

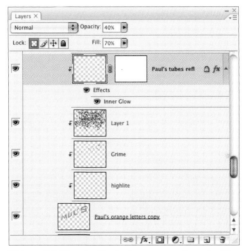

Figure 4.5 The duplicate layer was clipped with the layer of the orange plastic.

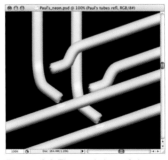

Figure 4.6 The end tips of the neon in the duplicate layer needed to be altered to act like a true reflection.

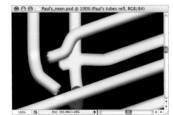

Figure 4.7 The tips in the duplicate layer were altered and recolored to look like a reflection.

Aged Neon

Another small detail that I needed to consider was the fact that these neon tubes were old. Years of glowing to attract customers have had their affect on the brightness of the neon tubes. Their glow is not consistent. There are sections of the tubes where the glows dim as the gases flow through.

The tubes were paths that were stroked with the Paintbrush Tool using a hard-edged tip and a color that was a soft, warm white (**Figure 4.8**). The brightness of the white created the effect of light being emitted from the tubes. Creating the glow of the lit neon tubes was a matter of applying a few layer styles. Inner Glow gave them the orange haze along the edges. I chose an orange color that was darker than the color of the tubes. It was necessary to change the Blend Mode to Multiply so that the color could be seen (**Figure 4.9**).

Bevel and Emboss gave the tubes their three-dimensional shape by adding a soft shadow along the bottom as well as an additional glow along the tops of the tubes (**Figure 4.10**).

To produce the effect of the fading light, in a separate layer, the paths that were used to create the tubes were stroked once more with a soft-edged brush using a bright white color (**Figure 4.11**).

This stroke was erased in certain areas to make it appear as if the light was brighter in some spots and less bright in others (**Figure 4.12**). The end result was a neon that had uneven brightness, as shown in **Figure 4.13**.

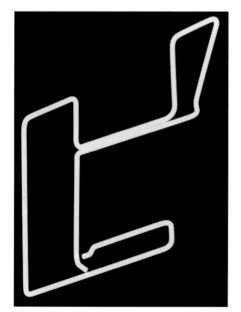

Figure 4.8 The tips were paths that were stroked with a warm white.

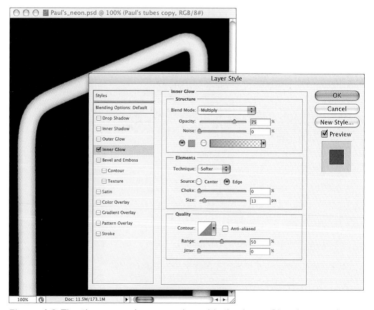

Figure 4.9 The tips were given an edge with the Inner Glow layer style.

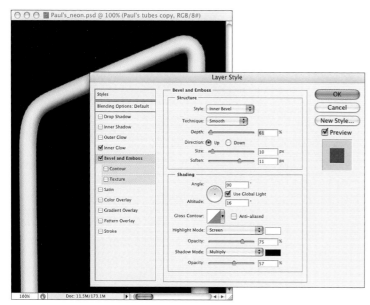

Figure 4.10 The tips were given their roundness with the Bevel and Emboss layer style.

Figure 4.12 The soft lines were erased in certain areas to simulate bright spots in the tubes.

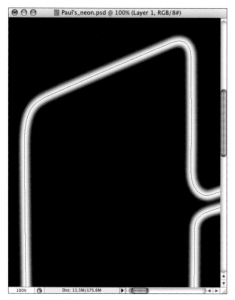

Figure 4.11 The tips were stroked in a new layer using a soft, white brush.

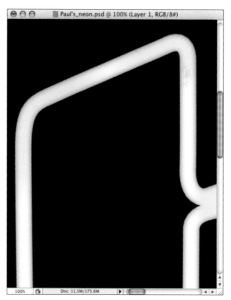

Figure 4.13 The final tubes with the uneven light flowing through.

Rust

Rust that had eaten away at the metal portions of the sign (**Figure 4.14**) was created using a modified brush tip. The basic tip is exactly the same as the one I used to create the damages on the stone wall in the painting "Oakland" and the stone wall in this painting (**Figure 4.15**). In fact, in many situations I often use this particular brush shape.

Because the damages on the stone surfaces were visible due to the affect of lights and shadows within the damaged areas, the Fill Opacity for the layer containing the strokes was lowered to zero, so the effect was created using the layer style.

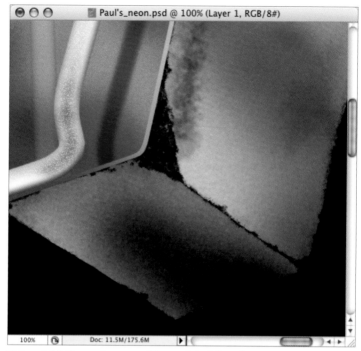

Figure 4.14 The rust areas of the metal of the sign.

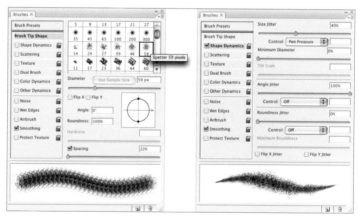

Figure 4.15 The brush tips have been modified to randomize the stroke.

For the rust on the signs, the Fill Opacity was left at 100% because the stroke needed to be visible. Color made the difference here. One function of the Brushes panel that was not used in the other instances was utilized here—Color Dynamics. In the Color Dynamics section the Foreground/Background Jitter was set to 100% (**Figure 4.16**). This feature randomly applies the colors assigned to the Foreground and Background to the brush tips as they paint over the canvas. Altering the Saturation and Brightness Jitters introduced further randomness to the colors being applied. Adjusting the Hue slider just a bit added even more randomness. Pushing the Hue slider too far produces unwanted colors, so I kept it low.

NOTE: The only problem with the Color Dynamics feature is that the preview box does not display the colors.

Setting the Foreground color to a brown and the Background to an orange (**Figure 4.17**) created the effect of rust when I stroked the canvas with the altered brush tip.

Figure 4.16 The Color Dynamics section of the Brushes panel.

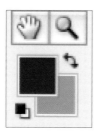

Figure 4.17 The Foreground and Background colors were set to simulate the colors of rust.

Fading Reflections

As you can see in **Figure 4.18**, reflections of lights and objects are visible in the ridges of the tiles on the building. These reflections lack detail due to the surface texture of the tiles and the limited area within the ridges. The reflections appear simply as tonal changes along the surface.

To achieve this effect, I employed the Other Dynamics portion of the Brushes panel. This section controls the Opacity and Flow Jitter of a stroke.

A more detailed explanation of the Other Dynamics portion of the Brushes panel can be found in the Brushes PDF file, which you can download at www.peachpit.com/ digitalpainting. **PDF**

I set the Opacity Jitter to Fade (**Figure 4.19**). I set an amount that would produce a stroke that was long enough to cover the area of reflection and then fade out to transparent as the reflection ended.

Figure 4.18 The reflections on the curved surfaces of the tiles.

Figure 4.19 The Other Dynamics section of the Brushes panel where the Opacity Jitter is set.

Choosing a dark blue color, I clicked once at the bottom of the ridge to be painted (**Figure 4.20**). Pressing the Shift key to connect one click of the Paintbrush to the next click, I clicked at the top of the wall of tiles. The result, visible in **Figure 4.21**, was a stroke that slowly faded as it reached the top of the wall.

The tiles are slightly rounded at the edges. This rounded surface disturbs the reflection. To get this effect, I added a layer mask where I painted the stroke with black to hide the areas of the stroke that fell over the edges of the tiles (**Figure 4.22**).

Figure 4.20 With a soft-edged, dark-blue brush tip, a single click is set at the bottom of the tiles to be painted.

Figure 4.21 The result is a streak that fades as it travels upward.

Figure 4.22 The portions of the stroke that fall over the tile edges were hidden with a layer mask.

Shadows

The strong shadow cast by a tree in front of the shop adds the drama that made the painting for me. Creating that shadow was a breeze. Photoshop has a brush tip that was perfect for this effect—Scattered Maple Leaves (**Figure 4.23**). If I may take a moment to brag, this is one of the brush tips that I created for the release of Photoshop version 7, the version where the Brushes engine was introduced.

In a layer, I stroked the brush using black for the Foreground color, filling the layer with leaves (**Figure 4.24**). The layer was blurred with the Gaussian Blur filter (Filter > Blur > Gaussian Blur), as shown in **Figure 4.25**. The mode for the layer containing the shadow was set to Multiply and the Opacity was lowered (**Figure 4.26**). This allowed the colors of the layers beneath to be affected, as would the colors in the real scene.

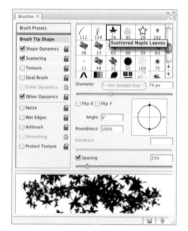

Figure 4.23 The Scattered Maple Leaves brush in the Brushes panel.

Figure 4.24 The scattered maple leaves fill a layer.

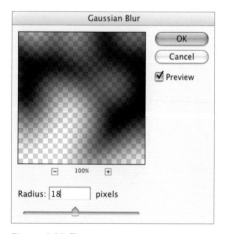

Figure 4.25 The layer with the scattered maple leaves was blurred.

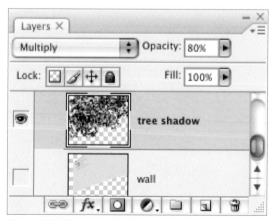

Figure 4.26 The mode for the scattered maple leaves layer was changed to Multiply, and Opacity was lowered.

In some cases, the shadows needed to be distorted as they traveled along angular surfaces, as shown on the sides of the letters in **Figure 4.27**. To get this effect, I distorted them using the Distort feature (Edit > Transform > Distort). I also applied the Motion Blur filter (Filter > Blur > Motion Blur) to stretch the shadow, as would be the case in a real-life situation.

Inside the orange, plastic letterforms, the shadow was created using a brown color (**Figure 4.28**).

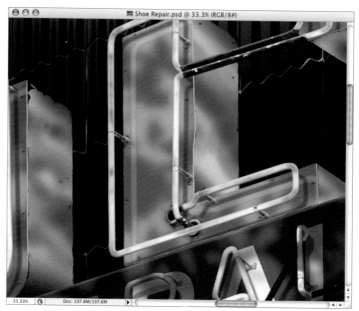

Figure 4.27 The layer with the shadow was distorted to travel along the sides of the letters.

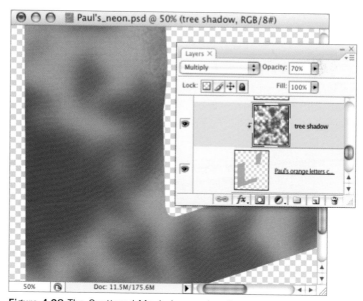

Figure 4.28 The Scattered Maple Leaves brush was applied using a brown color to cover the orange plastic of the letters.

Creating a Canvas Texture

Another technique used in this painting is the creation of the canvas awnings that appear above the entrance to the shop (**Figure 4.29**) and the stitching that holds them together.

The canvas texture is a pattern that I created to simulate the look of canvas. Again, I studied a piece of canvas to get it right.

I started by creating a series of vertical lines of varying thickness (**Figure 4.30**). These lines were given a layer style of Inner Glow to give them an edge.

Inner Glow adds a color evenly to the edges of the contents of a layer. Because it is a glow, the default blend mode is Screen, which makes a color lighter than the current color of the layer visible, thus simulating a glow. The color I needed to use had to be darker to make the edges look like they were curled inward. To make Inner Glow work the way I wanted it to, I simply changed the mode to Multiply, so when I chose a color that was darker than the color of the layer, it would be visible (**Figure 4.31**).

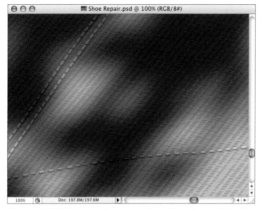

Figure 4.29 The awning over the door is made of canvas.

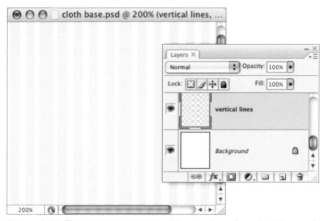

Figure 4.30 The pattern started with a series of vertical lines of varying thickness.

Figure 4.31 The lines were given a layer style to give them dimension.

Then in another layer I created a series of horizontal lines that also contained a modified Inner Glow layer style (**Figure 4.32**).

I created a new blank layer below each of the layers with the lines (**Figure 4.33**).

> **NOTE:** Creating a new layer will always put the new layer above the currently selected layer. To create the layer below the currently selected layer, hold the Command (Ctrl) key and press the Create New Layer button at the bottom of the Layers panel.

I targeted the layer with the lines and chose Merge Down from the Layers panel drop-down menu (**Figure 4.34**). This merged the layer into the blank layer, forcing the layer style to be flattened into the layer. I did this to each layer, the one with the vertical lines and the one with the horizontal lines. This was necessary because next I wanted to create the effect that the two sets of lines were interwoven. Masking or erasing the area where they intersect would have forced the layer style to reset itself to the new visible area and that would have destroyed the shape of the threads.

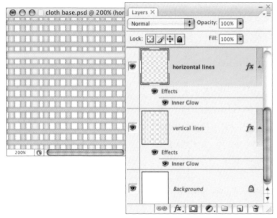

Figure 4.32 In a separate layer horizontal lines were generated and given a layer style.

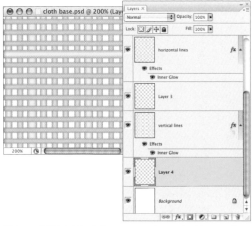

Figure 4.33 A blank layer was generated beneath each of the layers containing the lines.

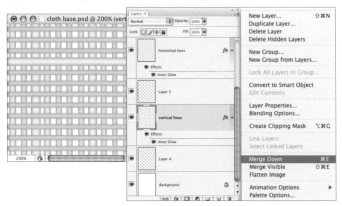

Figure 4.34 Each layer with the lines was merged with a blank layer to flatten its layer style.

I made the layer with the vertical lines a selection by Command-clicking (Ctrl-clicking) the preview icon for the layer in the Layers panel (**Figure 4.35**).

Using the Eraser Tool, I then eliminated the portions of the horizontal lines to simulate the interwoven quality of the cloth (**Figure 4.36**).

The entire image was then selected and Define Pattern was chosen from the Edit menu to make the fabric texture into a pattern.

The shapes of the awnings were filled with a solid color (**Figure 4.37**). In a separate layer, a large rectangular shape was filled with the canvas pattern (**Figure 4.38**). The pattern was then distorted to match the angle of the awnings (**Figure 4.39**) and then clipped with the layer of the awning shape (**Figure 4.40**).

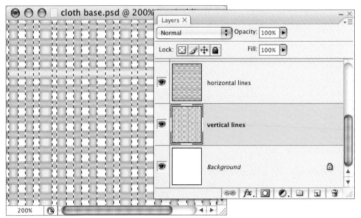

Figure 4.35 The layer with the vertical lines was made into a selection.

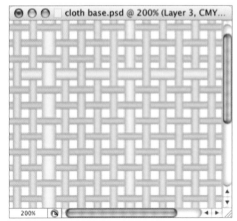

Figure 4.36 Portions of the horizontal lines were erased through the selection to create the look of interwoven fabric.

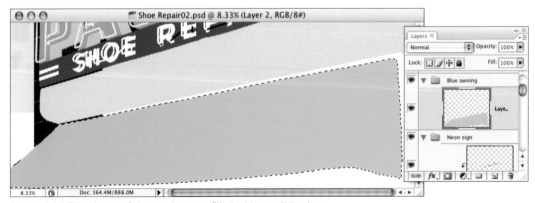

Figure 4.37 The shape of the awning was filled with a solid color.

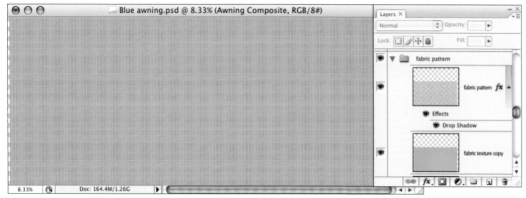

Figure 4.38 A layer was filled with the fabric pattern.

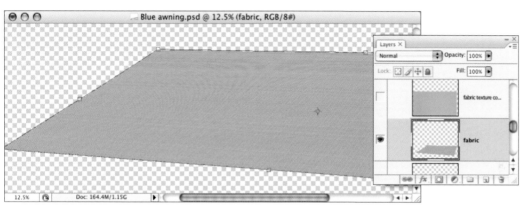

Figure 4.39 The pattern-filled shape was distorted to match the awning angle.

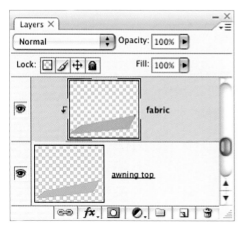

Figure 4.40 The layer with the fabric texture was clipped with the layer containing the awning shape.

The Stitching

The canvas over the awning was stitched, as shown in **Figure 4.41**. Creating the stitch was a snap thanks to the Brushes panel.

First, I created a single stitch by starting with a round brush tip (**Figure 4.42**). I clicked once with the brush. Then while pressing the Shift key to connect the clicks, I clicked a second time directly across from the first click (**Figure 4.43**). I turned the stitch into a brush (Edit > Define Brush Preset) and named it Stitch, as you can see in **Figure 4.44**.

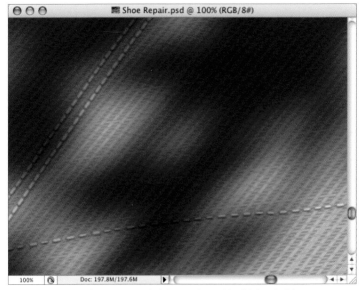

Figure 4.41 The Canvas was held together with thick stitching.

Figure 4.42 A single, round brush tip was applied.

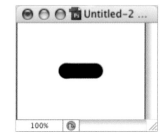

Figure 4.43 With the Shift key pressed a second tip connects to the first.

Figure 4.44 The shape is selected and turned into a brush.

In the Brushes panel I gave the brush tip enough spacing to simulate a stitch pattern (**Figure 4.45**). I set the Angle to Direction so the stitching would follow the angles of the canvas (**Figure 4.46**).

Paths were generated to represent the sew lines. The paths were then stroked with a Paintbrush using the Stitch tip (**Figure 4.47**).

For the final touch, a layer style of Drop Shadow was applied to give the stitching some dimension.

Years have gone by since I created this piece, but Paul's Shoe Repair still looks exactly the same as it did the day I decided to paint it. There is one tiny addition to the interior though—a print of "Shoe Repair" hangs proudly on the wall behind the register. Well, "hangs" might be the wrong word. Paul used tape to put it up and dust has settled on it to match the rest of the place.

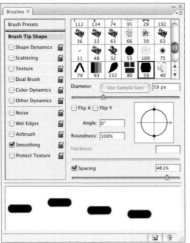

Figure 4.45 The Spacing amount is raised to give adequate separation to the tips to make it appear as stitching.

Figure 4.46 The Angle is set to Direction to make the brush tips follow the angle of the paths.

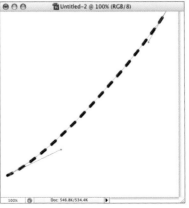

Figure 4.47 The path is stroked with the Paintbrush Tool to create the final stitching.

Figure 5.1 "old chair"

5 Old Chair

Another Shift

Some would call it an antique shop, and others would call it a junk shop. On San Pablo Avenue in Berkeley, there stood this tiny shop filled with some people's junk waiting to become somebody else's treasure. It was a beautiful sunny day and the shadows were razor sharp. This odd mixture of wares just begged to be captured.

The "old chair" painting (**Figure 5.1**) marked another shift in how I work—using the Wacom Cintiq. I don't want this to sound like a promotion for Wacom products, but the Cintiq did have a dramatic affect on my work.

From Mouse to Tablet

I was traditionally trained as an artist and learned to hold a pencil early in life. Like most moms, mine kept my earliest drawing from the age of two. Holding a paintbrush was a natural progression. With the introduction of the Apple Macintosh in 1984, I went digital. Although it was surprisingly easy for me to adjust to the mouse, which was the equivalent of holding a bar of soap to draw with, the awkward part of the transition was the fact that I was manipulating this bar of soap on the side while my eyes were looking at the screen in front of me.

Tablets had been around for some time, but I resisted. I was quite proud of being able to do what I was doing with a mouse. People used to say they could not believe I was still using a mouse.

It was the introduction of the optical mouse that forced me to switch to a tablet. I was working on two cinema displays at the time and found that moving across that much screen real estate was very difficult with a mouse. I was constantly lifting and dragging. I also found that the cursor would jump back to my starting point every now and then. That was annoying, but I could live with it. However, because I tend to work with tiny brushes, I kept losing my brush tip and found that I was wasting a lot of time dragging the mouse around to find my cursor. I would then, very slowly, move it down into position to continue working. Sound familiar?

So, I decided to try a tablet. I was ecstatic to say the least! Why I had resisted it for so long I don't know. I had full control over where my cursor was at all times. The feel of the stylus was also a lot more like what I was used to—a paintbrush. And there was less strain on my wrist.

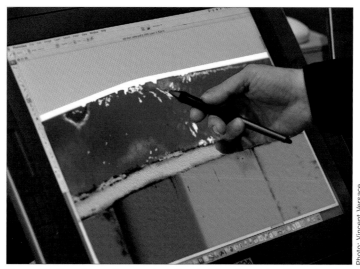

Photo: Vincent Versace

Figure 5.2 Here I am at my workstation holding the stylus like a brush.

The Cintiq

Then came the Cintiq! The Cintiq is a tablet that is built into the screen. Suddenly, I found myself full circle back to how I worked for most of my life—looking at my hand while painting. Being able to place my hand directly over the area I am working on makes a massive difference in how I work.

Up to this point, the majority of my pieces were composed of selections filled with colors. I created paths with the Pen Tool that were turned into selections and filled with gradients. With the Cintiq and the Brushes engine in Photoshop, I was back to working the way I was trained. Details were now brush strokes applied directly onto the screen because I could create specifically shaped brushes and then simply paint in the details.

I found myself holding the stylus the way I used to hold a brush. **Figure 5.2** shows me at work. Notice that I am holding the stylus like a traditional paintbrush, which is not always the case. But in certain situations it enhances the rhythmic movement of brush strokes and the creative flow process.

Consequently, the details in "old chair" were far more organic than anything I had previously created. The wear and tear on the edges of the table (**Figure 5.3**) and chair (**Figure 5.3a**) shows the freedom of movement that the Cintiq offered me. Unlike the small areas of brushwork that had previously appeared in parts of my paintings, freehand brush strokes made up the majority of this piece.

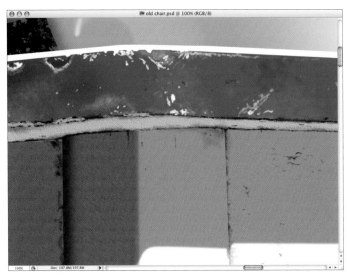

Figure 5.3 Painting on the Cintiq allowed the details in this painting to be more organic than in previous paintings.

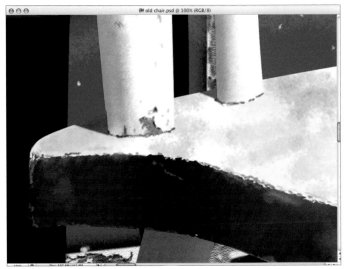

Figure 5.3a Another example of a more painterly style.

Techniques in Photoshop

It is difficult to teach hand work in the pages of a book. Rather than trying to educate you on how to swing a brush, I'll concentrate on certain techniques that will demonstrate how you can use certain aspects of Photoshop.

Finally a Purpose!

I'll start by describing a particular brush for which I could never find a use. I love telling this story because it is the only time I have ever used the Wet Edges feature in the Brushes panel. Wet Edges (**Figure 5.4**) sits in the lower section of the options in the panel. Unlike the features in the top left section of the panel, the features below the line have no controls. They are simply on or off. Wet Edges makes the central portion of a stroke transparent while concentrating the color at the outer edges.

So what use did I find for this feature? Dried spit! **Figure 5.5** shows a big stain of it on the ground. Sorry. I don't mean to gross you out, but what city street doesn't have a little dried spit on the ground?

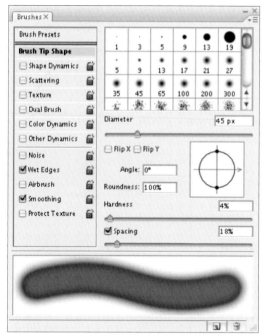

Figure 5.4 The Wet Edges feature in the Brushes panel.

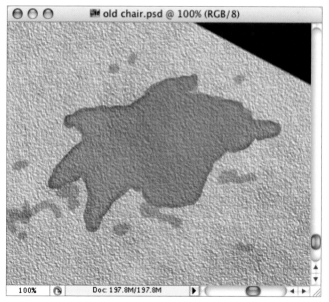

Figure 5.5 Wet Edges was used to create the stains on the pavement.

Damages

Another bit of brushwork that employed some special effects are the damages on the various items in the scene—the chair leg in **Figure 5.6** and the peeling paint between the tiles in **Figure 5.7**. These strokes not only employed the Spatter brush you've seen before but also used layer styles to complete the effect. This is similar to the damaged stonework in the "Oakland" painting. The difference is that in "Oakland" the brush strokes were invisible and the layer style created the effect. Here, in addition to the layer style, color was added to the stroke.

The two pink areas on the chair leg reveal where some light blue paint has chipped off exposing the pink paint beneath, plus a layer of white in between. This chair had many lives!

Due to the curvature of the leg, light affects each chip differently. The pink chips were created in two separate layers. In **Figure 5.8** you can see the chip on the right of the chair leg.

Figure 5.6 The detail of the damages on the leg of the chair.

Figure 5.7 The detail of the damages on the tiled wall.

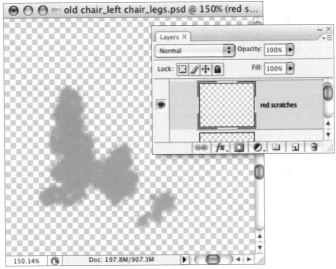

Figure 5.8 The shape for the chip was painted with pink.

The Transparency for the layer was locked. Using a soft-edged brush and a darker version of the pink, the edge of the chip was colored (**Figure 5.9**). I then applied the Texturizer filter in Sandstone mode (Filter > Texture > Texturizer) to the layer to add the texture (**Figure 5.10**). A layer style of Inner Glow (**Figure 5.11**) was applied to the chip to show the thickness of the paint exposed to full sunlight. In **Figure 5.12** you can see the chip in place simulating the thick blue and white paint chipped away exposing the pink underneath.

The chip on the left was created using the same technique as the chip on the right except that it used Bevel and Emboss (**Figure 5.13**). Here the angle casts a shadow along the edge where the paint layer is thick and away from the light. **Figure 5.14** shows the chip in place on the left side of the chair leg.

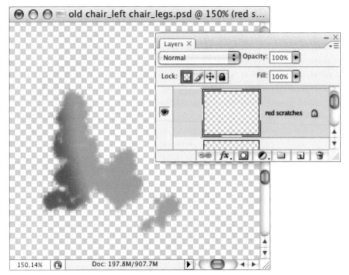

Figure 5.9 A dark edge was added to the edge of the pink chip.

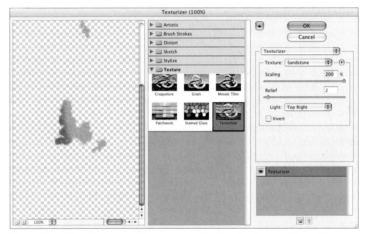

Figure 5.10 The Texturizer filter was applied to the layer of the chip.

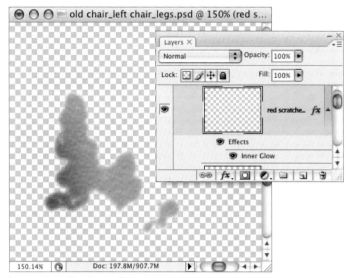

Figure 5.11 The Inner Glow layer style was applied to the layer.

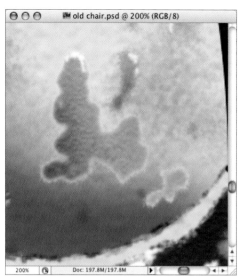

Figure 5.12 The pink chip on the leg of the chair.

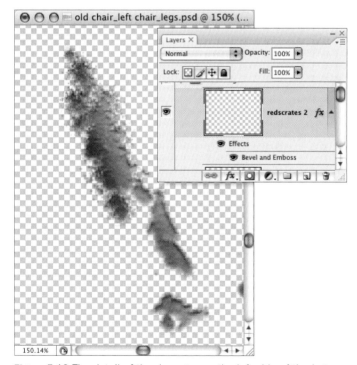

Figure 5.13 The detail of the damages on the left side of the leg.

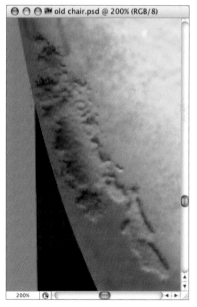

Figure 5.14 The Bevel and Emboss layer style was applied to the layer.

A similar technique of paint strokes working with a layer style was applied to the peeling paint over the grout between the tiles. Here a base layer contained the actual grout (**Figure 5.15**). Over the grout layer there are several layers of peeling paint. The layer of the grout was duplicated and colored a dark gray to simulate a stain over the grout. A Drop Shadow layer style was applied to the layer (**Figure 5.16**). As in the other cases, the modified Spatter brush tip was employed, but this time it was used with the Eraser Tool. The stain layer was chipped away with the Eraser Tool to expose the grout beneath.

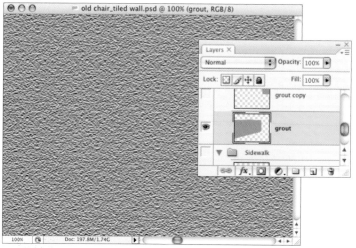

Figure 5.15 The layer containing the texture for the grout in between the tiles.

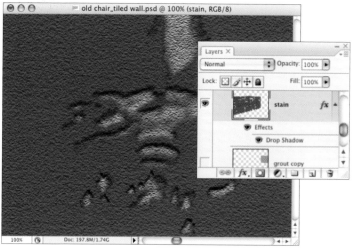

Figure 5.16 The contents of the layer containing the stains on the grout were erased to create the effect.

The same technique I used on the dark gray stain was applied to another duplicate of the grout that was colored white. This layer was to serve as a coat of white paint that covered the grout. With the Eraser Tool, the white paint was chipped away (**Figure 5.17**). **Figure 5.18** shows a section of the tiled wall with the damages.

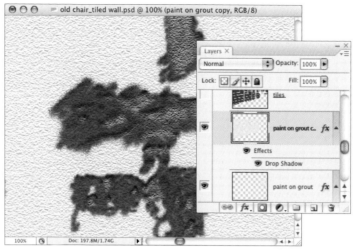

Figure 5.17 Portions of the layer containing the white paint on the grout were erased to create the effect of peeling paint.

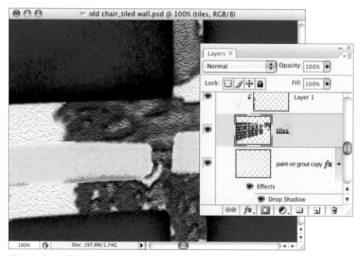

Figure 5.18 The detail of the damages on the tiled wall.

Other Dynamics

In the Other Dynamics section of the Brushes panel, Photoshop offers you the ability to adjust the Opacity and Flow of a stroke.

Opacity affects what its name implies—the opacity of the stroke. The Opacity is the level of translucency of the brush stroke that allows layers beneath it to show through. Flow affects the intensity of the stroke. Flow is the amount of paint being applied. Both of these options, as well as all the others, can be controlled by a stylus or Fade setting. The Fade setting lets you establish a given length at which the effect will be applied to the stroke. This is a feature I use quite often, but it is hardly noticed. **Figure 5.19** shows the Other Dynamics window where I have assigned a Fade to the Opacity of the stroke. This is similar to what you saw in Chapter 4, "Shoe Repair," where the Fade feature was applied to the Opacity to add reflections on the tiles.

The edge of the basin on the table has a small sheen of light on the side (**Figure 5.20**). This was created with the Paintbrush and a fading Opacity brush tip.

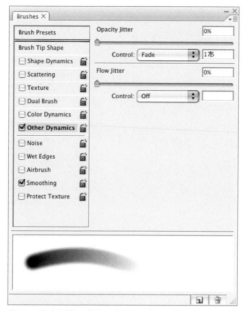

Figure 5.19 The Other Dynamics window.

Figure 5.20 The Opacity Fade was applied to the Paintbrush to create a reflection of light on the edge of the basin.

Personal Stock Library

In the Layers PDF file I mention using elements you've created in one painting in other places. By placing elements in separate layers you have the ability to repurpose those elements in other situations.

The items on display in the shop window demonstrate this concept. **Figure 5.21** shows a brass jug hidden behind a furniture leg. Its reflection is visible in the framed art next to it. The jug came from one of my earlier paintings "blue door," shown in **Figure 5.22**.

The small, framed painting in the window of the shop is from another, earlier painting "late afternoon" (**Figure 5.23**). No, the jug and print were not really in the window, I took a little artistic license and added my own touches.

The shop changed hands at one point, but the merchandise remained. I went into the shop to show the owner a print of the painting, and she was quick to point out that the chair was still available. At the time of this writing the shop sits empty. We'll never know the fate of that old chair.

Figure 5.21 The detail of the items displayed in the shop window.

Figure 5.22 The painting "blue door" from which the jug was taken.

Figure 5.23 The painting "late afternoon" that appears framed in the window.

Figure 6.1 "red truck"

6

Red Truck

Filters and Textures

The Berkeley Hills are honeycombed with tiny streets and pedestrian paths. I love walking and quite often find myself navigating through the maze of byways near our house. Not far from where we live is a house with a permanent fixture parked in its driveway—an ancient red truck. A Diamond T to be exact.

One day the sun bounced off the rim of the headlight and spoke to me. "YO, paint this!" it said. Well, maybe not in so many words, but you get the idea—inspiration hit.

I was on a new kick with my Cintiq and my regained painterly style. The red truck was to be my next piece (**Figure 6.1**). Textures became some of the most interesting aspects of this painting. All the rust and worn edges were perfect for the techniques I had developed in the painting "old chair." Yet there were plenty of new challenges afoot. Filters played a major role in the creation of this painting as well.

Spherize and the Negative Number

I'll start by discussing the creation of the reflections on the chrome rim of the headlamp (**Figure 6.2**). The Spherize filter (**Figure 6.3**) was key in completing this effect. Spherize distorts an image to make it appear as if it is wrapped around a spherical shape.

In **Figure 6.4** the headlamp is isolated in its own file named "Light." The shape for the rim area was placed in its own layer and called "outside rim."

To create the reflection on the chrome rim, an image of some trees and a cloud-filled sky was created (**Figure 6.5**). The various elements in the scene were created using a variety of brush shapes.

Since these elements were going to be greatly distorted to fit a narrow space, a tremendous amount of detail was not necessary.

A more detailed description of the Spherize process can be found in the Filters PDF file, which you can download at www. peachpit.com/ digitalpainting.

PDF

Figure 6.2 The reflection on the rim of the headlamp.

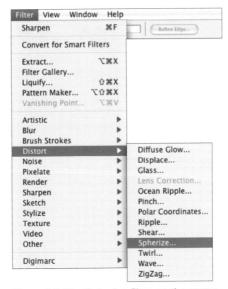

Figure 6.3 The Spherize filter on the menu.

The Spherize filter was applied to the scene (**Figure 6.6**). It is important to understand how the filter applies the effect. Though this concept is explained in the Filters PDF file, I want to explain it briefly here as well to help you understand how I applied this filter.

You can download the Filters PDF file from the Peachpit Web site at www. peachpit.com/digitalpainting.

PDF

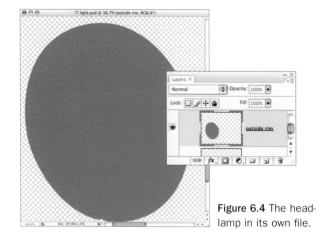

Figure 6.4 The headlamp in its own file.

Figure 6.5 The scene that served as the reflection in the chrome of the headlamp.

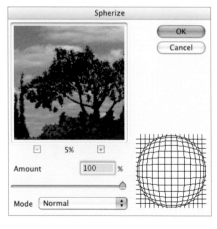

Figure 6.6 The Spherize dialog box.

Figure 6.7 shows a rectangular shape filled with a brick pattern placed at the center of the canvas. Applying the Spherize filter (**Figure 6.8**) produces the effect you see in **Figure 6.9**. The filter basically wraps the shape over the front edge of the sphere (**Figure 6.10**).

Looking closely at the filter's window you can see the small preview that it provides. Though it does not show the actual object being spherized, it does show the amount and how it will apply the effect. If you move the element to be spherized over to the side, as shown in **Figure 6.11**, the filter will treat the object as shown in **Figure 6.12**. The element gets wrapped around the side edge of the sphere (**Figure 6.13**).

If the canvas area is large enough so that an element being spherized falls beyond the boundaries of the sphere, you will get a distortion that affects only the parts of the element within the sphere, as visible in **Figure 6.14**.

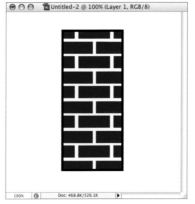

Figure 6.7 This brick-filled rectangle will demonstrate how Spherize works.

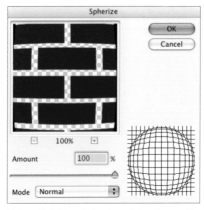

Figure 6.8 The Spherize dialog box with the brick-filled rectangle.

Figure 6.9 The result of applying the Spherize filter.

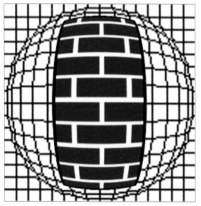

Figure 6.10 Spherize wraps a shape around a sphere.

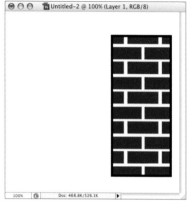

Figure 6.11 Spherize will have a different effect if an object is moved to the side.

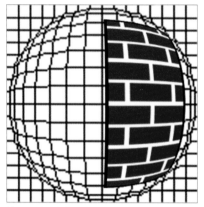

Figure 6.12 Spherize wraps a shape around the edge of the sphere.

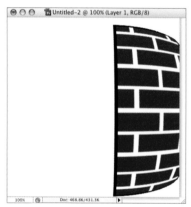

Figure 6.13 The result of applying the Spherize filter to an object that has been placed to the side edge of the canvas.

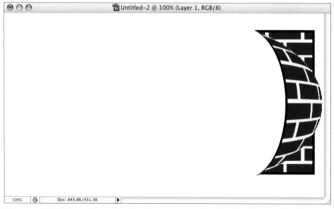

Figure 6.14 The distortion is far greater the farther the object is from the center of the image.

Figure 6.15 shows the tree and sky scene after it has been processed through the Spherize filter. Once the filter was applied, it was necessary to add some additional sky and foreground area to fill the space entirely. In **Figure 6.16** you can see the layer being clipped by the layer containing the shape of the headlamp.

Figure 6.17 shows the composite of all the layers for the front grill of the truck. The reflection of the grill in the head-lamp bends in the opposite direction of the surrounding environment. This distortion for the reflection needs to take on a different perspective. It needs to be pinched inward rather than bulge outward as you saw with the sky and trees.

Figure 6.18 shows the Spherize dialog box where I entered a −100 value. The filter will pinch rather than bloat the object, as illustrated in the preview graph.

In **Figure 6.19** you can see the twisted effect on the grill. In **Figure 6.20** the shape has been clipped by the headlamp.

The final headlamp with all the reflections is shown in **Figure 6.21**. Look closely and you will notice the speckling effect caused by the erosion of the chrome. You will learn about that effect later in this chapter. But first let's look at one more instance of the Spherize filter at work in "red truck."

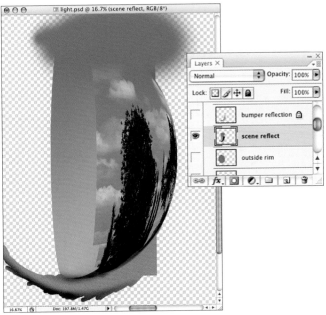

Figure 6.15 Here you can see the tree and sky scene after it was processed through the Spherize filter. Some additional tones were added to the top and bottom.

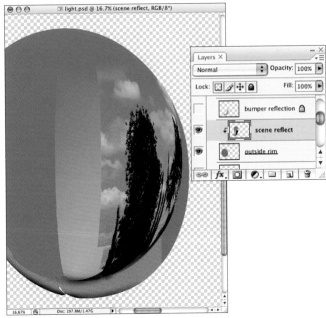

Figure 6.16 The distorted scene is clipped by the layer of the headlamp rim.

Figure 6.17 The front grill of the truck.

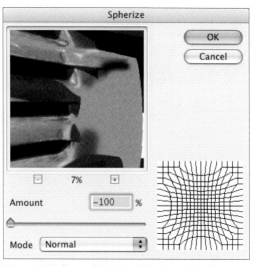

Figure 6.18 The grill in the Spherize dialog box where a negative value has been entered.

Figure 6.19 The distorted grill in place over the headlamp rim.

Figure 6.20 The distorted grill is clipped by the layer of the headlamp rim.

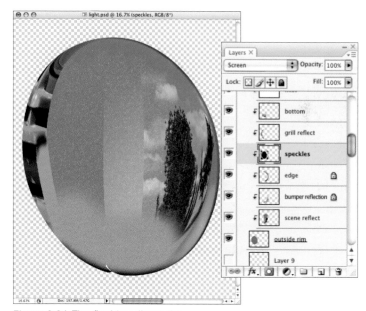

Figure 6.21 The final headlamp rim.

Aging the Truck

In **Figure 6.22** you see the fender before textures were applied to it to make it look worn. **Figure 6.23** shows one of the many textures that make the truck look worn and corroded. The texture was processed through the Spherize filter. Prior to applying the filter, the texture was placed into a separate file and positioned at the top of the canvas, as shown in **Figure 6.24**. This created the effect of the texture wrapping over the top of a sphere.

The Spherize filter was applied once (**Figure 6.25**) and then applied again a second time to exaggerate the effect (**Figure 6.26**).

The layer with the texture was then imported into the file with the truck. The mode for the layer was set to Lighten (**Figure 6.27**). This made only the lighter tones visible over the red of the truck. The layer was then clipped onto the fender for the final look (**Figure 6.28**).

Figure 6.22 The fender without the texture.

Figure 6.23 One of the textures that simulates the wear on the fender.

Figure 6.24 The texture is placed at the top of the canvas.

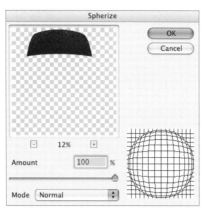

Figure 6.25 The texture is Spherized.

Figure 6.26 The texture is Spherized a second time.

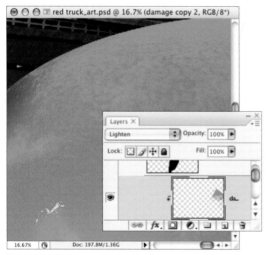

Figure 6.27 The mode for the layer containing the texture is set to Lighten.

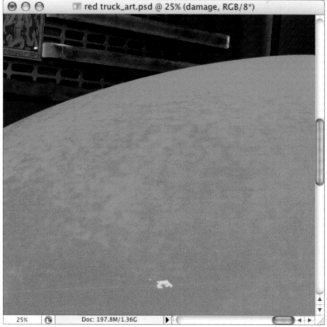

Figure 6.28 The final texture in place.

Creating a Worn Metal Texture

The texture that I used in the preceding technique was created with a collection of filters. But now the new Smart Filters feature in CS3 makes that process an easy task. Though this feature was not available at the time I created the painting, I want to show you how it works. To use this feature, convert the layer or Background to a Smart Filter layer by choosing Filter > Convert for Smart Filters. This allows you to apply as many filters as you want without committing them to the image. You can change the parameters, hierarchy, and the amount for the filter or eliminate the filter entirely at any time. The image will adjust to reflect any changes applied to the filters.

Figure 6.29 A gradient is applied with the desired colors for the texture.

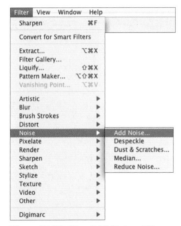

Figure 6.30 The Add Noise filter.

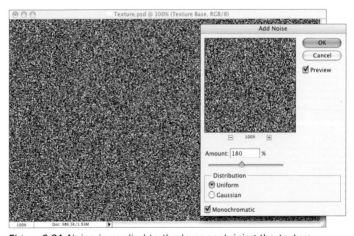

Figure 6.31 Noise is applied to the layer containing the texture.

I started by laying down a gradient (**Figure 6.29**). The first filter to be applied was Add Noise (**Figure 6.30**). An amount large enough to produce a strong noise was used in Monochromatic mode to keep the noise within the specified color ranges (**Figure 6.31**).

Using the Levels command (Image > Adjustments > Levels), I gave the noise more contrast (**Figure 6.32**).

Next, I applied the Motion Blur filter to the layer (**Figure 6.33**). This made the noisy texture start to streak down, as you can see in **Figure 6.34**.

The Filters PDF file explains the Smart Filters feature in more detail. Download it at www.eachpit.com/ digitalpainting.

PDF

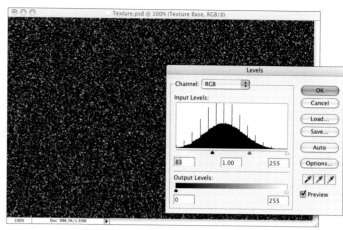

Figure 6.32 Levels increased the contrast for the noise texture.

Figure 6.33 The Motion Blur filter.

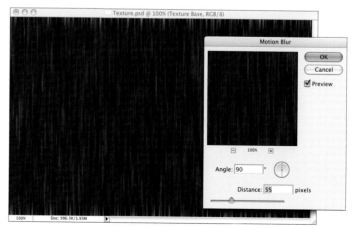

Figure 6.34 Motion Blur streaks the texture.

Once again, Levels was used to increase the contrast (**Figure 6.35**).

The final filter to be applied was the Spatter filter (**Figure 6.36**). The Spatter filter added the additional randomness to the texture (**Figure 6.37**). **Figure 6.38** shows the Layers panel where all the filters can be seen as Smart Filters applied to the layer.

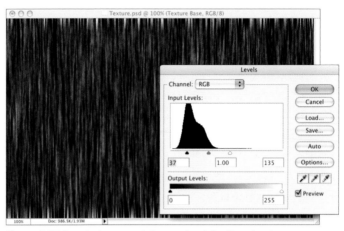

Figure 6.35 Levels increased the contrast for the streaks.

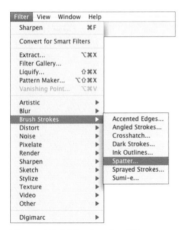

Figure 6.36 The Spatter filter.

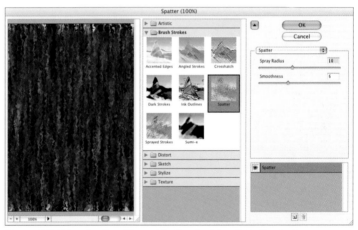

Figure 6.37 The Spatter filter adds the final touch to the texture.

Figure 6.38 The texture in a Smart Filter layer.

Using the Displace Filter

The same worn metal texture I just created also appeared along the top of the truck hood (**Figure 6.39**). To get this effect, the texture was given another filter—Displace (**Figure 6.40**).

> The Displace filter is described in more detail in the Filters PDF file, which you can download at www. peachpit.com/digitalpainting.
> **PDF**

The Displace filter works with two files. The first is the image you want to distort and the second is the image that is used to create the distortion. The second image is called a Displacement Map. The filter uses the luminosity values (lights and darks) of the Displacement Map to distort the image. Where there is a 50% gray value or neutral density in the Displacement Map, there will be no displacement (distortion). Any values lighter than 50% gray will distort the pixels of an image up and to the left. Any values that are darker than 50% gray, will distort the pixels of an image down and to the right.

Figure 6.39 The texture was used to depict the wear on the hood of the truck.

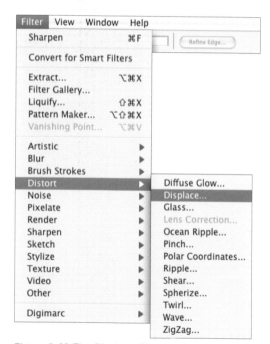

Figure 6.40 The Displace filter.

Now that you have an idea of what displacement is, let's look at how I used it in this case. I rotated the file containing the texture. To create the Displacement Map, I checked the dimensions of the texture file (**Figure 6.41**) by pressing the Option (Alt) key and clicking in the Document Size box on the lower left of the document window. I then created a second file that was the same size as the file with the texture. The second file was given a gradient from 50% gray to white (**Figure 6.42**).

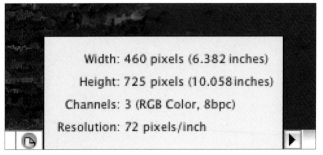

Figure 6.41 The dimensions of the file are made visible.

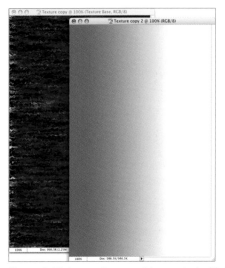

Figure 6.42 A new document is created with the identical dimensions as the texture document and filled with a gradient.

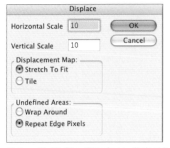

Figure 6.43 The Displace dialog box.

The Displace filter was called up (Filter > Distort > Displace). The settings were left at the default (**Figure 6.43**). In the second window that pops up requesting the Displacement Map, the file with the gradient was chosen (**Figure 6.44**). The result was the subtle twist of the texture (**Figure 6.45**).

The texture was then rotated back and flipped horizontally to get the curvature to go in the same direction as the truck hood. The final touch was to skew it (Edit > Transform > Skew), which lined it up with the hood, as shown in **Figure 6.46**.

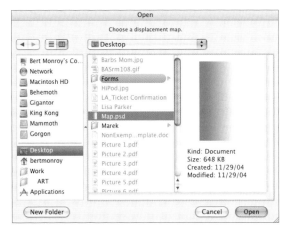

Figure 6.44 The second window of the Displace filter where you choose the file to be used as a Displacement Map.

Figure 6.45 The result of the Displace filter.

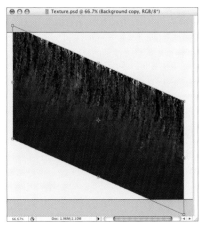

Figure 6.46 The texture is skewed to match the curvature of the truck hood.

Tiny Speckles

Earlier in this chapter I mentioned the speckles on the chrome edge of the headlamp (**Figure 6.47**). A similar effect is visible on the windshield, which is shown in a close-up in **Figure 6.47a**. The technique I used to create this is a very versatile effect that I use often and in various situations.

I started out by adding a large amount of noise with the Add Noise filter (Filter > Noise > Add Noise), as shown in **Figure 6.48**. This created a strong, static-looking pattern of black and white noise. To be able to modify the noise to get the needed results, it was necessary to introduce some gray into the mix. Applying the Blur or Blur More filters found on the Blur menu (Filter > Blur) would do it. If you choose the Gaussian Blur as I did in **Figure 6.49**, it will also work, but make sure you use a very low radius. You just want to introduce some gray, not throw the whole thing out of focus.

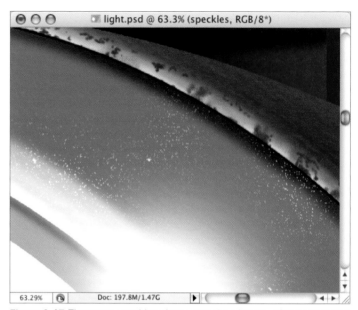

Figure 6.47 Tiny wear speckles that cover the chrome of the headlamp.

Figure 6.47a A speckle effect on the windshield caused by time and the elements.

Once you have gray, the Levels command will do the rest (Image > Adjustments > Levels). **Figure 6.50** shows how I have pushed the shadow and mid-tone sliders over to the far right. As you can see in the figure, the noise has been reduced to what appears to be a star field. Placing this layer over your image and setting the mode to Screen allows only the white speckles to show, thus creating the effect I achieved in the painting.

I mentioned the versatility of this effect earlier. It can start as a star field. Blurring it with the Blur More filter again will create the effect of falling snow. Blurring it with the Motion Blur filter (Filter > Blur > Motion Blur) will create falling rain. I'll use the falling rain effect in the next chapter.

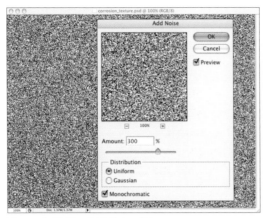

Figure 6.48 The Add Noise filter.

Figure 6.49 The Gaussian Blur filter softens the noise by adding grays to the black and white noise.

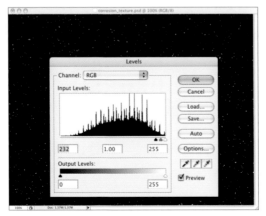

Figure 6.50 The Levels command reduces the amount of noise.

The Headlamp

The main focus in the painting of the red truck is the headlamp. At least to me it is. The intricate detail of the glass cover took some effort.

The glass is a collection of many layers working in concert to form the realistic look of the glass that covered the headlamp caught in the rays of the sun. The first of the layers was a simple, white elliptical shape that would serve as a mask for all the layers above it (**Figure 6.51**).

Using the Pen Tool, I created a series of paths that matched the cut lines in the glass of the actual headlamp (**Figure 6.52**). The lines, as they appear on the real truck, are rounded where they cross each other. Considering the amount of lines in the headlamp, it would have taken far too much time to create all the rounded edges. That's where Photoshop makes things easy.

I created an Alpha channel for the document by clicking the Make New Channel icon at the bottom of the Channels panel. Since nothing was selected, this created a black Alpha channel.

For a more detailed description of what Alpha channels are, refer to the Channels PDF file, which you can download at www.peachpit.com/ digitalpainting.

PDF

Figure 6.51 A layer containing the elliptical shape of the headlamp.

Figure 6.52 A series of paths were created with the Pen Tool for the lines on the face of the glass.

In the Alpha channel I stroked the paths with the Paintbrush Tool using a small, hard-edged brush tip (**Figure 6.53**).

I applied the Gaussian Blur filter to the channel to soften the edges. As you can see in **Figure 6.54**, the edges are soft, and where the lines intersect they have become rounded. I then applied the Levels command to the channel to sharpen it up (**Figure 6.55**). A second Levels adjustment gave me thick lines with rounded edges where the lines intersect (**Figure 6.56**).

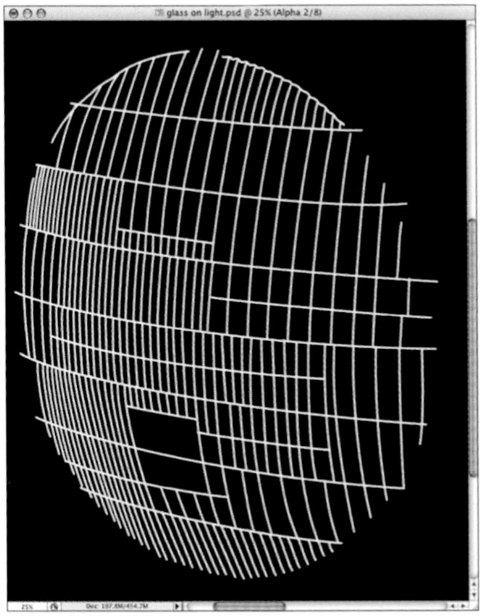

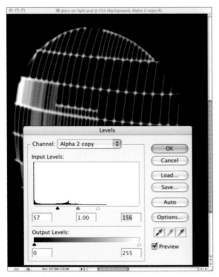

Figure 6.53 In an Alpha channel the paths were stroked with a white Paintbrush.

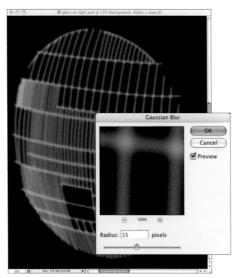

Figure 6.54 The Alpha channel was blurred to round out the lines.

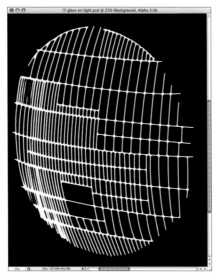

Figure 6.55 The Levels command reduces the amount of blur.

Figure 6.56 A second application of the Levels command sharpened the lines.

I made the Alpha channel a selection (Select > Load Selection) and filled a layer with a dark gray color through the selection (**Figure 6.57**). Using the Dodge and Burn Tools, I lightened and darkened parts of the grid lines to add highlights and shadows (**Figure 6.58**).

In a new layer, behind the layer with the lines, I created a gradient going from a medium blue to a light blue (**Figure 6.59**). This layer laid the foundation for the color inside the headlamp.

Figure 6.57 A layer was filled with gray through the selection of the Alpha channel.

Figure 6.58 Using the Dodge and Burn Tools, highlights and shadows were added to the grid lines

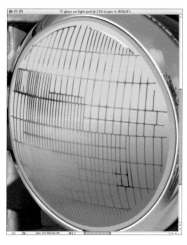

Figure 6.59 A gradient was laid down in a layer behind the layer with the grid lines.

A new layer was inserted between the layer with the lines and the layer with the gradient. In this layer I started to add the reflections in the glass. I first created a series of white lines, like those shown in **Figure 6.60**. To soften the lines, I applied a Gaussian Blur filter to them and lowered their Opacity (**Figure 6.61**).

I then dragged the Smudge Tool down over each section between the grid lines to curve the lines (**Figure 6.62**). This was a fairly freehand kind of treatment, and I varied it from section to section as you can see in **Figure 6.63**.

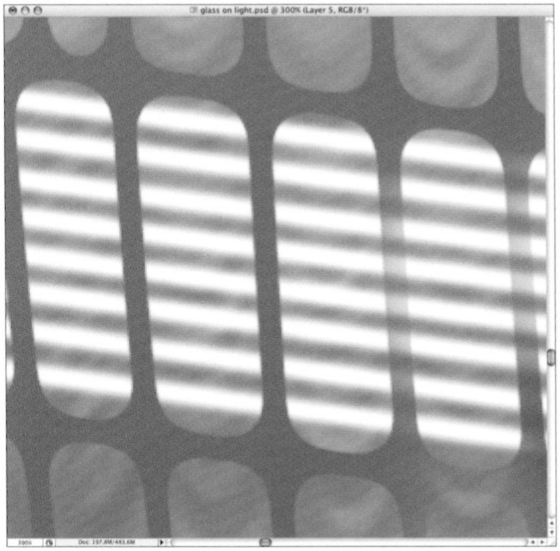

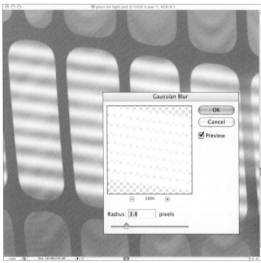

Figure 6.60 In a new layer, over the layer with the gradient, a series of lines were created.

Figure 6.61 The lines were blurred.

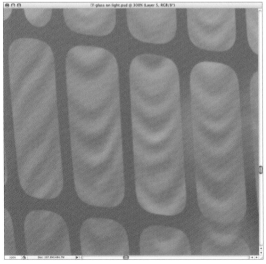

Figure 6.62 The lines were distorted using the Smudge Tool.

Figure 6.63 Distorted lines were added over the entire face of the headlamp glass.

In a second new layer, I laid down broad swatches of colors and applied the same smudging effect (**Figure 6.64**).

In a third new layer, I placed dark areas of color to simulate deep shadows cast onto and through the glass (**Figure 6.65**).

Finally, I added the strong highlights of the sunlight reflecting on the glass (**Figure 6.66**) by using loose brush strokes applied with a sharp-edged Paintbrush in specific spots, as shown in **Figure 6.67**.

To get the rim that holds the glass in place, I created a gray rectangle in a new layer and cut out the shape of the glass. To do this, I made the layer of the glass shape a selection and deleted the gray center of the rectangle. Then I applied the Satin layer style to add some soft reflections to the edge (**Figure 6.68**).

All the layers were then clipped with the base layer that contained the white ellipse for the overall shape of the glass headlamp (**Figure 6.69**).

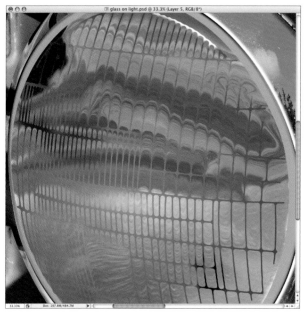

Figure 6.64 Large blotches of color were applied and distorted in various areas of the glass face.

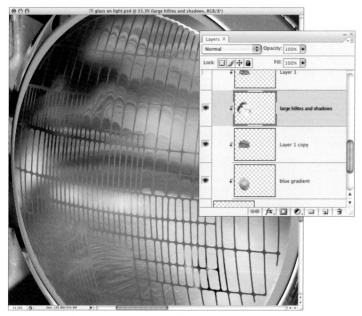

Figure 6.65 Dark tones were added in spots to simulate shadows cast inside the headlamp.

Figure 6.66 Strong highlights were added to the glass to simulate reflections of the sun.

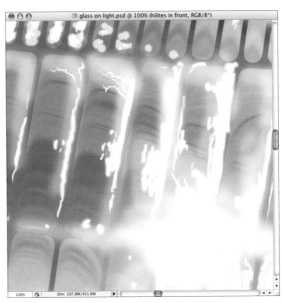

Figure 6.67 The highlights were made with loose strokes of the Paintbrush Tool.

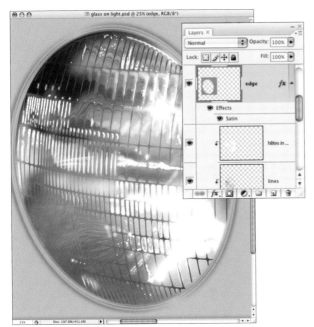

Figure 6.68 A gray rectangle was created with a hole cut in the center and a Satin layer style was applied. This was the rim of the glass.

Figure 6.69 All the layers that made up the glass of the headlamp were clipped with the base layer containing the shape of the headlamp.

Rust, Dirt, and Grime

Yes, the modified Spatter brush that I've used in so many other paintings made a grand appearance in this painting as well. By using different colors for the Foreground and Background, the brush was used to create the rust that appears all over the truck, a portion of which is shown in **Figure 6.70**. It was also used to make the dirt and wear on the front grill of the truck (**Figure 6.71**).

Figure 6.70 The rust visible throughout the body of the truck was created with a modified Spatter brush tip.

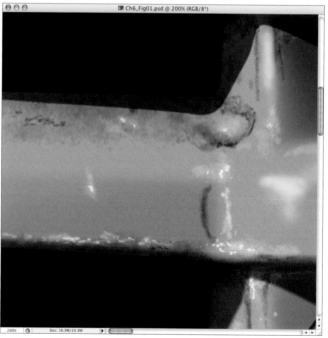

Figure 6.71 The dirt and wear on the grill was also created with the modified Spatter brush tip and different colors.

The Minor Details

No detail is ever too small to be left unattended. No matter how small, every detail brings the total image to life. Neglecting to properly handle some part of an image will draw the eye to the imperfection, thus distracting the viewer away from the whole experience. With this in mind, I want to draw your attention to the tiny hole visible above the headlamp. **Figure 6.72** shows a close-up of the detail. I'm not sure what that little hole was for, but the truck had one. Not just a hole, but also a slight bulge around the hole.

The hole started out as an elliptical path (**Figure 6.73**). In a layer, the path was filled with black (**Figure 6.74**).

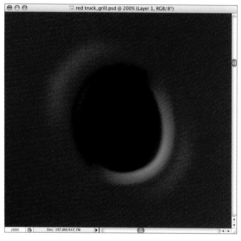

Figure 6.72 A tiny hole sits above the headlamp.

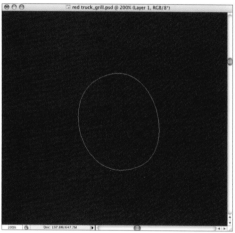

Figure 6.73 An elliptical path was drawn to create the shape of the hole.

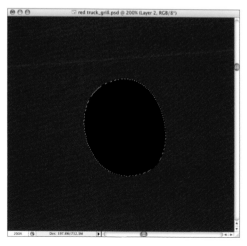

Figure 6.74 The path for the hole was filled with black.

The layer was given a layer style of Bevel and Emboss using an Outer Bevel for the Style. This created the highlights and shadows that started to give the hole some dimension (**Figure 6.75**).

The layer was blurred (**Figure 6.76**) to soften the edges of the hole and lighting effects.

The layer with the hole was made into a selection by Command-clicking (Ctrl-clicking) on it in the Layers panel. The selection was expanded (Select > Modify > Expand). Expand will enlarge your selection by the amount you specify. In another layer the selection was filled with black (**Figure 6.77**). This layer was also given a Bevel and Emboss layer style and its Fill Opacity was lowered to zero (**Figure 6.78**). As before, the layer was blurred to soften the effects.

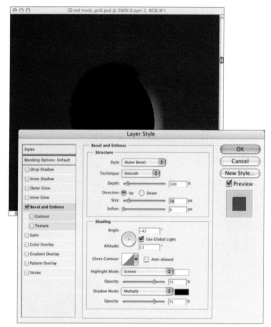

Figure 6.75 A layer style of Bevel and Emboss was applied to add dimension to the hole.

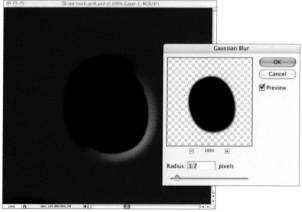

Figure 6.76 The layer for the hole was blurred slightly to soften the edge.

Keep in mind that the steps outlined in this chapter should be studied for what they do and not necessarily how I have used them. You may not have to create worn metal textures. However, the processes described here coupled with slight modifications to colors, modes, and the like will produce varying effects that can help solve many imaging challenges you might be faced with.

The truck, by the way, is still there. I saw it the other day. The red is a little more faded than when I painted it, but it still sits there enjoying its retirement basking in the warm rays of the sun.

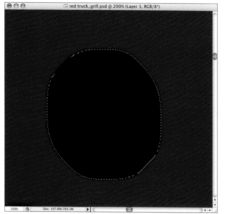

Figure 6.77 The layer of the hole was made into a selection. The selection was expanded and filled with black.

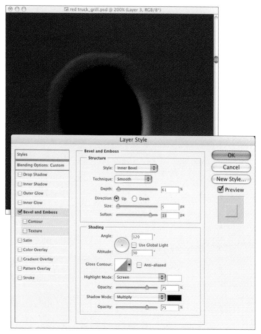

Figure 6.78 The Fill Opacity for the layer was lowered to zero and the layer style of Bevel and Emboss was applied to add dimension.

Figure 7.0 "Oyster Bar"

7

Oyster Bar

Complexity and Precision

The Oyster Bar restaurant is a little hole-in-the-wall place in midtown Manhattan. I first got the inspiration to paint it in 2001 while on a trip to my old hometown of New York City. When in New York, I often stay at my friend John's apartment overlooking Times Square. Across the street sits the Oyster Bar restaurant. The red glow from its neon sign miraculously beats the competition of all the other lights on that stretch of 7th Avenue and 54th Street.

I planned the painting (**Figure 7.0**) for years. In fact, I did not paint it until 2005. The complexity of the scene kept me from attempting it sooner than I did. The vast number of layers needed for each detail made the file sizes far too great for earlier machines. When I got my hands on a dual 2.5 GHz G5, I felt I was ready to tackle the job. Even with all that power certain functions still took what seemed like an eternity.

As with all my paintings, to alleviate the memory constraints, the image was composed of multiple sections. Each section was created in its own file: the wooden façade of the restaurant, the awning, the brick building, chalkboard, sidewalk, street, street signs, Oyster Bar neon, Sea Food neon, and the interior of the restaurant. Plus, many other files were used for such things as the silverware on the tables and the manhole covers. A lot of stuff! Each file contained all the layers, paths, and Alpha channels needed for that particular section. Some of the files were as large as 2 GB in size. Saving alone was an exercise in patience.

The distance from the subject required me to abandon the freedom of paint strokes that the last two paintings had offered me with the Cintiq and return to the precision of thousands of vector paths. After all, getting involved in those details is what I love to do most. This painting presented me with a whole new set of challenges.

Needless to say, a return trip to New York was needed to get additional reference shots of the details, sketch the scene, and take notes. The number of years since I had been there had brought about some dramatic changes in the scene. The awnings had changed (**Figure 7.1**). The kiosks were different. Even the streetlights were new. Sometime during those years New York City had switched from the WALK/DON'T WALK signs to the international hand signaling STOP and the little generic walking man.

The hardware and software were ready and so was I.

Figure 7.1 Besides a new awning, the years saw many changes in the scene.

Creating Rain and Puddles

One effect that I had never used in any painting prior to this one was the effect of rainfall. I had created rain for commercial illustrations but never for my personal work. All my work usually deals with strong lights and shadows. This one was overcast and rainy.

Figure 7.2 shows the streaks of rain as they pass over a section of the awning of the restaurant. I needed the rain to seem completely random—no two drops the same size. I mentioned in Chapter 6 that the effect of the star field could become rain by streaking it with the Motion Blur filter. The same process would be applied here, but I needed the raindrops to be larger than those produced by modified noise. The rain you see is close to you. It is not a heavy downpour.

I chose a hard-edged tip for the Paintbrush Tool and brought up the Brushes panel (Window > Brushes). In the panel, the tip spacing was increased, as shown in **Figure 7.3**.

Figure 7.2 The streaks of rain falling over the awning.

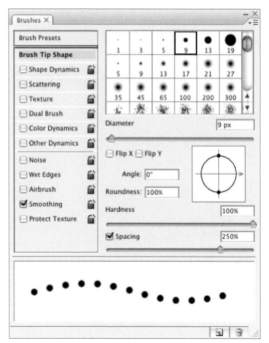

Figure 7.3 The tip spacing was increased to allow more room between the raindrops.

I randomized the size of each tip in the Shape Dynamics section of the Brushes panel (**Figure 7.4**). This guaranteed that each time the Paintbrush laid down a brush tip it would be a different size than the previous tip, thus making each drop appear different. Finally, in the Scattering section of the panel (**Figure 7.5**) I scattered the tips away from the stroke to hide the actual stroke being applied, thus adding more randomness to the raindrops.

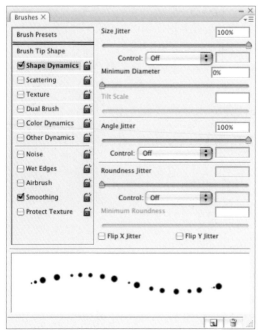

Figure 7.4 The size of each brush tip was randomized.

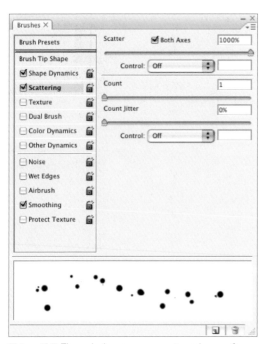

Figure 7.5 The raindrops were scattered away from the brush stroke.

A layer was created for the rainfall. Using white for my color, I stroked the canvas with the modified brush to create a random pattern of drops (**Figure 7.6**).

To make the dots appear as falling rain, the Motion Blur filter was applied (Filter > Blur > Motion Blur), as shown in **Figure 7.7**. Wanting to make the rain seem totally random, all of the previous steps were applied to a second layer. The difference in this layer was that the Distance amount for the Motion Blur filter was lowered to make the drops in this layer possess different lengths. In **Figure 7.8** you can see the rain over the wooden façade of the restaurant.

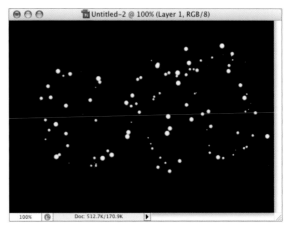

Figure 7.6 The canvas was stroked with raindrops.

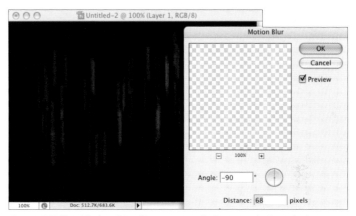

Figure 7.7 The Motion Blur filter was applied to streak the raindrops.

Figure 7.8 The rain falling in front of the restaurant.

When the Rain Stops Falling

The puddles required a different approach. For one thing, they are not in motion. Unlike the falling rain, their stationary status also caused reflections. Let's first look at a simple puddle, as shown in **Figure 7.9**. In **Figure 7.10** you see the actual strokes applied in a layer with the Paintbrush Tool using a gray color. Note the little red edges on the shapes on the lower right. These were added because the water is highly reflective, and the edges of the puddles needed to reflect the red neon sign visible over the edge.

To make the puddles appear wet, it was necessary to show the effect of light on the shapes. Applying a layer style was all that was needed.

> **NOTE:** Studying the effects of light on a wet surface made it easy to re-create that wet effect. I sprinkled a little water on a hard surface and then lit it with a desk lamp.

Water is transparent, but it does have mass. That mass casts a shadow. So I double-clicked on the layer containing the puddles in the Layers panel to bring up the layer style. The first style applied was the Drop Shadow (**Figure 7.11**).

Figure 7.9 The puddle over the sign case.

Figure 7.10 Simple strokes were applied to represent the puddle shape.

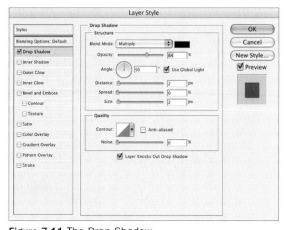

Figure 7.11 The Drop Shadow.

It is a slight shadow, so the Opacity was lowered from the default setting to lighten the effect of the shadow. Due to the small size of the puddle area, the Distance and Size parameters were lowered.

Next, an Inner Shadow was applied to add an edge to the puddles (**Figure 7.12**). The Mode was set to Overlay to vary the effect of the shadow as it passed over different tones in the metal sign. The Distance and Size parameters were lowered here as well.

Finally, applying Bevel and Emboss completed the effect by adding dimension to the puddles (**Figure 7.13**). The Size was lowered as before. The Highlight color was changed to a light blue to represent the sky above. The Shadow color was changed to white and its Mode to Color Dodge. This had the effect of increasing the saturation of the colors of the metal sign in the layer below, thus acting the way water works when lying on surfaces. In **Figure 7.14** you see the final puddles over the sign.

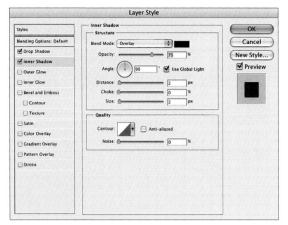

Figure 7.12 The Inner Shadow.

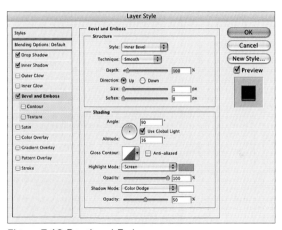

Figure 7.13 Bevel and Emboss.

Figure 7.14 The final puddles.

Creating Large Puddles

The puddles that accumulated on some of the other surfaces required a bit more work. **Figure 7.15** shows the puddles on top of the Learning Annex kiosk. They reflect the neon sign above them.

The shapes and basic effects for these puddles were done exactly as in the previous example. But I needed to add the reflections. A copy was made of the layer containing the neon for the Oyster Bar. That layer was then flipped upside down (Edit > Transform > Flip Vertical). The Ripple filter was applied to the layer (Filter > Distort > Ripple), as shown in **Figure 7.16**.

The rounded edges of the puddles have an additional distorting effect on the reflections, so one more step was needed. The layer containing the puddles was made into a selection by Command-clicking (Ctrl-clicking) on the layer in the Layers panel. Making the layer with the reflection the target, I summoned the Liquify filter (Filter > Liquify). Having the selection of the puddles active, it created a Quick Mask mode (red tint) over the layer, making it easy to identify the areas that needed to be distorted. Note that the Quick Mask mode is visible with irregularly shaped selections. Using the Warp Tool in the filer, I pushed the edges of the reflection to simulate the effect that would happen in real life, as shown in **Figure 7.17**.

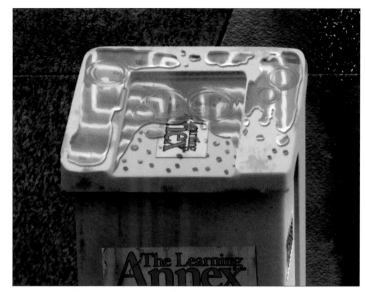

Figure 7.15 The puddles on top of the kiosk.

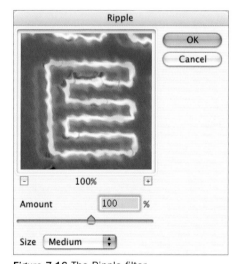

Figure 7.16 The Ripple filter.

The layer with the reflection was turned into a Clipping Group with the layer of the puddle. A Clipping Group uses the opacity of the base layer (in this case the layer with the puddles) as a mask for the other layers in the group. The other layer in this case is the one containing the reflection. A Clipping Group is created by clicking between two layers in the Layers panel while pressing the Option (Alt) key. In **Figure 7.18** you see the final puddle with the distorted reflection.

A more detailed description of a Clipping Group is in the Layers PDF file. Download it at www.peachpit.com/digitalpainting.

PDF

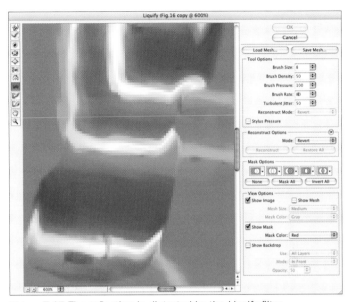

Figure 7.17 The reflection is distorted by the Liquify filter.

Figure 7.18 The distorted edges of the reflection in the final puddle.

Puddles on the Street

Let's look at another effect as a result of the rain ending its downfall—the little ripples in the puddles that accumulated on the street (**Figure 7.19**). There are many factors to consider if you want to make the ripples look real. Note that most of the ripples are blue, and the ripples on the right pick up the lights from the restaurant.

What is happening here? The flat surface of the water is being bent into a number of curved mirrors. Objects off to the side become visible within the side walls of the ripples that face them. All the blue ripples on the left of the figure lack other colors because they are reflecting the sky and the darkness of the unlit kiosks. The ripples that form within sight of the restaurant above them sparkle with reflected light.

Let's start with a simple blue ripple. These ripples pick up the blue sky above. Here I used the ZigZag filter. It worked with the existing colors that fell within the selected area in the scene. **Figure 7.20**

shows the surface of the street without the ripples. The Background layer was duplicated into a second layer. The need for working on a duplicate layer will become obvious later.

In the duplicate layer, using the Elliptical Marquee Tool, a small oval shape was selected (**Figure 7.21**).

Using the Paintbrush Tool, two rough circles were drawn within the selected area using a blue color selected to represent the unseen sky (**Figure 7.22**).

The ZigZag filter was chosen (**Figure 7.23**) to distort the selected area to simulate the impact of a falling raindrop. I played with the settings until I got the desired effect, as shown in **Figure 7.24**.

Only the outer ripples were needed for the effect. A layer mask was applied to the layer, and with a black paintbrush I eliminated the central portion of the ripple, as shown in **Figure 7.25**. This exposed the original, unfiltered layer below.

Figure 7.19 The ripples in the puddle from the falling rain.

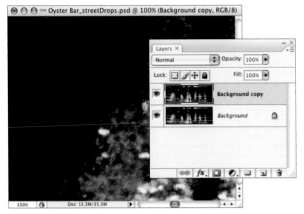

Figure 7.20 The flattened image of the street.

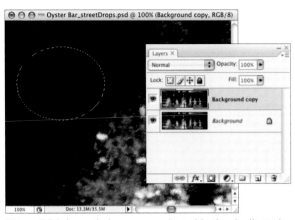

Figure 7.21 An oval shape was selected in the duplicated Background layer.

Figure 7.22 Blue to represent the sky was painted into the selected area.

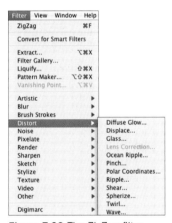

Figure 7.23 The ZigZag filter.

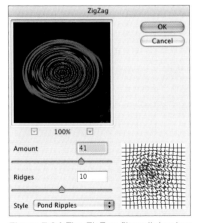

Figure 7.24 The ZigZag filter dialog box.

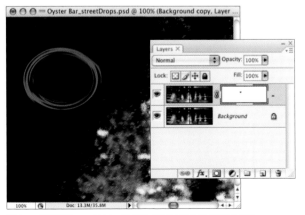

Figure 7.25 The center of the drop was masked out to better simulate the splash effect of a raindrop.

A second, smaller oval was selected that partially overlapped the first ripples. It was painted with blue circles as in the larger selection (**Figure 7.26**). The ZigZag filter was applied again, but the parameters were altered to make it different from the previous drop (**Figure 7.27**). As before, the center was masked (**Figure 7.28**).

In **Figure 7.29** a third oval was selected. This one, however, fell in an area where the light from the restaurant was being reflected as was the sky above. In this instance, three more colors needed to be added to the mix—yellow, orange, and white. To have full control over how the colors would be distorted, the dark areas of the selected area were cloned over the light tones, as shown in **Figure 7.30**. The colors were painted, as shown in **Figure 7.31**. **Figure 7.32** shows the ZigZag filter's effect on the selection. **Figure 7.33** shows the final ripples.

With a large, soft-edged, white paintbrush, small highlights were added to the ripples to make the reflections of light shine like the real thing (**Figure 7.34**).

Following these steps over and over again with varying sizes of selections and parameters for the ZigZag filter, the balance of the drops were created throughout the painting.

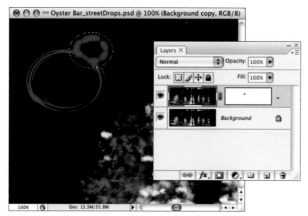
Figure 7.26 A second oval was selected.

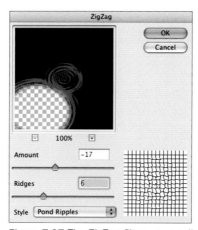
Figure 7.27 The ZigZag filter was applied.

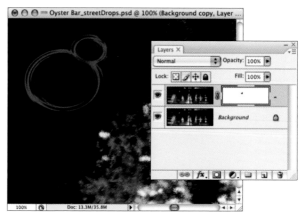
Figure 7.28 The center of the drop was masked.

Figure 7.29 A third oval was selected. This one overlapped an area of reflected light.

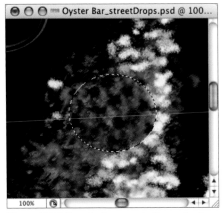

Figure 7.30 The dark areas in the selection were cloned over the bright tones.

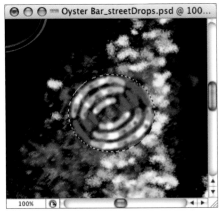

Figure 7.31 Colors were added—blue for the sky, the others for the reflected lights.

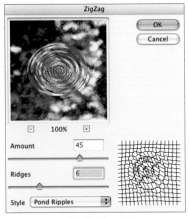

Figure 7.32 The ZigZag filter was applied.

Figure 7.33 The final ripples.

Figure 7.34 Tiny highlights were added to make the reflected light sparkle.

Creating the Manhole Cover

The manhole cover shown in **Figure 7.35** is one of those intricate details that required some of the features that exist in Adobe Illustrator. Illustrator plays a very important role in the creation of my artwork. It is the place where most of the elements are first created. I can't discuss the manhole cover without covering Illustrator.

But before I start, let me digress to prove a point made earlier in the book—the need for additional reference shots. **Figure 7.36** shows a close-up of the manhole cover in the original reference shot. Not much detail to work with there! Hence, the need for the detail shot shown in **Figure 7.37**.

Figure 7.35 The manhole cover.

Figure 7.36 The manhole cover in the original reference shot.

Figure 7.37 The reference shot used to study the details of the manhole cover.

Transform Again

The pattern on top of the manhole cover was easy to duplicate using Adobe Illustrator. In Illustrator I created a small path to represent the basic shape of the pattern on the cover (**Figure 7.38**). This path would become the source for the entire pattern. I did not want to create an actual pattern. I needed the paths to be actual paths so that I could use those paths for various selection functions once they were imported into the Photoshop file. The path was duplicated to the right (**Figure 7.39**) by pressing the Option (Alt) and Command (Ctrl) keys and dragging the selected object. The Shift key was also pressed to constrain the duplicate directly across from the original.

The two paths were duplicated again, rotated, and placed in position below the original, vertical paths, as shown in **Figure 7.40**. Selecting all four paths, I duplicated them and moved them down to a position just below the originals (**Figure 7.41**). Here is where the Transform Again feature in Illustrator makes it simple. By pressing Command-Y (Ctrl-Y) the action is repeated as many times as I press the keys. This allowed me to create an entire column of shapes in less then three seconds (**Figure 7.42**). Next, the entire column was selected and duplicated to the right, and aligned in position next to the original column (**Figure 7.43**). The Transform Again feature once again allowed me to effortlessly fill the entire area needed for the pattern in very little time (**Figure 7.44**).

Figure 7.38 The path for the basic shape of the pattern.

Figure 7.39 The path was duplicated to create two paths.

Figure 7.40 The two paths were duplicated and rotated below the original paths.

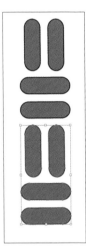

Figure 7.41 All four paths were duplicated and positioned below the originals.

Figure 7.42 Using the Transform Again feature, the shapes were duplicated many times.

Figure 7.43 The entire column of paths was duplicated and positioned to the right of the originals.

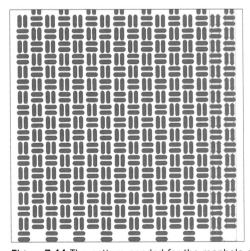

Figure 7.44 The pattern needed for the manhole cover.

Additional paths were then created for the other parts of the manhole cover. The text was created with another Illustrator feature that allows you to create text on a circular path, as shown in **Figure 7.45**. Once all the elements were in place, rotating the entire artwork gave me the final art (**Figure 7.46**).

I grouped all the paths that made up the manhole cover. Using the Free Distort filter in Illustrator (**Figure 7.47**), I twisted the paths to conform to the angle of the manhole cover to fit the scene, as shown in **Figure 7.48**. The final paths were ready to be exported into Photoshop (**Figure 7.49**).

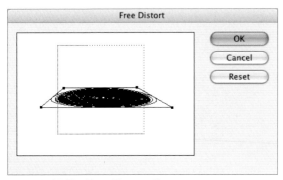

Figure 7.47 The Free Distort effect.

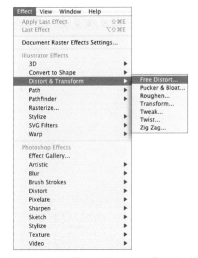

Figure 7.48 The paths were distorted to match the angle in the scene.

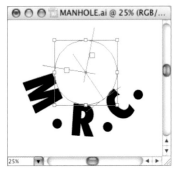

Figure 7.45 The text was created on a circular path.

Figure 7.46 The final paths for the manhole cover.

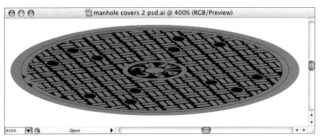

Figure 7.49 The final paths for the manhole cover ready to be exported into Photoshop.

Making the Manhole Cover Come to Life

The actual details of the manhole cover were achieved in Photoshop. Each part of the manhole cover was selected separately and filled with a color in individual layers. **Figure 7.50** shows the Layers panel containing all the layers that make up the manhole cover. In **Figure 7.51** you can see the completed manhole cover in Photoshop.

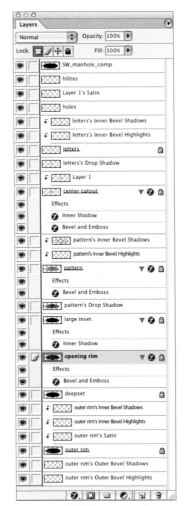

Figure 7.50 All the layers that make up the manhole cover in Photoshop.

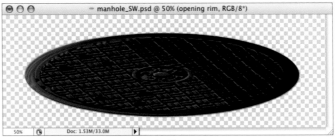

Figure 7.51 The manhole cover in Photoshop.

Calculations

Calculations is a feature I use a lot in my paintings. I use it to create specific masks based on multiple Alpha channels. It is through these Alpha channel masks that I apply most of my filters and other effects. With Calculations I manipulate those Alpha channels.

The Channels PDF file discusses Alpha channels in more detail. Download it at www.peachpit.com/digitalpainting.

PDF

Calculations works with two Sources at one time. These two Sources can be in the same file or in separate files. The Sources can be a component color channel or an Alpha channel. An active selection can also be used as a Source. Photoshop treats the selection as an Alpha channel; the selected area becomes white and the unselected area becomes black. If a layer is selected as a Source, the values of that layer are used as a mask.

For example, in **Figure 7.52** you see the Calculations dialog box where Source 1 is set to a different file than Source 2. The only requirement for using two different files is that they both have the exact same dimensions and resolution.

The Channel for Source 1 is the Red component channel. In Source 2, an Alpha channel called Alpha 1 is being used for the Channel.

Blending can be set to any of the modes on the list. The Add and Subtract modes available in Calculations and Apply Image do not exist anywhere else in Photoshop.

Modes are outlined in the Layers PDF file. Download it at www.peachpit.com/digitalpainting.

PDF

The Opacity setting is applied to Source 1 over Source 2. Mask uses a channel as a mask for Source 1. It works exactly as a layer mask: It masks parts of Source 1 so that parts of Source 2 can show through.

In Result you decide the destination of the result of your Calculation parameters. The result can be sent to a New Channel, a New Document, or a Selection in the current document.

Let's study how Calculations played a part in the creation of the manhole cover. **Figure 7.53** zooms in to see the details of the manhole cover. Note all the different tones that give the surface its three-dimensional look. Also note the reflections of the neon signs. All the colors and tones were applied through specific masks that exposed the shapes where and how I needed them.

In **Figure 7.54** the layer that contains the actual shapes of the texture has been turned into a selection. The selection was saved to the Alpha channel shown in **Figure 7.55**. The Alpha channel was duplicated and blurred, as shown in **Figure 7.56**. The Sharp channel will serve to constrain the effects to be in register with the original shapes. The blurred channel will be used to create the soft edges where the colors can be applied to the shapes.

With the Move Tool the blurred channel was nudged over to the left and down to intersect the Sharp channel. This is exactly the same procedure you saw used for the neon tubes described in Chapter 3.

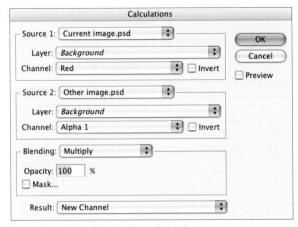

Figure 7.52 The Calculations dialog box.

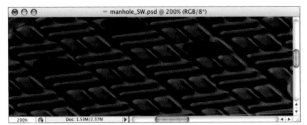

Figure 7.53 Zooming in you see the detail on the manhole cover.

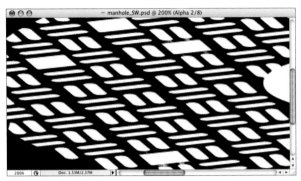

Figure 7.55 The Alpha channel for the cover shapes.

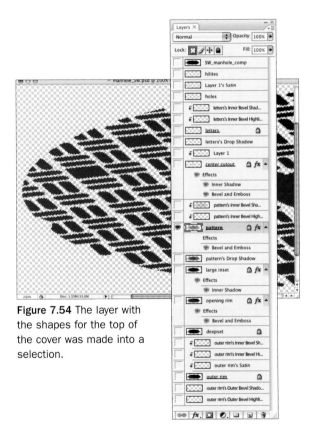

Figure 7.54 The layer with the shapes for the top of the cover was made into a selection.

Figure 7.56 The duplicate Alpha channel was blurred.

PHOTOSHOP STUDIO WITH BERT MONROY : DIGITAL PAINTING

In **Figure 7.57** you see the Calculations dialog box. Source 1 was set to Alpha 1. That was the blurred channel. Source 2 was the Sharp channel. Subtract was used for the Blending mode. Since the Preview check box was on, you can see what the result will be. It is easy to see that the upper-right edges of the shapes are being exposed. The Result was sent to a New Channel. This New Channel was an Alpha channel that could then be made into a selection to colorize the edges of the shapes.

Another channel calculation was made to add some color and texture below the shapes. In **Figure 7.58** an additional calculation was performed. The Sources were reversed. Blending was set to Difference. This exposed the area of the two channels where they were different. This affected the tops of the shapes as well as the areas below the shapes (**Figure 7.59**). To protect the basic shapes, a Mask was used. Alpha 1 was selected to serve as the Mask. Looking back at Figure 7.58 you see how the mask turned the basic pattern shapes to black, thus protecting them and exposing only the areas that needed to be affected. The Result was also sent to a New Channel for later use.

The different Blending modes coupled with Masks and specific channel information give you unlimited possibilities to create many kinds of masks.

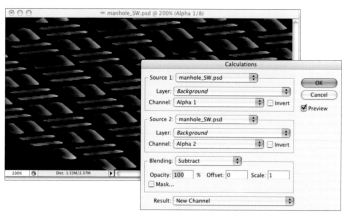

Figure 7.57 A new channel was created in the Calculations dialog box.

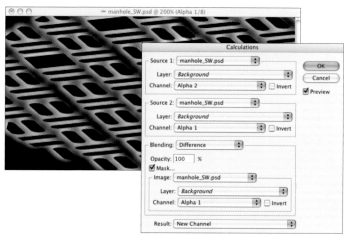

Figure 7.58 Another new channel was created using different parameters set in the Calculations dialog box.

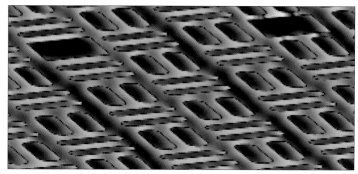

Figure 7.59 The result of this Calculation affects the area within the shapes.

Warping with a Mesh

Another really cool feature in Illustrator is the ability to warp vectors using a mesh. A similar warping feature was added to Photoshop with the release of version CS2—the Warp command found on the Transform menu (Edit > Transform). However, the feature is far more powerful in Illustrator. In Photoshop you are limited to a distortion mesh that is three columns by three rows. In Illustrator you can determine the number of columns and rows.

Figure 7.60 is a close-up of the trash can in the scene. The can has a wire net body that needs to conform to the curvature of the can. The basic shapes were generated in Illustrator. **Figure 7.61** shows the frame for the can. **Figure 7.62** shows the wire net created for the can. The wire net was created in a separate layer. Yes, Illustrator has layers too.

Figure 7.60 The trash can on the sidewalk.

Figure 7.61 The basic frame of the trash can in Illustrator.

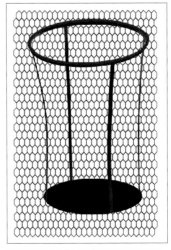

Figure 7.62 The wire net pattern over the trash can.

I selected the entire wire net and went into the Envelope Distort function (Object > Envelope Distort > Make with Mesh) shown in **Figure 7.63**. The dialog box that pops up allows you to determine the number of sections the mesh for warping will contain. I chose a total of ten rows with ten columns (**Figure 7.64**). This gave me sufficient space for distorting the net of the can to achieve the three-dimensional effect I was looking for.

Figure 7.65 shows the mesh for warping over the net of the can. **Figure 7.66** shows some of the sections of the mesh where they have been moved, causing the net to distort.

Figure 7.63 The Envelope Distort feature.

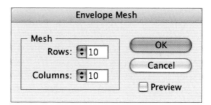

Figure 7.64 The Make with Mesh dialog box.

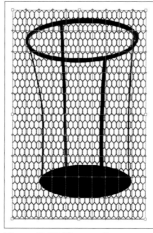

Figure 7.65 The mesh over the wire net.

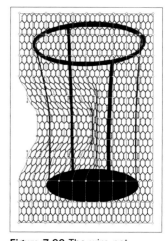

Figure 7.66 The wire net being warped.

The Easy Way Out

The main reason I turn to Illustrator to create the shapes for Photoshop is because Illustrator is resolution independent. I can work at any size, and the edges will be clean. I can put in as much detail as I want and then reduce the image to fit the size and resolution of the Photoshop document.

It is also much easier to work in vectors than in pixels for creating basic, simple shapes. For instance, look at the tiny clips that attach the neon tubes to the sign in **Figure 7.67**. Creating these shapes in Illustrator was a snap because there are more controls in Illustrator for altering vectors than there are in Photoshop. For example, the Scissor Tool allows you to cut a path. That tool does not exist in Photoshop.

The shapes for the little clips were created in Illustrator, as shown in **Figure 7.68**. Via the clipboard, these paths were then imported as paths into the Photoshop file. In Photoshop the paths were turned into selections and filled with the appropriate color and texture.

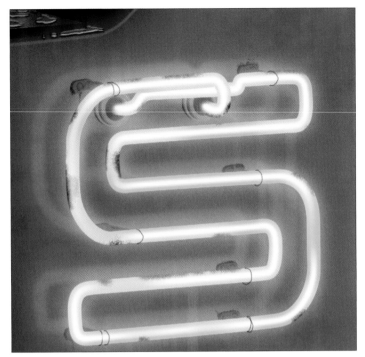

Figure 7.67 The tiny clips that attach the neon tubes to the sign.

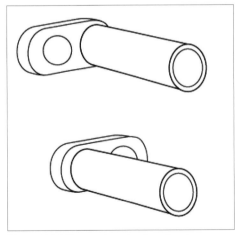

Figure 7.68 The vectors for the clips in Illustrator.

The parking restriction signs in **Figure 7.69** were also done in Illustrator. Illustrator has better text controls. The Illustrator file is shown in **Figure 7.70**. Note that there are two sets of signs. The large signs on the left were created to get the maximum detail. The smaller signs on the right have been resized to match the size needed for the Photoshop file. In this particular case, because the color had been added in Illustrator, the smaller Illustrator file was not imported via the clipboard as paths but rather as pixels.

Little details are the most crucial—like the tiny salt and pepper shakers that sit on the various tables in the restaurant (**Figure 7.71**). They also started as vectors created in Illustrator (**Figure 7.72**).

The ability to add minute details that are impossible to do in the Photoshop file can make for some silly additions. In **Figure 7.73** you see a close-up of the tiny manufacturer's label on the placard sign outside the restaurant. **Figure 7.74** shows the Illustrator file where you can see the contents of the label. I worked on the large version at the bottom. It has the name of the subject, my signature, and where I got my inspiration. The tiny version at the top of the file is the resized version for export to Photoshop.

Figure 7.69 The parking restriction signs in Photoshop.

Figure 7.70 The vectors for the signs in Illustrator.

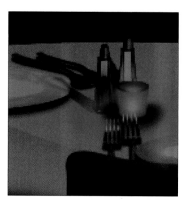

Figure 7.71 The salt and pepper shakers.

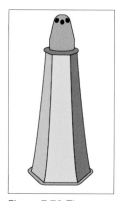

Figure 7.72 The vectors for the salt and pepper-shakers in Illustrator.

Figure 7.73 The tiny manufacturer's label on the placard in Photoshop.

Figure 7.74 The vectors for the manufacturer's label in Illustrator.

Creating Perspective Guides with the Blend Tool

Another feature that Illustrator has that Photoshop doesn't is the Blend Tool (**Figure 7.75**). The Blend Tool is one tool that I find myself using over and over again. Its effect can be used for a myriad of situations, from animation in-betweens to perspective foreshortening. This tool interpolates or morphs one path into another for all of the attributes: fill color, stroke weight and color, shape, and so on.

But in this example, I want to show foreshortening. In **Figure 7.76** you can see two lines that were generated to be the outer and inner edges of the concrete slabs in the sidewalk. I needed to create the edges in between these two while conforming to the perspective that had been established.

Double-clicking the Blend Tool in the tool panel popped up the Blend Options for this tool (**Figure 7.77**).

The Spacing was set to Specified Steps, and the number of steps desired was entered.

Clicking on a specific anchor point on each of the two elements (top anchor points) resulted in the creation of all the steps in between.

Figure 7.78 shows the final result that was imported into a Photoshop file to serve as guides for the creation of the sidewalk.

Figure 7.75 The Blend Tool in the Illustrator tool panel.

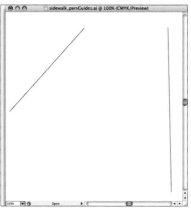

Figure 7.76 The two lines to represent the edges of the sidewalk in Illustrator.

Figure 7.77 The Blend Tool options window.

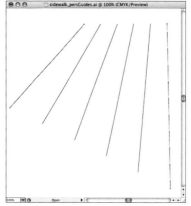

Figure 7.78 The result of the blending between the two lines.

The Textures

I'll finish up this chapter by discussing the creation of some of the textures that are in the painting.

Cutting Wood

Let's start with the material that the restaurant's façade is made of—wood. Wood is a complex, grain texture made up of long undulating lines. And of course there are the occasional knot and burl that must be introduced to complete the look of real wood. This might sound like a tough process to replicate but not for the savvy Photoshop user.

In **Figure 7.79** you see a close-up of the wooden planks that make up the wall of the restaurant. I created a new file to work on the basic wood texture. In a new layer, I selected a large rectangle and filled it with a color that I wanted the wood to be, as shown in **Figure 7.80**.

Figure 7.79 The wall of the restaurant shows the wood texture.

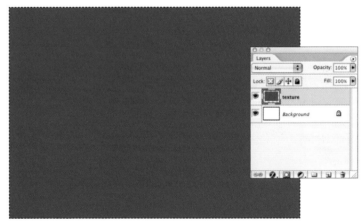

Figure 7.80 A rectangular shape is filled with a brown color for the wood.

In **Figure 7.81**, noise has been added to the brown rectangle (Filter > Noise > Add Noise). Note that I set the amount to a large number. This created a lot of noise that became a great starting point for the wood grain.

To stretch the noise to better simulate the grainy texture of wood, the Motion Blur filter (Filter > Blur > Motion Blur) was applied (**Figure 7.82**). The Motion Blur filter lightened the color so a little adjustment was made using the Levels command (Image > Adjustments > Levels). **Figure 7.83** shows the Levels command doing its job to bring out the luster of the wooden grain.

The result up to this point is fine for most woods, but I wanted burls and knots and more flow to the wood grain, so one last procedure was necessary— Liquify (Filter > Liquify). This filter produces the exact effects I was looking for. Using a combination of three of the tools within the filter, I was able to distort the motion-blurred lines to achieve a better looking wood grain.

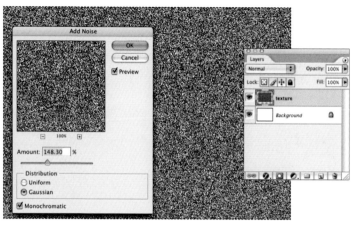

Figure 7.81 The Add Noise filter was applied to the brown rectangle.

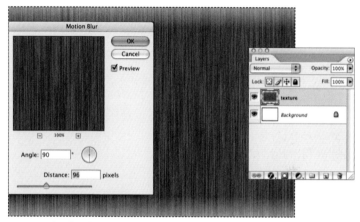

Figure 7.82 The Motion Blur filter stretched the noise to a wood grain look.

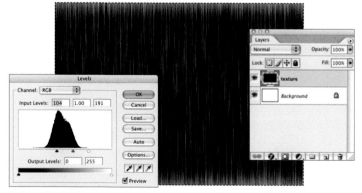

Figure 7.83 The Levels command was used to intensify the wood grain color.

With the Forward Warp Tool, the first tool at the top of the toolbar, I pushed the lines up and down at slight angles. This gave me the distortions you see in **Figure 7.84**. The Turbulence Tool, the eighth tool in the toolbar, created the look of burl in the wood. Finally, the Bloat Tool, the fifth tool down, allowed me to create the knotholes in the wood. Holding the tool in one place slowly starts to bloat the area, creating the perfect knot. The color directly beneath the center of the brush shape will be the color expanded into the knot. Moving the cursor back and forth within an area alternates the color being used, allowing you to fine-tune the color of your knot.

Transferring the finished texture over to the painting was not a simple drag and drop. One very important consideration had to be taken into account—each plank of wood on the building was unique. Dragging the entire texture over would look like the façade was constructed of large sheets of wood. No, each plank had to be thin and look as if it was not cut from the same tree. To get this effect, I selected a long, vertical, rectangular shape, as shown in **Figure 7.85**. This selected shape was dragged over to the painting. The process was repeated many times for each plank of wood. The variety was created by moving the rectangular selection to a new position each time before copying over to the painting. The result was the wooden façade of the restaurant.

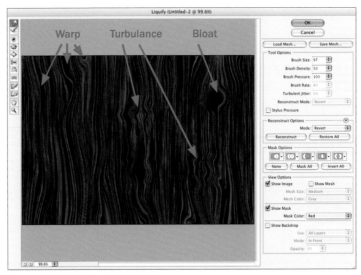

Figure 7.84 The Liquify dialog box.

Figure 7.85 A rectangular selection to represent a single plank of wood was made and put in position over the texture.

Pouring Concrete

Next is that tiny bit of concrete at the base of the light pole (**Figure 7.86**). This texture, as the one I just covered, required the use of multiple filters to get the desired effect.

In a layer the shape was created using the Pen Tool. The shape was filled with a gray color to simulate the color of concrete. The Filter Gallery (Filter > Filter Gallery) was called up and Craquelure was chosen from the Texture folder (**Figure 7.87**).

To enhance the effect, the Craquelure filter was applied once again, as shown in **Figure 7.88**. For the final touch, the Texturizer filter was applied in Sandstone mode, as shown in **Figure 7.89**. This last filter added the roughness of the surface, whereas the others added the cracks and dents usually present in concrete. Keep in mind that in CS3 you have Smart Filters that allow you to apply many filters. The Filter Gallery does allow the application of multiple filters, but not all filters are present and they are not editable after they are applied.

Sections of the concrete base were selected separately and lightened or darkened to give the concrete base a three-dimensional look. A slight red was added to the far, top edge to simulate the reflection of the neon sign above. This was accomplished by using a soft-edged Paintbrush in Color mode, which allowed me to add color without affecting the existing detail of the texture.

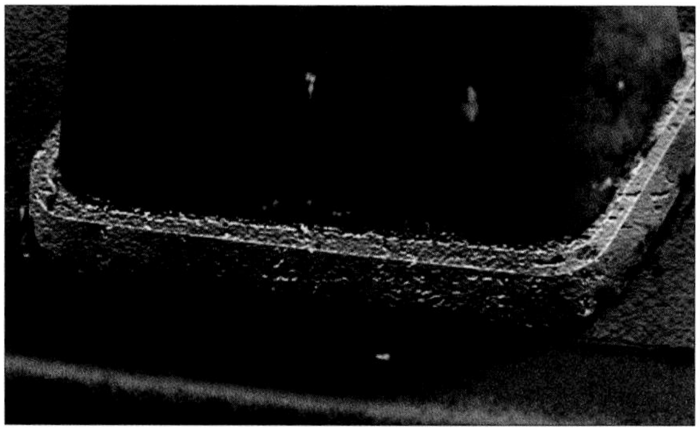

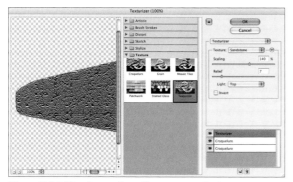

Figure 7.86 Concrete at the base of the light pole.

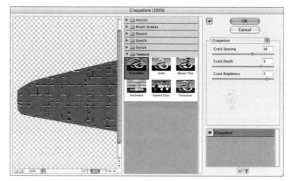

Figure 7.87 The Craquelure filter was applied in the Filter Gallery.

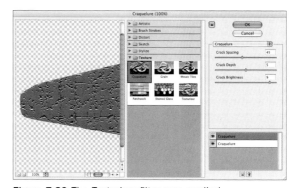

Figure 7.88 The Craquelure filter was applied a second time.

Figure 7.89 The Texturizer filter was applied.

Getting Slick

A lot of water is on the ground due to the rainfall. The puddles show ripples as the raindrops hit them, as described earlier in this chapter. The sidewalk, however, needed to show this wetness as well. **Figure 7.90** shows a close-up of the street on the lower left of the art. The texture picks up colors and reflections that are very random in nature. Here is another instance where a combination of filters was necessary to do the job. **Figure 7.91** shows the first of the filters. It is the same Texturizer filter that I used

for the concrete, but in this case the Relief has been heightened to exaggerate the effect.

The second filter used to create this effect was the Sumi-e filter shown in **Figure 7.92**. **Figure 7.93** shows the third and final filter—Fresco. These three filters gave me the effect I was looking for to create the look of moisture on the street. The texture was applied to a layer that was then colorized in certain areas where color was needed for reflections.

Figure 7.90 Looking closely at the street you can see the wet surface caused by the falling rain.

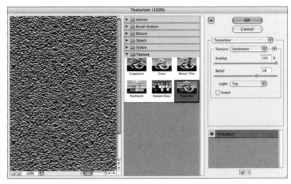

Figure 7.91 The Texturizer filter was applied to start the process.

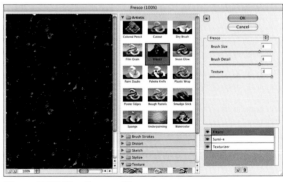

Figure 7.93 The Fresco filter.

Figure 7.92 The Sumi-e filter.

That Little Extra Oomph

One final note on this piece—the additional 10%. I often stress the need to add that little extra something to make an image come to life. It might be something that no one will notice, but in the grand scheme of things, it will make everything work together. **Figure 7.94** shows a puddle along the curb on the side street. The water was created exactly as I described in all the exercises in the beginning of this chapter. But there was one difference—the reflection. Though the building being reflected is not visible in the scene, it would cast a reflection based on the observer's angle of view.

I created the simple building façade that is shown in **Figure 7.95**. The building was distorted (Edit > Transform > Distort) to match the angle of the street and the perspective of a reflection at that angle. Why bother? Because when re-creating reality, every detail counts.

Then in a last minute effort I just had to add one more element of authenticity. Think about it: It is raining in the painting. When people go into the restaurant, they probably stamp their feet on the entrance mat to shake off the rain. That tiny little ripple in the mat shown in **Figure 7.96** makes it real.

The "Oyster Bar" brought me back to my previous method of painting where paths made up the shapes rather than free-form brush strokes. It was a wonderful experience, but thereafter I was on to the next set of challenges!

Figure 7.94 The puddle on the side street.

Figure 7.95 The building façade created to serve as a reflection in the puddle.

Figure 7.96 A little ripple in the mat provides genuine detail.

Figure 8.0 "Lunch in Tiburon"

8

Lunch in Tiburon

Capturing Sunlight

At the time of this writing, "Lunch in Tiburon" was my latest painting. "Damen" was painted prior to "Lunch in Tiburon." So far, each chapter has dealt with a painting in the order in which it was created. But here I'll stray from the chronological order that I have followed until now in the book. I'll make "Damen" the last chapter due to its unique, monumental size and the fact that it appears on the cover. I trust you will not mind my taking a little artistic license on this sequencing matter.

"Lunch in Tiburon" was inspired by what its name implies—a lunch in the city of Tiburon, California (**Figure 8.0**). My good friend Arne owns a wonderful yacht called "Summer Breeze." On occasion we'll go out for a spin around San Francisco Bay that usually involves lunch at a well-known restaurant in Tiburon called Sam's. We dock the boat to Sam's pier and spend a leisurely hour or so at the outside dining area enjoying great conversation and an equally great meal.

The sun always seems to shine brighter on that side of the bay. The famous San Francisco fog doesn't make it to this corner of Marin County that often. On this particular day the table looked so comfortable during our visit (**Figure 8.1**). Waiting for the check, it seemed to beg us to stay just a little longer. It was then that the painting appeared before my eyes.

I was very excited to start this one. Maybe it was because I was still in the middle of working on "Damen" and was feeling weary after spending so many months on the same subject. I couldn't wait to start this new journey! The brightness of the sun bouncing off so many textures was a challenge.

I wanted to capture the sun so that those looking at the painting would feel the need to put on sunglasses. "Lunch in Tiburon" also presented me with the opportunity to return to the painterly style that I had rediscovered in the creation of "old chair" and "red truck." The reflections dancing through the various surfaces cried out for the fluid motions of brushes gliding over the Cintiq canvas.

Though the scene was a simple still life, there was a complexity to the elements in the scene that posed a tremendous challenge for the powers of Photoshop. It is the solutions to those challenges that I will share with you in this chapter.

Figure 8.1 An outing with a group of friends inspired the painting "Lunch in Tiburon."

The Tablecloth

Let's start with the base of the image—the tablecloth. Not only does it travel back in the expanse of the tabletop, it buckles here and there from the remnants of an active meal shared by friends.

I first had to create the pattern of the table-cloth. It is a pattern that I am sure you have come across many times. I have seen it in red in dozens of Italian restaurants. Blue seems to be popular everywhere else. Many of these patterned tablecloths are made from fabric, but the ones used at Sam's are made of plastic.

The basic pattern is composed of four distinct squares that contain specific designs. Since symmetry is crucial in creating a pattern, I created a set of guides, as shown in **Figure 8.2**. Within these guides the four design elements were created (**Figure 8.3**).

> The Pen Tool and Patterns PDF file, provides a more detailed description of creating patterns. Download it at www.peachpit.com/digitalpainting. **PDF**

Normally, the four squares would be sufficient to create the pattern. The complexity and, most important, the randomness within the pattern details required me to take a few additional steps in the creation of this pattern. First and foremost is the fact that I worked within a grid of fifteen squares (**Figure 8.4**).

Let's get into the creation of the elements for each square.

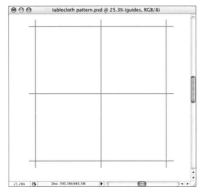

Figure 8.2 The basic four-square grid of the pattern.

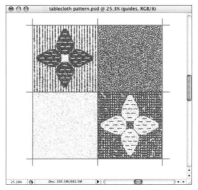

Figure 8.3 The pattern design elements within the grid.

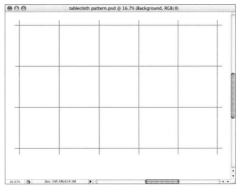

Figure 8.4 The nine-square grid.

The Florets

The floret design started in Adobe Illustrator. In a new document, a vertical line was drawn and converted into a guide (View > Guides > Make Guides). This guide would ensure the symmetry of the floret petal. A shape was created to serve as the side of one of the floret petals, as shown in **Figure 8.5**.

The entire shape was selected. The Reflect Tool was chosen and the cursor was placed centered on the guideline. The position of the cursor determines from where the reflection will be performed. Pressing the Option (Alt) key, I clicked to bring up the dialog box for the Reflect Tool (**Figure 8.6**). Vertical was chosen for the axis and the Copy button was clicked to make a copy of the original shape shown in **Figure 8.7**.

The two anchor points at the top were selected and joined (Object > Path > Join). Smooth was chosen as the type of joint (**Figure 8.8**). Where the two paths were joined, Smooth gave the edges the round quality I was looking for.

To create the other three petals, the Rotate Tool was selected. As with the Reflect Tool, the position of the cursor determines the point of rotation. The cursor was placed directly below the petal shape, and with the Option (Alt) key pressed, the Rotate dialog box was brought up, as shown in **Figure 8.9**.

Ninety degrees was entered for the Angle and the Copy button was clicked. The result was a copy of the original floret that was angled (**Figure 8.10**). The Transform Again function (Object > Transform > Transform Again) repeats the last action performed. Pressing Command-D (Ctrl-D) twice, the keyboard shortcut for Transform Again, two more petals were generated to complete the floret (**Figure 8.11**).

The tiny indents in the center of each petal were then created (**Figure 8.12**).

With the overall shape for the floret complete, two copies were made. One was colored white, the other blue. They were now ready to be exported to the Photoshop file.

Figure 8.5 Half of the shape for the floret was created in an Illustrator file.

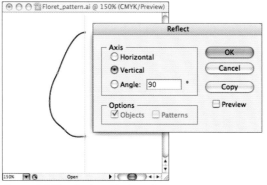

Figure 8.6 The Reflect Tool made a copy along the chosen axis.

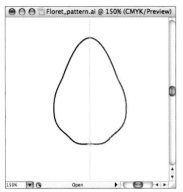

Figure 8.7 The second side of the floret.

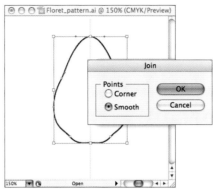

Figure 8.8 The two sides of the floret were joined to make a single, closed path.

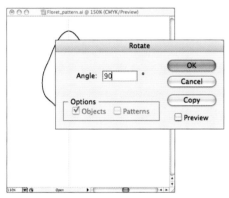

Figure 8.9 The Rotate dialog box where the angle for rotation was determined.

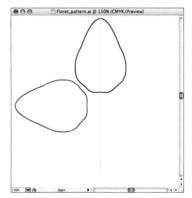

Figure 8.10 The first, rotated copy was generated.

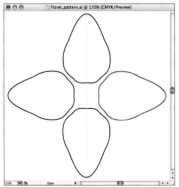

Figure 8.11 Using the Transform Again command, additional copies were made.

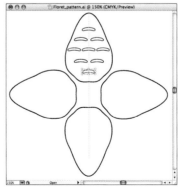

Figure 8.12 The tiny shapes inside the petals were created.

The Background

In the Photoshop file, a guide was created in a layer to determine where each of the various boxes that make up the pattern would fall (**Figure 8.13**). The florets appear on top of squares. One square has crisscrossed lines. The second square has vertical lines of irregular thickness in the background. For the first square, a series of vertical and horizontal blue lines were created. Random cross sections of the lines were erased to vary their lengths, as shown in **Figure 8.14**. Though it is a repeating pattern, every tiny floret seems to be different from its neighbor. This required the pattern to possess a certain amount of randomness. The pattern with the blue lines was duplicated, and the erased sections were done differently from the original. The white florets were placed into the two boxes (**Figure 8.15**).

The blue floret was placed into another section of the grid (**Figure 8.16**). This floret had the vertical lines of irregular thickness. These lines are simple strokes created with a brush tip that changes in size and shape along the length of the stroke.

The Paintbrush Tool was selected with a hard-edged round tip. In the Brushes panel, the tip was modified to create the needed effect.

Figure 8.17 shows the Brushes panel with all the necessary modifications. In the Shape Dynamics section, the Size Jitter was set to 100%. This feature randomized the diameter of the brush tip as it was stroked across the canvas.

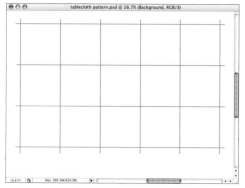

Figure 8.13 A grid was created to serve as a guide for positioning the square of the pattern.

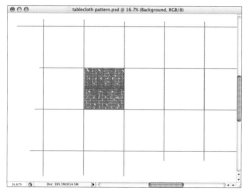

Figure 8.14 Random, intersecting lines made up the first square of the pattern.

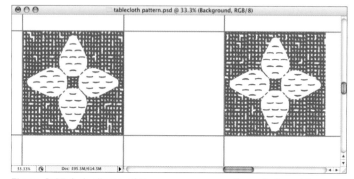

Figure 8.15 A duplicate of the square was made and altered to make it different from the original. The white florets are in place.

A Minimum Diameter was set to limit how small the smallest brush tip would be.

The Angle Jitter was set to 100% to randomize the angle of the brush tip. Since the brush tip at that point was a round brush, angle would have no effect until the next control—Roundness.

Roundness randomly changed the shape of the tip from a circle to an ellipse as a stroke was applied. A Minimum Roundness was set to limit the amount of flattening.

Spacing was increased slightly to clearly see the different shapes within the stroke (**Figure 8.18**).

With the tip set to behave the way I wanted it to, a bright blue color was chosen and a dot was placed at the top of the canvas (**Figure 8.19**). Pressing the Shift key to connect from one click to the next, I clicked at the bottom of the canvas to complete the line (**Figure 8.20**).

Several additional lines were created on either side to complete the background for the pattern in (**Figure 8.21**).

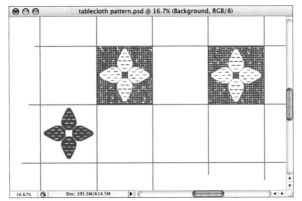

Figure 8.16 The blue floret was imported into the pattern.

Figure 8.17 The Size, Angle, and Roundness Jitters were set to randomize the look of the stroke.

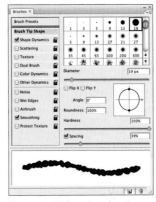

Figure 8.18 Spacing was increased to make the randomization of the brush tips easy to see. This is purely for demonstration purposes.

Figure 8.19 A dot was created at the top of the canvas.

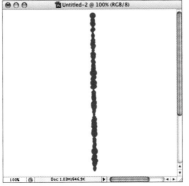

Figure 8.20 With the Shift key pressed, a second click at the bottom of the canvas completed the line.

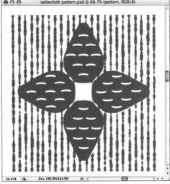

Figure 8.21 The completed lined background for the blue floret.

Speckled Texture

Next, I created the speckled texture that you see in **Figure 8.22**.

In a separate layer, an area was selected to contain the texture. The area was filled with a 50% gray (Edit > Fill > Use > 50% Gray).

The Add Noise filter (Filter > Noise > Add Noise) was then applied to the area with a high Amount to produce a lot of noise. **Figure 8.23** shows the layer filled with the noise. The Pointillize filter was then applied to the area (**Figure 8.24**). This turned the noise into the little dots shown in **Figure 8.25**. This layer was duplicated because it would later serve another purpose in its current state.

To turn the dots into a mesh of lines, the Find Edges filter was applied (**Figure 8.26**). The result was the texture shown in **Figure 8.27**. This texture needed to match the blue of the tablecloth. The blue color was chosen as the Foreground color. Fill was chosen from the Edit menu and the Mode was set to Color (**Figure 8.28**). This turned all the unwanted colors that resulted from the Pointillize filter into the required blue, as shown in **Figure 8.29**. Some dark values were still present, so the Fill command was applied again, but this time the Mode was set to Lighten (**Figure 8.30**). The result was the texture that was needed for the tablecloth (**Figure 8.31**).

The appropriate squares in the grid were filled with the new texture, as shown in **Figure 8.32**.

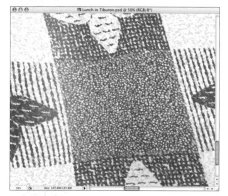

Figure 8.22 This texture was created next.

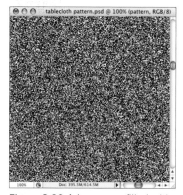

Figure 8.23 A layer was filled with a lot of noise.

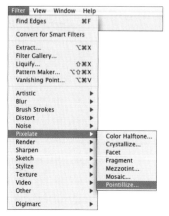

Figure 8.24 The Pointillize filter.

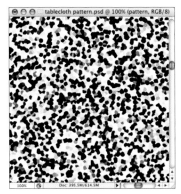

Figure 8.25 The effect of the Pointillize filter.

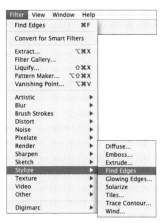

Figure 8.26 The Find Edges filter.

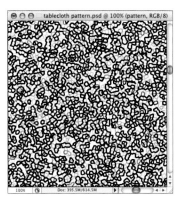

Figure 8.27 The effect of the Find Edges filter.

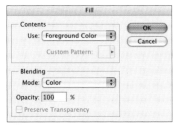

Figure 8.28 The Fill dialog box where the Mode was set to Color.

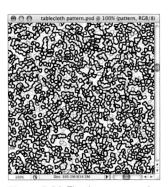

Figure 8.29 The layer was colorized to blue tones.

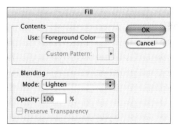

Figure 8.30 The Fill dialog box where the Mode was set to Lighten.

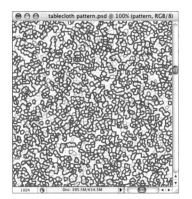

Figure 8.31 The pattern now had a consistent blue tone.

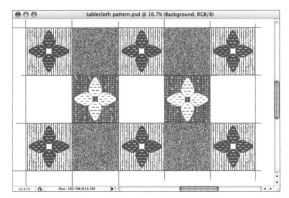

Figure 8.32 The pattern with all the basic squares in place.

The Overall Texture

An overall texture runs through the tablecloth that consists of tiny bumps. To simulate this texture, I used the duplicate texture that was created earlier when the Pointillize filter was applied. The layer was desaturated to make it gray, as shown in **Figure 8.33**.

The layer was placed in front of all the other layers that contained the stripes and florets. The Mode for the layer was set to Hard Light, which made it appear as a soft texture over the stripes and florets (**Figure 8.34**).

Creating the Pattern

With all the elements complete, the pattern could finally be defined. It is crucial that the step and repeat process of a pattern be seamless. Where the pattern ends it must then repeat.

> A more detailed explanation of creating a pattern can be found in the Pen Tool and Patterns PDF file, which you can download at www.peachpit.com/digitalpainting. **PDF**

The grid was made visible to facilitate the symmetrical selection of the pattern (View > Show > Grid) and the Snap to Grid option was made active (View > Snap to > Grid) to ensure an accurate selection.

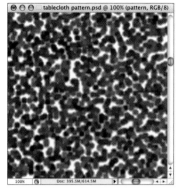

Figure 8.33 The duplicate layer of the Pointillized noise was desaturated.

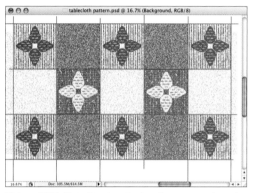

Figure 8.34 The desaturated pattern was placed over the floret squares and set to Hard Light.

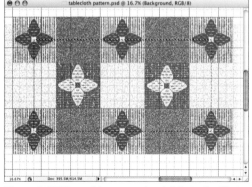

Figure 8.35 The grid was made visible to facilitate the symmetrical selection of the pattern. The area for the pattern was then selected.

An area was selected that started from the center of the floret on the upper left to the center of the floret on the lower right, as shown in **Figure 8.35**. Define Pattern was chosen (Edit > Define Pattern). In the Pattern Name dialog box that popped up the pattern was given a name (**Figure 8.36**).

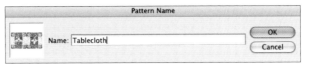

Figure 8.36 The pattern was named.

The painting measures 20 inches by 15 inches. To have enough tablecloth to distort into the necessary shape, I needed the pattern to be larger than the painting. The canvas size for the pattern file was increased to 30 inches by 20 inches. A new layer was filled with the pattern (Edit > Fill > Use > Pattern), as shown in **Figure 8.37**.

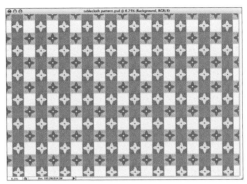

Figure 8.37 A layer was filled with the finished pattern.

The layer containing the finished pattern was dragged and dropped into the file for the painting. I zoomed out to view the work area and chose Edit > Transform > Distort. The bounding box became visible in the work area (**Figure 8.38**).

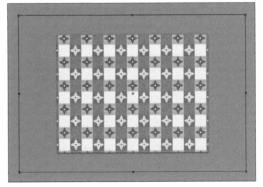

Figure 8.38 The layer with the tablecloth pattern was copied to the art file.

The handles were manipulated until I achieved the 3D perspective I wanted the tablecloth to have (**Figure 8.39**).

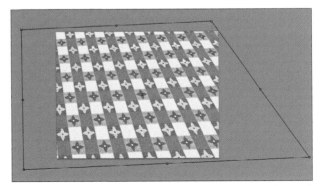

Figure 8.39 The layer with the tablecloth pattern was distorted to look three dimensional.

Soft Folds

After a bunch of guys having lunch and pushing glasses and plates around the table are done, the tablecloth no longer lays flat. A few folds were evident here and there. **Figures 8.40** and **8.41** show two close-ups of the tablecloth where these folds existed. Notice that there is a slight bend to the cloth where it is not lying flat against the table. To get these folds, I relied on an often-overlooked filter that I love using—Displace (**Figure 8.42**).

A more detailed explanation of the Displace filter is in the Filters PDF file, which you can download at www.peachpit.com/digitalpainting.

PDF

Displace

The Displace filter works with two files. The first is the image you want to distort, and the second is the image that is used to distort it. This second image is called a Displacement Map. The filter uses the luminosity values (lights and darks) of the Displacement Map to distort the image. Where there is a 50% gray value or neutral density in the Displacement Map there will be no displacement (distortion). Any values lighter than 50% gray will distort the pixels of an image up and to the left. Any values that are darker than 50% gray will distort the pixels of an image down and to the right.

Keeping this in mind, you can create very elaborate Displacement Maps to distort images in a variety of ways. I employ the Displace filter many times during the creation of my paintings.

Figure 8.43 shows the tablecloth before any details have been added. I filled a new layer with a 50% gray (Edit > Fill > Use 50% Gray). As mentioned earlier, this will have no effect on the image. Using a large, soft-edged paintbrush, swaths of black and white were applied to the canvas. These tones would distort the tablecloth based on their tonal value. **Figure 8.44** shows the image that served as the Displacement Map.

The Displacement Map must be a separate document. The entire layer was selected (Select > All). The selection was copied to the clipboard (Edit > Copy). A new document was created (File > New).

NOTE: To stress the concept of staying organized, note that the Displacement Map file in Figure 8.44 is named "map for tablecloth."

When the new document opened, the contents of the clipboard were pasted into it (Edit > Paste). This document was then saved as the Displacement Map for the tablecloth.

NOTE: When creating a new document in Photoshop, the New Document window will reflect the size and resolution of the contents of the clipboard.

In the actual tablecloth file, the Displace filter was chosen. The parameters were set for the desired amount (**Figure 8.45**). In the second window that popped up, which asks for the selection of the Displacement Map, the map for tablecloth.psd file was chosen (**Figure 8.46**).

Figure 8.47 shows the rumpled tablecloth.

Figure 8.40 The tablecloth in the painting "Lunch in Tiburon" does not lie flat but has folds.

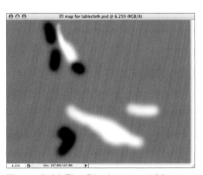

Figure 8.41 Another section of the tablecloth that has a slight fold.

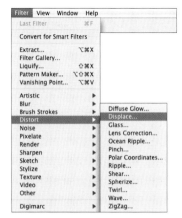

Figure 8.42 The Displace filter in the menu.

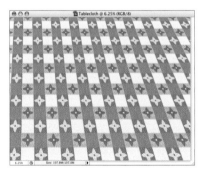

Figure 8.43 The tablecloth before displacement.

Figure 8.44 The Displacement Map for the tablecloth.

Figure 8.45 The Displace filter was chosen.

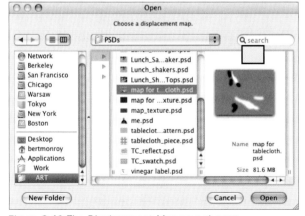

Figure 8.46 The Displacement Map was chosen.

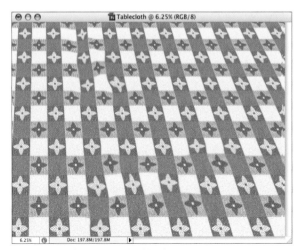

Figure 8.47 The rumpled tablecloth.

Because the tablecloth was made of plastic instead of cloth, additional displacement of the tablecloth was needed. **Figure 8.48** is zoomed into the image to see the pattern on the tablecloth. You can see how sharp and even the edges are. The very same texture that I used to create the complex blue background on one of the tablecloth squares a few pages back (**Figure 8.49**) was also used here to add texture to the overall tablecloth. You guessed it! I made the texture into a pattern. An entire canvas was filled with the textured pattern. The pattern was then used as a Displacement Map for the tablecloth. **Figure 8.50** shows the ragged distortion of the tablecloth caused by the Displace filter.

Figure 8.48 A close-up of the tablecloth showing the details prior to adding a texture.

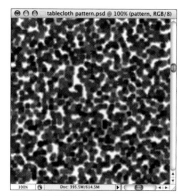

Figure 8.49 The Displacement Map that was used to add a rough texture to the tablecloth.

Figure 8.50 The ragged texture of the tablecloth after the Displace filter was applied.

The Pepper Flake Brush

Let's move on to the pepper shaker, which is filled with coarse pepper flakes. **Figure 8.51** shows a close-up of the pepper shaker. The flakes are different colors and shapes. **Figure 8.52** zooms into the pepper granules inside the shaker.

To create all the pepper flakes, I relied on a custom brush and a few layer tricks. Let's start by looking at the process for making the custom brush that was created for the pepper.

You first need to consider what constitutes a brush. Any selection can be turned into a brush. It can be an eye on a person's face, a signature, or a cloud—whatever. You also need to consider that the values of the colors within the brush will determine its opacity. Where the brush tip is black, it will be 100% opaque. Anything other than black, be it red, green, or a gray, will be transparent based on the value of that color. Where the brush tip is white, it will be completely transparent. This brush tip behavior is the same regardless of the Opacity setting for the tool that is using the brush tip. Let's say you created a brush with a 50% gray. If the Paintbrush Tool is set to 100% Opacity, the stroke will have an opacity of 50%. If the Opacity of this particular brush is lowered to 50%, the resulting stroke will have an opacity of 25% because the original brush tip was created with a 50% gray.

Figure 8.51 The pepper shaker in "Lunch in Tiburon."

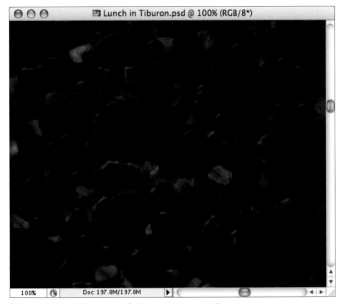

Figure 8.52 A close-up of the pepper granules.

A more detailed explanation of the Brushes panel can be found in the Brushes PDF file, which you can download at www.peachpit.com/digitalpainting.

PDF

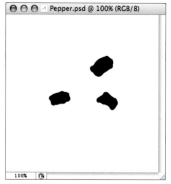

Wanting my pepper granules to be opaque, I chose a solid black for the Foreground color. Using a rounded, hard-edged brush tip shape, I created three shapes to represent three flakes of pepper (**Figure 8.53**).

Figure 8.53 The brush tip started as three shapes to represent three individual pepper flakes.

The shapes were selected and defined as a Brush Preset (**Figure 8.54**). I named the brush "pepper" in the Brush Name dialog box that pops up when you create a Brush Preset (**Figure 8.55**).

With the Paintbrush Tool selected, I then selected the tip. A newly created brush will appear at the bottom of the list (**Figure 8.56**). The Brushes panel (Window > Brushes) was opened (**Figure 8.57**). In the Brush Tip Shape section, Spacing was increased, as shown in **Figure 8.58**. This separated the brush tips, making them appear as distinct flakes.

To further randomize the brush, in the Shape Dynamics section (**Figure 8.59**) the Size Jitter and Angle Jitter were adjusted. After this adjustment each brush tip had a different size and angle than the tips on either side of them.

Figure 8.60 shows the Scattering section of the Brushes panel. Scattering distributes the brush tips away from the actual stroke being applied to the canvas.

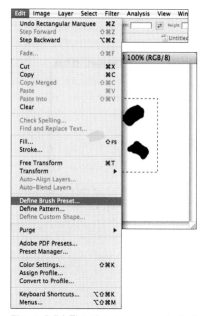

Figure 8.54 The shapes were selected and defined as a Brush Preset.

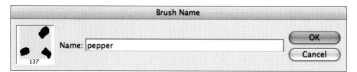

Figure 8.55 The brush tip was named in the Brush Name dialog box that pops up when a Brush Preset is created.

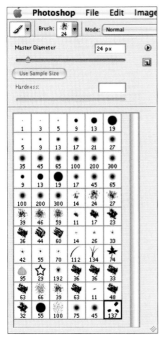

Figure 8.56 The brush tip was selected from the drop-down menu.

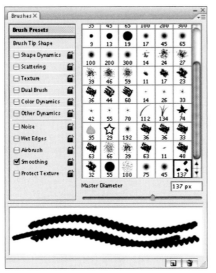

Figure 8.57 The Brushes panel.

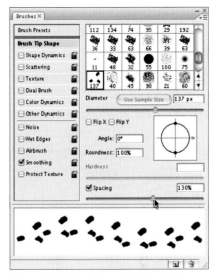

Figure 8.58 Spacing was increased.

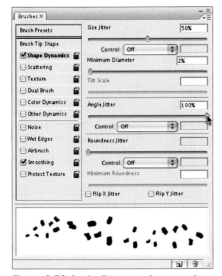

Figure 8.59 Angle Jitter was increased.

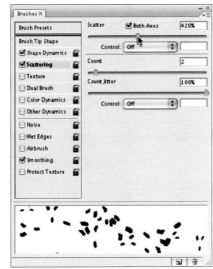

Figure 8.60 Scattering was applied.

The higher the percentage, the farther they will travel. The scatter will be applied up and down from where the stroke is drawn. The scatter can be applied to both axes, which causes the tips to be applied to the left and right as well as above and below.

NOTE: All the brush functions can be controlled by a stylus input device like the Wacom tablets using pen pressure, tilt, and so on.

The Count was raised slightly. Count controls the number of brush tips that are generated. A high number makes a brush stroke dense. If the Count is left at 0, the stroke uses the current Spacing parameters set in the Brush Tip Shape section, which is controlled by the input device. Count Jitter was set to 100% to randomize the Count amount along the stroke as it was applied to the canvas. To complete the pepper granules brush, Color Dynamics were altered, as shown in **Figure 8.61**. This made each tip a different color than the neighboring tips.

Figure 8.61 Color Dynamics were altered.

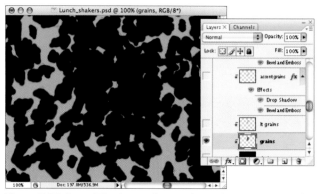

Figure 8.62 One of the layers that made up the pepper granules.

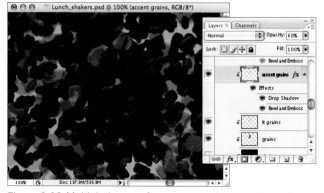

Figure 8.63 Multiple layers of pepper granules were turned on. The selected layer has layer styles applied to it.

Figure 8.62 shows one of the various layers that make up the pepper where the brush was used. In **Figure 8.63** you can see multiple layers of pepper flakes. The currently selected layer has a layer style applied to it that starts to give the illusion of depth and shape to the granules. Some of the layers have also had the Add Noise filter (Filter > Noise > Add Noise) applied to them.

To add the final touch of texture, another brush was employed. **Figure 8.64** shows the selection of one of the Spatter brushes. **Figures 8.65** and **8.66** show the alterations to the tip in the panel.

Figure 8.67 shows a close-up of the granules with the details added to the edges, making them rough and three dimensional.

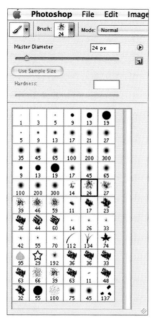

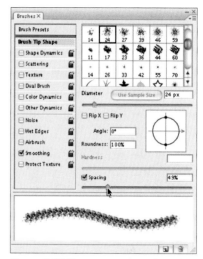

Figure 8.65 The spatter was altered.

Figure 8.64 One of the Spatter brushes was selected.

Figure 8.66 Additional alterations to the Spatter brush.

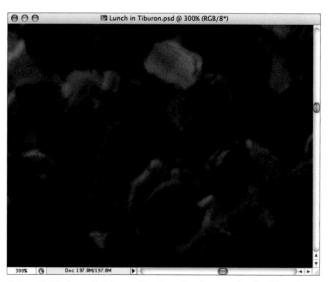

Figure 8.67 Zooming in on the granules to see the final touches of detail added with the Spatter brush.

A Touch of Light

One of the most challenging aspects of creating "Lunch in Tiburon" was re-creating the brightness of the sunlight. So many reflective surfaces called for a multitude of glistening hot spots.

Creating the basic hot spots was simply a matter of using a hard-edged brush tip and adding tiny spots here and there with the Paintbrush Tool. Making them glow was also an easy task—using layer styles.

Figure 8.68 shows a dab of white painted onto the canvas in a layer. This dab became a glint of light when the layer style shown in **Figure 8.69** was applied. In **Figure 8.70** you can see the effect of the glow.

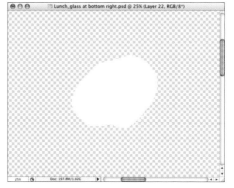

Figure 8.68 A spot of white to simulate a glint of the sun on the edge of the glass.

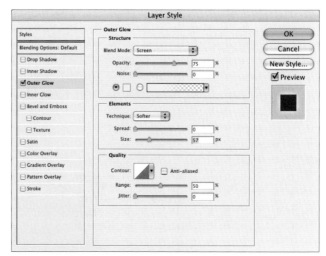

Figure 8.69 The Outer Glow layer style.

Figure 8.70 The spot with the glow.

In some cases additional color glows were needed. Due to refraction and the reflection of other elements in the scene, some glows had dual colored glows. Note in **Figure 8.71** that both a yellow and a blue glow surround some of the glints of light. This effect required an additional step to the layer style process.

Figure 8.72 shows a spot of light that has been given a blue glow. It is possible to separate the layer style from a layer to modify it independently from that layer. **Figure 8.73** shows the Layer menu choice that separates the layer style into its own layer.

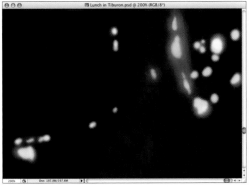

Figure 8.71 Some glints of light have dual colored glows around them.

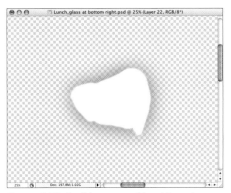

Figure 8.72 A white spot with a blurred outer glow.

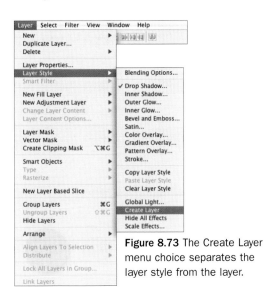

Figure 8.73 The Create Layer menu choice separates the layer style from the layer.

Note that in **Figure 8.74** you see two versions of the Layers panel. The one on the left shows the layer with the layer style. The one on the right shows how the layer style is now in its own layer.

With the blue glow separated, it was moved over to the left of the spot of light (**Figure 8.75**). A yellow outer glow was applied to the layer with the spot of light (**Figure 8.76**). The yellow glow was separated in the same manner as the blue glow and then repositioned to the right of the spot (**Figure 8.77**).

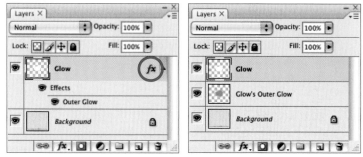

Figure 8.74 The panel on the left shows the layer with the layer style. The panel on the right shows the style in its own layer.

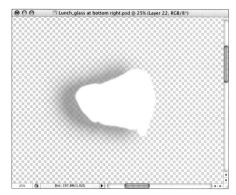

Figure 8.75 The blue glow was moved to the left of the white spot.

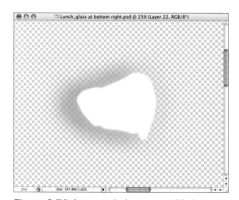

Figure 8.76 A second glow was added using yellow.

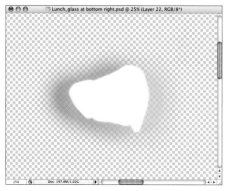

Figure 8.77 The yellow glow was separated to its own layer and moved to the right of the spot.

Refractions

Some elements when viewed through shaped glass become distorted beyond recognition. The more contours a glass possesses the heavier the distortions will appear.

Red Straw Through Glass

Figure 8.78 shows a close-up of the straw in the glass on the lower right of the painting. As you can see, it is being distorted as it passes through the curves of the glass. The actual shapes were created as individual paths with the Pen Tool and filled with the appropriate red tones. Adding the texture and fade was a little trickier.

The layer that contained the red swirl was given a layer mask (Figure 8.79). In the layer mask, gray tones were applied to partially hide the swirl (Figure 8.80). Using the modified Spatter brush, strokes were applied to texture the red swirl. (You saw this technique used in many situations throughout the book.)

The result, as shown Figure 8.81, was a swirling refracted view of the red straw.

Figure 8.78 The straw is refracted behind the glass.

Figure 8.79 The red shape was created with the Pen Tool.

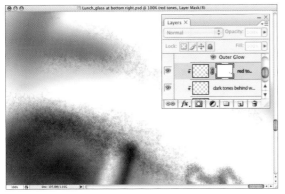

Figure 8.80 The layer mask for the red shape of the refracted straw.

Figure 8.81 The masked straw.

Tablecloth Through Glass

A distorted view of the tablecloth can also be seen through all the glasses on the table. To create this distortion, a small section of the tablecloth pattern was copied into a layer (**Figure 8.82**). Using the Warp command (**Figure 8.83**), the section of pattern was distorted in many directions, as shown in **Figure 8.84**.

The distorted tablecloth pattern was then blurred slightly using the Gaussian Blur filter (Filter > Blur > Gaussian Blur), as shown in **Figure 8.85**.

The final shape was then clipped by the base layer that contained the overall shape of the glass (**Figure 8.86**).

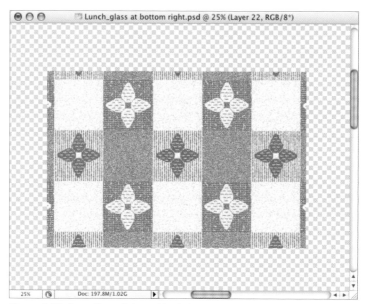

Figure 8.82 A section of the tablecloth pattern.

Figure 8.83 The Warp command.

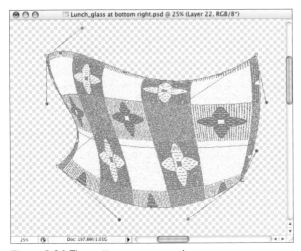

Figure 8.84 The pattern was warped.

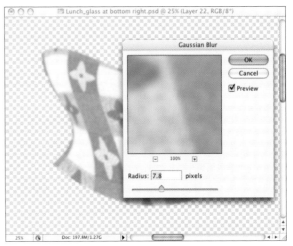

Figure 8.85 The warped pattern was blurred using the Gaussian Blur filter.

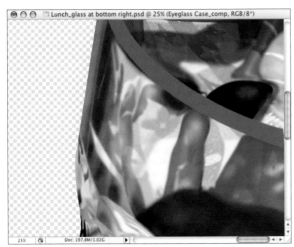

Figure 8.86 The final tablecloth seen through the edge of the glass.

The Fine Text

The labels on the mustard and vinegar bottles were created in Illustrator because the Text Tool in Photoshop has always been limited. The main reason for the limitation is that a pixel-based program is not where you create text. Headline text is fine. You can use Photoshop to create text that is on fire or made of ice. But for body copy, well, that kind of text is best done in applications like Illustrator or InDesign because they are designed for that.

Figure 8.87 shows the mustard bottle, and **Figure 8.88** shows the Illustrator document where the back of the label was generated. The larger label is the original. As previously stated, working larger makes it easy to get the detail. The text on the left has been resized to export to the Photoshop file.

In Photoshop the label was distorted using the Warp command (Edit > Transform > Warp).

Figure 8.87 The label on the mustard bottle.

Figure 8.88 The mustard bottle label in the Illustrator file.

Figure 8.89 The front of the mustard label in the Illustrator file.

Figure 8.89 shows the front of the mustard bottle. I only needed to create the part of the word that was visible. I did not use an actual font. The letters were created to match the font that appeared on the bottle. As with the back of the label, the front was exported into Photoshop and distorted with the Warp command.

The back of the vinegar bottle label was a bit more complex. Because it was seen through the edge of a drinking glass, it was heavily distorted (**Figure 8.90**). The label was created in Illustrator (**Figure 8.91**). All the same procedures that were used for the mustard label were used for this label as well, plus one added step. To get all those twists and smudges, the label was processed using the Liquify filter (Filter > Liquify). **Figure 8.92** shows the label being distorted in the filter.

Figure 8.90 The back of the vinegar bottle label.

Figure 8.91 The vinegar bottle label in the Illustrator file.

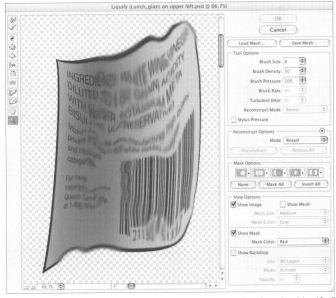

Figure 8.92 The vinegar bottle label was distorted using the Liquify filter.

Free-form Painting

Many of the details throughout the balance of the painting were created with free-form strokes of the Paintbrush Tool with different brush tips gliing over the Cintiq. Layer styles were applied to various strokes to add glows and such. **Figure 8.93** shows a detail of the glass on the lower left. **Figure 8.94** shows a detail of the glass on the lower right. **Figure 8.95** shows the bottom of the saltshaker. As you can see, all the details are rough brush strokes.

I'd like to share with you one last story about the creation of this piece. When I started doing research for the details, I could not find any reference for the vinegar bottle. I went to the Four Monks Web site, the manufacturer of the vinegar. Every label was different from what was in my original reference shot.

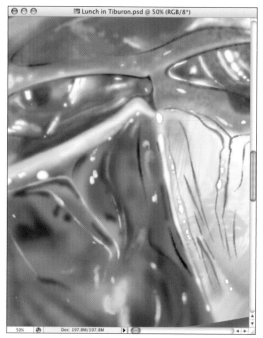

Figure 8.93 Detail of the edge of the glass on the lower left of the painting.

Figure 8.94 Detail of the bottom of the glass on the lower right of the painting.

Arne and I made a special boat trip back to Sam's to research the bottle. It was a great excuse for a day off! I asked for a vinegar bottle, but it was not the same bottle as the one at the lunch that prompted the painting. I showed the waitress the painting in progress. She brought the owner over to the table. He gave me the disappointing news that the labels had been changed quite a few months before. Unfortunately, the new design did not work as well with my composition. The back label had all the information at the top with no detail at the bottom. Needless to say, I had to make it up as best as I could, given the lack of detail in my original shot.

As I watched the first print come off my Epson 9800, all I could think about was the next challenge.

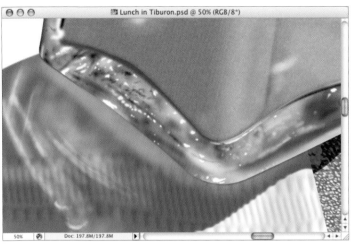

Figure 8.95 Detail of the bottom of the saltshaker in the painting.

Figure 9.1 "Damen"

9

Damen

The Greatest Challenge

"Damen" was the greatest challenge I ever encountered in my personal work (**Figure 9.1**). It went beyond the power and features found in Photoshop and Illustrator. It was a challenge on a personal level as well because it was a test of my patience and determination. To force myself to devote almost an entire year to one project was a task I was not prepared for. I never considered what effect time would have on me, or my work.

Time played a role in my commercial work in the form of deadlines. This was different—there was no deadline. There was only the monumental task of completing a painting that was not only complex in nature but also massive in scale.

As I stated in Chapter 1, I was thinking about panoramas when I started this project. It was also the first painting I created with the print in mind. The size was equal to four of my previous paintings.

I started the painting by completing the platform on the left (**Figure 9.2**). The amount of time that it took to complete that section of the image was longer than many of my other works. The sheer thought of what was left to do started to frustrate me. I began to grow impatient. I started thinking that if I completed the city in the background and the tracks on the side, I would consider it a finished work. I was ready for the next project. I was getting bored with this painting.

The thought came to me that perhaps if I worked on another section I might be able to continue. I started to work on the city (**Figure 9.3**). This would complete the image or set me on the road to do the rest.

Each building was painstakingly reproduced for accuracy. **Figure 9.4** shows the AT&T building in its own file. I treated each as a separate image, trying not to think of the overall panorama.

When the city was completed, I decided to make a bold move and start the platform on the right. **Figure 9.5** shows the shelter on the platform. **Figure 9.6** shows the platform plus the area below it. It was the completion of that part of the painting that gave me the desire to complete the panorama. The platform on the right gave the painting a border. It tied the whole piece together. It was the inspiration and motivation to see the entire project through to completion.

Figure 9.2 The completed platform on the left of the panorama.

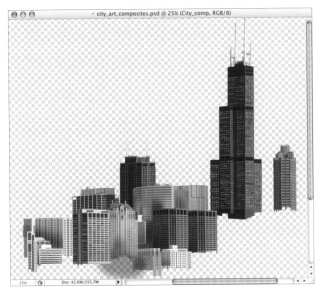
Figure 9.3 The skyline of downtown Chicago.

Figure 9.4 The AT&T building in its own file.

Figure 9.5 The shelter on the right platform.

Figure 9.6 The platform on the right and the area below it.

Individual Documents

Each element, like the trash can on the platform, was created in its own file. Upon completion of each element, it was exported to the composite file where the individual parts were assembled. Once all the elements were in place, the file was flattened and named "Damen_OnceOver." It is in this file that I scanned the image inch by inch looking for imperfections or additional details needed. I was not sure how much would be lost or gained in the print, so I spent a day with my friend Stephen Johnson so he could print out a test copy on his printer. It took four hours to print.

Returning to my studio, I tacked up the print. Needless to say it took up the entire back wall and covered all of my bookcases. I was then able to comb every inch of the print looking to see what had been lost. Every detail was there! I could actually add more. I sat at my machine and was ready to finalize the art!

When I unveiled the print at Photoshop World, I was amused to watch people's reactions. Here was this massive, ten-foot print, and people were standing six inches away looking at the tiniest of details.

Figure 9.7 The orange building in the center of the "Damen" painting.

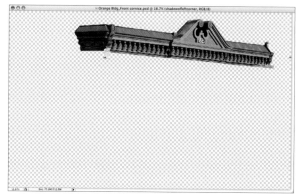

Figure 9.8 The first main file for the cornice at the top of the building.

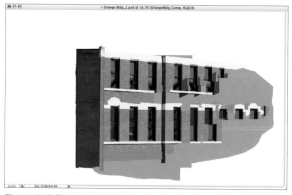

Figure 9.9 The second main file for the front facade.

15,000 Layers

One of the facts about "Damen" that caught worldwide attention was the claim that the painting was composed of over 15,000 layers. However, the 15,000 layers did not exist in a single file. All the individual objects in the painting were created in separate files. Each file contained all the layers, alpha channels, and paths that were necessary to create that particular piece of the overall painting. There were about 50 main element files and hundreds of subfiles. In reality, if you were to take into account all of the files and subfiles that were created for the image, the number would far surpass the stated quantity of 15,000 layers.

Files and Subfiles

To illustrate the concept of files and subfiles, let's look at the orange building that dominates the central portion of the painting (**Figure 9.7**). The building was made up of three main files. **Figure 9.8** shows the file for the cornice that runs along the top of the building. **Figure 9.9** shows the front façade of the building. **Figure 9.10** shows the side of the building. Multiple files were involved in their creation as well. **Figure 9.11** shows the brick texture that was created in a separate file. It will be discussed later in this chapter.

Figure 9.12 shows one of the subfiles—an Illustrator file for the floral design on the cornice. In **Figure 9.13** you can see the final design as it appeared in the Photoshop file.

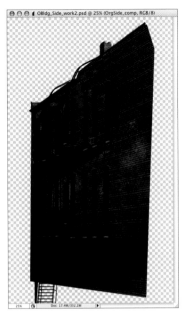

Figure 9.10 The third main file for the side of the building.

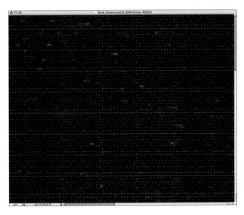

Figure 9.11 The brick texture in a separate file.

Figure 9.12 A subfile that was used to create one of the details for the painting.

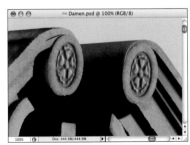

Figure 9.13 The subfile of the floret in the painting.

The Train

To give you an idea of how there could be so many layers, let's take a look at the layers that went into the creation of a single element within the painting. In **Figure 9.14** you can see the face of the train that is leaving the station. **Figure 9.15** shows the face of the train in its own document.

It is important to note that the reflections of the platforms visible in the front windows of the train (**Figure 9.16**) are not in the actual train document. Those details were added later, once the train was in position and I was able to decide what parts of the station would be viewed reflected in the glass

Figure 9.14 The train leaving the station.

Figure 9.15 The file containing the front face of the train.

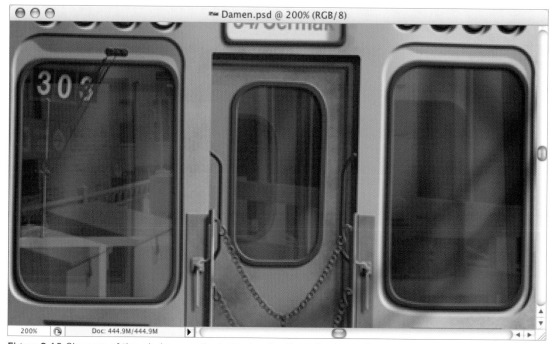

Figure 9.16 Close-up of the windows on the train showing the reflections of the station.

Organization

Figure 9.17 shows the Layers panel with all the individual layers that made up the face of the train. Note that every element is in its own layer. Also note that many of the layers contain layer styles and that many are contained within a Clipping Group. There are also many groups and subgroups of layers as indicated by the folders in the panel. Some of the groups have been assigned colors to make them more visible. Another important fact is that every layer is named. When you deal with that many layers, keeping them organized is crucial. Naming them and placing them within pertinent folders is a way to stay organized.

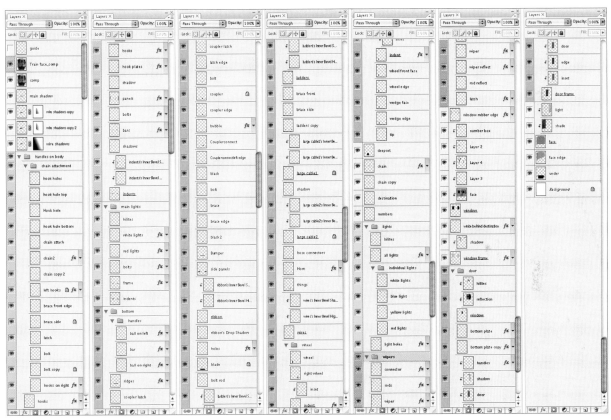

Figure 9.17 The Layers panel for the file of the face of the train.

Layer Styles

Throughout this book, you've seen that layer styles play an important role in the creation of my paintings. Looking at the Layers panels for the train, note that more than half of the layers have a layer style applied. Needless to say, I use them a lot.

Zooming into the window section of the train, you see a comparison in **Figure 9.18** of the effect of layer styles. On the left is the train window as it appears in the painting. On the right is the exact same window but with the layer styles turned off for all the layers. Note how flat everything becomes. As I mentioned in Chapter 2, highlights and shadows are what gives a two-dimensional image the appearance of the third dimension—depth.

One very important fact to keep in mind with layer styles is what they do to the image and where. Blend modes are available for the styles (**Figure 9.19**). You also have the ability to change their color. There are times when a slight modification to the default settings will make the style behave in extraordinary ways.

The Layers PDF file that you have probably downloaded by now has a more detailed description of the layers features. Download it at www.peachpit.com/digitalpainting.
PDF

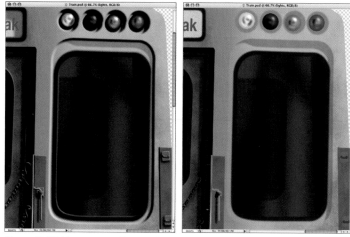

Figure 9.18 You can easily see the difference when comparing an image with layer styles applied (left) to one that has no layer styles (right).

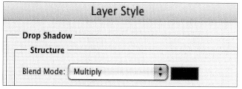

Figure 9.19 The mode and color of a layer style will afafect the result they produce.

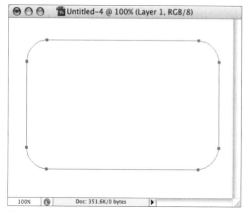

Figure 9.20 A path was created with the Pen Tool to serve as the shape of the window frame.

The Windows

Let's look at how layer styles created the third dimension in various parts of "Damen." The frames around the windows of the train are nothing more than basic, stroked lines. The addition of highlights and shadows made them pop from the surface. **Figure 9.20** shows a path for a simple window frame created with the Pen Tool. In **Figure 9.21** the path has been stroked in a layer with a hard-edged paintbrush using a dark gray color.

The Layer Style dialog box was called up by double-clicking the layer in the Layers panel. The first style I applied was the Drop Shadow (**Figure 9.22**). This made the frame appear to rise from the surface. The Drop Shadow has many controls, and most of the controls are obvious in what they do.

The Bevel and Emboss layer style (**Figure 9.23**) gave the frame the curvature it needed for the edges by adding a shadow along the inside edge and a highlight along the outside edge.

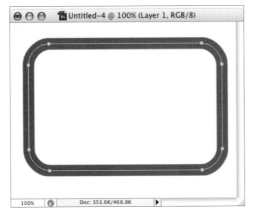

Figure 9.21 The path was stroked with a gray, hard-edged paintbrush.

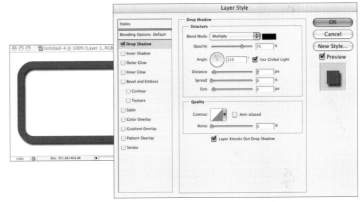

Figure 9.22 A Drop Shadow layer style was applied to the frame and added depth.

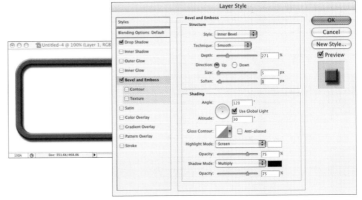

Figure 9.23 Bevel and Emboss made the frame appear to be thick and raised from the surface.

The Rivets

The rivets on the girders that appear on the platform (**Figure 9.24**) were created in a similar way to the windows with a slight addition.

Scratching the Surface

Before getting into creating the actual rivets, I'll first discuss the overall texture of the girders. Many of the surfaces in my paintings were created with a single filter—Texturizer.

Years of wear and tear over countless layers of paint have given the sufaces of the girders on the platform in "Damen" a bumpy quality. The texture started as a gradient applied in a layer, as shown in **Figure 9.25**. The Texturizer filter was applied to the layer (**Figure 9.26**). **Figure 9.27** shows the Texturizer filter dialog box. This filter has several textures that can be used. Sandstone is the one I use most often to create these types of textures. In Figure 9.27 you can see that I have chosen Sandstone for the Texture. I pushed the Scaling up quite a bit to enlarge the texture. I lowered the Relief to minimize the height of the texture. Relief, coupled with the direction of the Light source will elevate or lower the texture, making it rough or smooth.

Figure 9.24 The rivets that appear over the girders on the platform.

Figure 9.25 A simple color gradient for the girders.

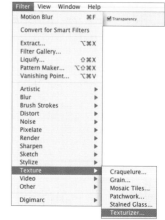

Figure 9.26 The texturizer filter on the Filter menu.

Figure 9.28 shows the result of the filter. **Figure 9.29** shows another instance where Texturizer was used to create the texture on the roof over the platform on the right.

In **Figure 9.30** you can see Texturizer used in the same area with two different settings. The basic setting gave me the texture. Selecting specific areas with a feathered selection allowed me to create the extra damages that appear on the pole and the wall in back. In the selected areas the Texturizer filter was applied with a higher Relief. The feathering made a seamless transition from one texture to the other.

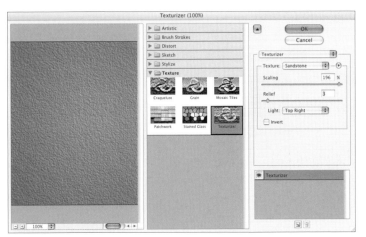

Figure 9.27 The Texturizer filter dialog box.

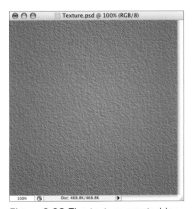

Figure 9.28 The texture created by the Texturizer filter.

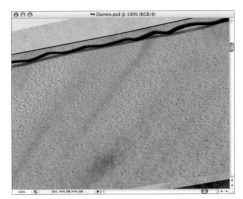

Figure 9.29 The texture appears in other parts of the painting. Here it is on the roof of the platform shelter.

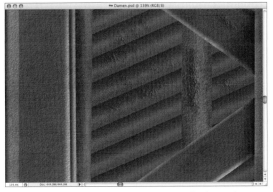

Figure 9.30 The same texture was applied to other parts of the walls. The additional damage was created using the same filter applied with different settings through feathered selections.

Back to the Rivets

In a separate layer to contain the rivets, a circular selection was made and filled with a color, as shown in **Figure 9.31**. It does not matter what color is used because it will not be seen. In the Blending Options section of the Layer Style dialog box, I lowered the Fill Opacity to zero (**Figure 9.32**).

Next, I applied the Drop Shadow, as shown in **Figure 9.33**. The angle was changed for the Light source. The light comes from below right because it is the sunlight that is being reflected off the platform.

As with the window frame, I then applied Bevel and Emboss (**Figure 9.34**). In this case the color of the Highlight was changed to a beige color to closely match the color of the paint on the girders.

One final touch was needed and that was to make the rivet appear as if it was coated with layer upon layer of paint. To achieve this effect, I simply blurred the layer using the Gaussian Blur filter (Filter > Blur > Gaussian Blur), as shown in **Figure 9.35**.

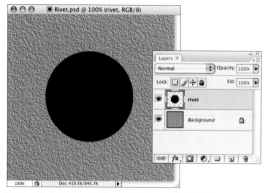

Figure 9.31 The rivets started as filled circles in a layer.

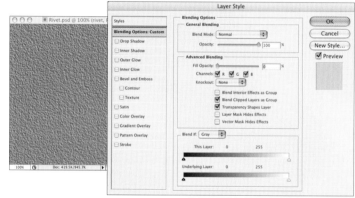

Figure 9.32 In the Blending Options section of the Layer Styles dialog box, the Fill Opacity was reduced to zero, making the black circle invisible.

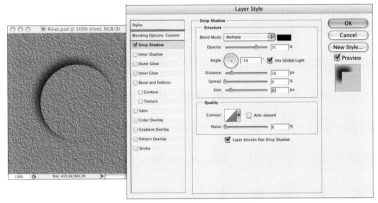

Figure 9.33 A Drop Shadow was applied to the circle.

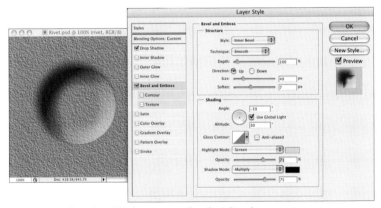

Figure 9.34 Bevel and Emboss gave the rivet its shape.

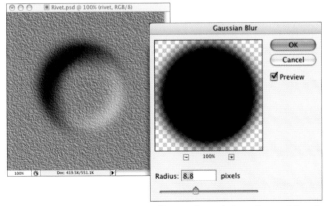

Figure 9.35 The Gaussian Blur filter softened the edges of the rivet, making it look like it was covered with years of paint.

Rusty Railings

Bevel and Emboss was also used to create the rust visible on the railings shown in the close-up in **Figure 9.36**. In a layer I used a Spatter brush that was modified to create rust spots (**Figure 9.37**). (This brush technique was used to create the rust in Chapter 4, "Shoe Repair.") What makes the rust different in this painting is the addition of Bevel and Emboss, which made the rust look like it had eaten through the paint, as shown in **Figure 9.38**.

Figure 9.36 The railings on the platform are old and rusty.

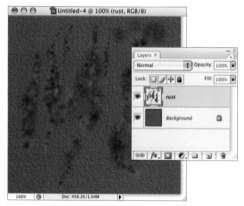

Figure 9.37 Tones were created to simulate rust by using a modified paintbrush.

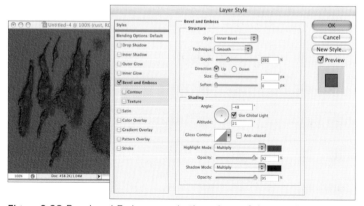

Figure 9.38 Bevel and Emboss made the edges of the rust look deep— as if the outer paint had been eaten away.

Dirt and Grime

Since I touched on brushes in the previous example, let's dig deeper into their use in other parts of "Damen."

Figures 9.39 and **9.40** show close-ups of details where there is considerable dirt and grime on the surfaces of the station platform. For these textures I used one of the Spatter brushes in Photoshop (**Figure 9.41**). I added some spacing to the stroke. Having a specific set of dots in the tip makes it appear to have a pattern when Spacing is increased, as indicated in the preview box (**Figure 9.42**). Playing with the Size and Angles for the tips (**Figure 9.43**), the pattern is eliminated, leaving behind a stroke that resembles the dirt I wanted to apply to the platform.

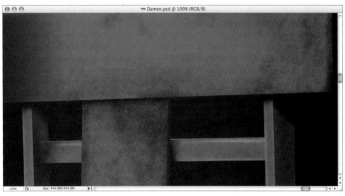

Figure 9.39 Dirt and grime on the structure of the platform.

Figure 9.40 Dirt and grime on the sign below the platform.

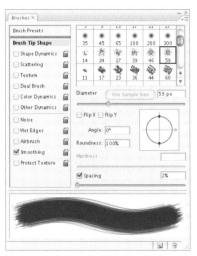

Figure 9.41 The Spatter brush tip was selected in the Brushes panel.

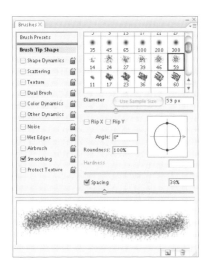

Figure 9.42 When Spacing is increased for the Spatter brush tip, it creates a pattern.

Figure 9.43 Altering the settings added the randomness needed for the effect of the dirt and grime.

Trees

Another example of a custom brush is the one I created for the trees visible in the distance beyond the platform (**Figure 9.44**). The leaves started as a simple shape created with a rounded brush (**Figure 9.45**). Besides the various Shape Dynamics (as you saw in the previous examples), Scattering was applied to the brush (**Figure 9.46**) to give the brush tip additional randomness.

Color Dynamics played a crucial role in creating the trees. Assigning differing shades of green to each tip made the trees seem more realistic. In **Figure 9.47** you can see a stroke applied where the Foreground color is a bright green and the Background color is a dark green. By shifting the Hue and Saturation sliders slightly, a variety of additional shades of green appear for individual brush tips.

Figure 9.48 shows one of the trees in the original working file with all the layers that made up that tree.

Figure 9.44 The trees at the far end of the platform.

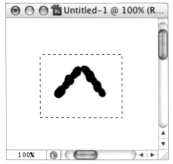

Figure 9.45 The brush starts as a simple shape to represent two hanging leaves.

Figure 9.46 Scattering plus other Dynamics made the strokes totally random in nature.

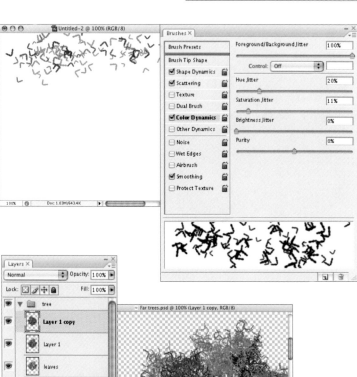

Figure 9.47 A stroke applied with two shades of green varies widely due to the adjustments in the Brushes panel.

Figure 9.48 The trees in the original file showing all the layers.

Patterns

A pattern is usually used to fill large areas with a repeating motif. Patterns have many uses. In this section you will learn about the role patterns played in the creation of "Damen."

Figure 9.49 shows the brick wall on the side of the orange building in the scene. I have outlined the creation of a brick wall in other books and videos, but this one is a bit different.

The difference in the brick wall on the building in "Damen" is that this wall has been ravished over time. The severe weather conditions of Chicago, coupled with a continuous rattle of trains next door, have reshaped the bricks into crumpled reflections of their former appearance.

To get this effect, it was necessary to make every brick look different from the others around it. I started with four differently shaped bricks (**Figure 9.50**). These four bricks were duplicated, repositioned, and rotated 180° (**Figure 9.51**). The building has a façade that consists of six rows of bricks with rows of half bricks in between. Additional bricks were added and modified. I created the basis for the pattern with a complete section of bricks, as shown in **Figure 9.52**.

Figure 9.49 The brick wall on the side of the orange building.

By looking at the basic pattern with the grid on, I made sure that I had half the grout area on either side of the half bricks at the top, as indicated by the arrows at the top of **Figure 9.53**. I also matched half the grout at the top of the half bricks on top and the full bricks at the bottom. This guaranteed that I would get an invisible seam where the pattern repeated. Likewise, I made sure I had full bricks cut precisely so they would repeat as full bricks, as indicated by the arrows at the bottom of Figure 9.53.

I then defined the pattern (**Figure 9.54**).

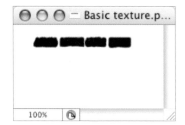

Figure **9.50** The pattern started with four distinct brick shapes.

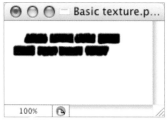

Figure **9.51** The four bricks were duplicated, repositioned, and rotated to make them appear different from the original four.

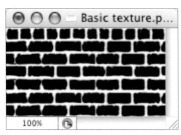

Figure **9.52** The bricks for the pattern were completed.

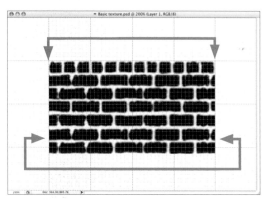

Figure **9.53** The bricks were adjusted so they would step and repeat properly, thus creating a seamless pattern.

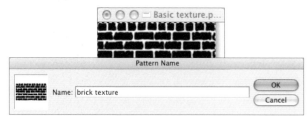

Figure **9.54** The brick pattern was defined.

I created a new file with a very large canvas size. I filled a separate layer with the pattern shown in **Figure 9.55**. I needed plenty of wall space to cover the entire building at the proper scale.

Then came the tedious part of creating further damage to the individual bricks. I zoomed into the texture to get a close look at a section of bricks. With the Dodge and Burn Tools I lightened and darkened bricks randomly, as shown in **Figure 9.56**. As I completed one section, I scrolled down to the next. Upon reaching the bottom I scrolled to the right and continued upward. Needless to say this took some time. This is one of the many reasons "Damen" took 11 months to complete.

I employed layer styles to give the bricks dimension. Drop Shadow (**Figure 9.57**) pulled the bricks out of the wall. Inner Shadow gave the bricks an edge. Note in **Figure 9.58** that Use Global Light is turned off. This gave me control over where the darkness of the edge would affect the bricks without affecting the drop shadow.

I filled the Background layer with an appropriate color for the grout and gave it some noise (**Figure 9.59**).

Figure 9.60 shows the completed wall texture. **Figure 9.61** zooms out to show about a third of the total wall texture.

In **Figure 9.62** you can see the wall after it has been distorted. Additional wear and tear was added once the wall was in place. **Figure 9.63** shows the completed wall on the side of the building.

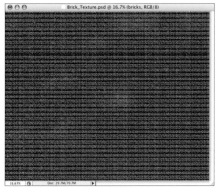

Figure 9.55 In a file with a canvas size large enough to contain the wall, the brick pattern was filled in a separate layer.

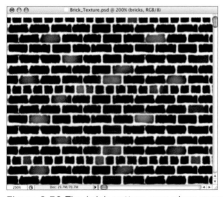

Figure 9.56 The brick pattern was given more randomness with the Dodge and Burn Tools.

Figure 9.57 To give the bricks a three-dimensional look, a Drop Shadow layer style was applied.

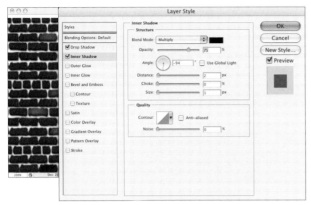

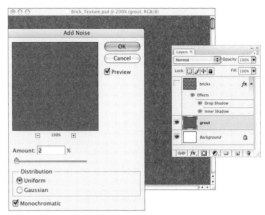

Figure 9.58 The shape of the bricks was further distorted with the Inner Shadow layer style. Use Global Light was turned off to control the Inner Shadow independently of the Drop Shadow.

Figure 9.59 The grout was created in a new layer.

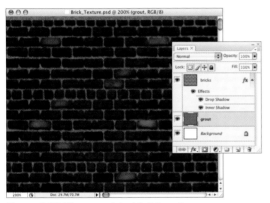

Figure 9.60 The completed brick pattern.

Figure 9.61 The completed brick wall.

Figure 9.62 Additional wear and tear was added to the brick once it was in place.

Figure 9.63 The finished brick wall.

Repurposing Layers

The brick pattern is a perfect example of reusing elements created in layers. Creating the complex brick wall was very labor-intensive. Why do it twice?

In the Layers PDF file I talk about re-using elements that have been created. Download it at www.peachpit.com/digitalpainting.

PDF

Since the bricks and grout were in separate layers it was very easy to change their colors and any layer styles that were applied. Doing exactly that, I repurposed the wall for another building in the scene. The only necessary modification besides the color shifts was to scale down the pattern in size. **Figure 9.64** shows one of the buildings in the Chicago skyline in the distance—same bricks, different colors.

The additional train cars are another example of the reuse of elements. **Figure 9.65** shows the original file containing the side of the train car. Since every element was in its own layer it was easy to make each car appear different. The reflections in the windows were changed. The dirt on the walls of the car was changed. The numbers on the cars were changed. Everything else was the same. The only additional change was to slightly rotate each car to make the train look as if it is traveling along a downward curve. In **Figure 9.66** you can see the three train cars made from one original.

Figure 9.64 The finished brick wall was colorized and reduced in size to make up the façade of another building.

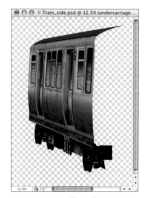

Figure 9.65 The finished side of the train car.

Figure 9.66 The additional train cars were made by duplicating the original train car and changing certain layers.

The Illustrator Connection

Throughout this book I've mentioned that Adobe Illustrator always plays a strong role in the creation of my work because some tools in Illustrator do not exist in Photoshop. I'll show you three of those tools and how they were crucial in the creation of "Damen."

The Blend Tool

The Blend Tool is a very useful feature in Illustrator that I use often. It interpolates or morphs two objects. The tool creates and distributes shapes evenly between the two objects, blending their shape, fill color, and stroke weight and color. The Blend Tool simplifies many of the tasks that would normally require a lot of calculating and experimentation.

Figure 9.67 shows a close-up of the trash receptacle on the platform.

> **NOTE:** If a shape is made up of multiple objects, the objects must be grouped (Object > Group) for all of them to be blended together. If they are not grouped, you must perform the blend for each object. If the amount of blend steps and position of the starting and ending objects are the same, all subsequent steps generated by the blend will be in register with each other.

Figure 9.67 The trash can on the platform.

The many slats that make up the sides were created using the Blend Tool that exists in Illustrator but is missing from Photoshop. **Figure 9.68** shows the center slat and the slat on the outer edge. The center slat is straight on from the viewer's perspective. The outer slat is viewed at an angle and shows the rounded edge at the top. This rounded edge needs to become less visible as it travels around the rim of the can.

Figure 9.69 shows the Blend Options dialog box for the Blend Tool where the desired amount of steps has been entered using the Specified Steps option found under Spacing.

I then clicked the upper-left anchor point of the slat on the left and the upper-left anchor point of the slat on the right. The result was the creation of all the slats in between, as shown in **Figure 9.70**.

> **NOTE:** It is crucial to use the same relative anchor point on each object if the objects are the same shape or a close approximation of relative anchor points if objects are not the same shape (for example, from the leftmost top edge of the starting object to the leftmost top edge of the ending object). If you do not select relative points, the result will be quite different from what you might expect.

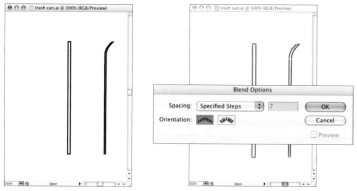

Figure 9.68 The two outer slats were created in Illustrator.

Figure 9.69 The Blend Options dialog box for the Blend Tool.

Figure 9.70 The additional in-between slats were generated with the Blend Tool.

Figure 9.71 The Expand command.

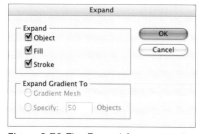

Figure 9.72 The Expand feature settings.

When the blend is completed, the resulting objects are grouped with the originals and can't be accessed individually. Note the appearance of the objects in Figure 9.70. The two outer objects are selected, but those in between appear within a horizontal line connecting the two outer shapes. To be able to select specific slats, it was necessary to Expand (Object > Expand) the object (**Figure 9.71**). In the Expand dialog box that popped up I specified which attributes would be kept (**Figure 9.72**). The result was nine individual slats.

Creating the opposite side was a simple matter of copying and flipping. All the objects were selected with the exception of the center slat. Selecting the Reflect Tool, I placed the cursor at the center slat to establish the point from which the reflection would be generated. I then clicked while pressing the Option (Alt) key to bring up the options for the Reflect Tool (**Figure 9.73**). With the Vertical option selected I clicked the Copy button. This made a copy of the slats to the left of the center slat, completing the trash can, as shown in **Figure 9.74**.

A few additional vectors (paths) were generated to represent the horizontal plates and top of the trash can (**Figure 9.75**). These vectors were then exported to Photoshop where they were used to make selections that were filled with colors and textures.

Figure 9.73 The Reflect options dialog box.

Figure 9.74 The additional slats on the left side of the trash can.

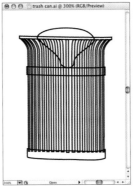

Figure 9.75 The completed vectors that were exported to Photoshop.

The Railings

The Blend Tool was also instrumental in creating the railings that border the structures on the platform (**Figure 9.76**). The decorative arches that line the tops of the railings started as a single shape in Illustrator. The shape was duplicated and scaled down in size to create the illusion of depth, as shown in **Figure 9.77**. The Blend Tool then created all the in-between arches, as shown in **Figure 9.78**.

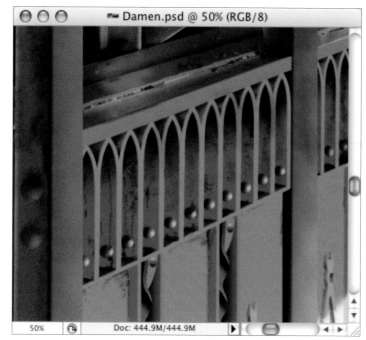

Figure 9.76 The railings on the platform.

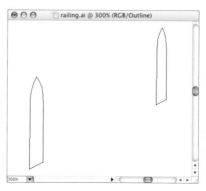

Figure 9.77 The arches started as simple shapes in Illustrator.

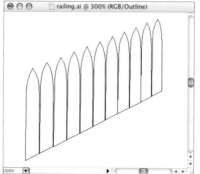

Figure 9.78 Additional arches were generated with the Blend Tool.

The Springs

The third example of using the Blend Tool in "Damen" is the set of tiny springs that are hardly visible under the train (**Figure 9.79**). A line was generated and stroked with a gray color and rounded end tips to represent a coil in the spring. The line was duplicated below the original to represent the bottom of the spring, as shown in **Figure 9.80**. Using the Blend Tool, the two lines were blended to form the interim coils (**Figure 9.81**).

To create the back portion of the spring, the layer with the gray lines was duplicated and placed in back of the original. The duplicate was flipped horizontally, and the stroke color was changed to black (**Figure 9.82**). The result was the spring you see in **Figure 9.83**.

Figure 9.79 The tiny spring is visible behind the ladder under the train car.

Figure 9.80 A line was generated and duplicated below the original.

Figure 9.81 The additional coils for the spring were generated with the Blend Tool.

Figure 9.82 The coils were duplicated, flipped, and colored black.

Figure 9.83 The final spring.

Transform Again

Another feature of Illustrator that is lacking in Photoshop is Transform Again. In Chapter 7, "Oyster Bar," I mentioned this feature in the creation of the manhole cover. In "Damen" it is used in a different situation.

Multiple Windows

The Civic Opera House that is a part of the visible Chicago skyline has many windows, as you can see in **Figure 9.84**.

To create all those windows, I only needed to create one (**Figure 9.85**). The window was made up of multiple shapes, so I selected all of them and grouped them (Object > Group). I then duplicated the window over to the right, as shown in **Figure 9.86**.

> **NOTE:** In Figure 9.84 you can see a tiny outline of the building shape to the left of the actual building. That tiny shape is the final size that was needed for the Photoshop document. In the Illustrator document the details were created in an enlarged size and later reduced in size for export to Photoshop.

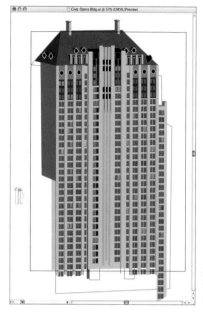

Figure 9.84 The drawing of the Civic Opera House in Illustrator.

Figure 9.85 The drawing for a single window of the Civic Opera House in Illustrator.

Figure 9.86 The window was duplicated to the right of the original.

The two windows were duplicated directly below (**Figure 9.87**). Using the Transform Again feature a few times (Command-D/Ctrl-D), many copies of the two windows were created (**Figure 9.88**).

To add randomness to the windows, individual panes of glass were selected with the Direct Selection Tool and assigned different colors, as shown in **Figure 9.89**.

Multiple Conductors

A similar process was used for generating multiple shapes like those shown in **Figure 9.90**. These shapes are the conductors that appear in various places along the power lines visible in **Figure 9.91**.

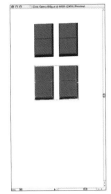

Figure 9.87 The two windows were duplicated below the originals.

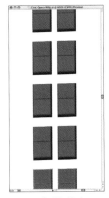

Figure 9.88 Using the Transform Again feature in Illustrator, multiple copies were made of the windows.

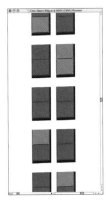

Figure 9.89 Individual window panes were recolorized.

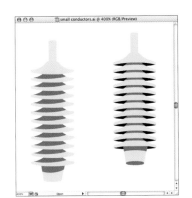

Figure 9.90 The electrical conductors in Illustrator.

Figure 9.91 The electrical conductors in the painting.

Advanced Text Features

The Blend Tool and Transform Again function coupled with the advanced text features found in Illustrator made the creation of the various signs throughout the image a breeze to create.

The hazard sign shown in **Figure 9.92** has repeating shapes, like the stripes along the sides. It also has some symbols that are simple, hard-edged shapes. **Figure 9.93** shows the Illustrator file where the basic elements for the sign were generated and then reduced to two different sizes needed for the final image.

Because they are vectors in Illustrator, resizing has no damaging effect on the objects. When they were imported into the Photoshop document, they rasterized to the resolution of the Photoshop file.

The recycle sign shown in **Figure 9.94**, the two signs in **Figure 9.95**, plus the sign in **Figure 9.96** were all done in Illustrator. **Figure 9.97** shows the single Illustrator file that contained all the signs. Shadows, dirt, and the necessary distortions for perspective were all carried out in the Photoshop file.

Figure 9.92 The hazard sign over the tracks.

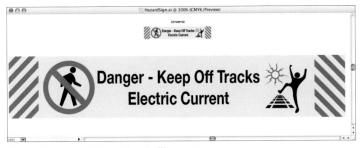

Figure 9.93 The hazard sign in Illustrator.

Figure 9.94 The recycle sign in the painting.

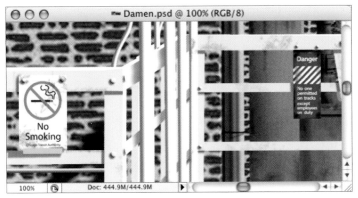

Figure 9.95 Two more hazard signs in the painting.

Figure 9.96 The rider information sign in the painting.

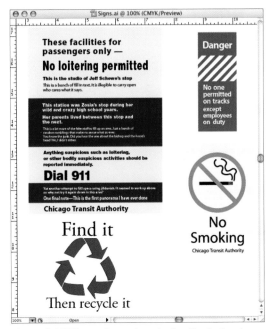

Figure 9.97 The various signs in the Illustrator document.

The Clipping Group

Every feature that Photoshop has to offer was put to use in the creation of "Damen." The Layer Clipping Group that I've discussed in other chapters in this book was employed hundreds of times in this painting.

The small portion of the Layers panel for the face of the train (**Figure 9.98**), outlined at the beginning of this chapter, shows four Clipping Groups out of the many that made up this element. **Figure 9.99** shows the windows with all the layers that are clipped by the shape of the windows. **Figure 9.100** shows all the layers without the clipping mask.

Figure 9.101 shows one of the windows in the orange building. **Figure 9.102** shows the various layers unclipped. **Figure 9.103** shows the shelter on the platform. **Figure 9.104** shows the textures for the metal unclipped.

"Damen" was a real test of my knowledge of the features in Illustrator and Photoshop, and it forced me to use them all.

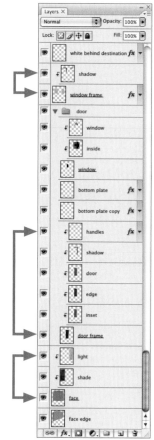

Figure 9.98 A small section of the Layers panel for the face of the train.

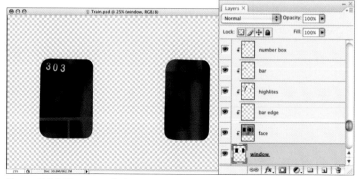

Figure 9.99 The two windows on the front of the train with all the layers clipped.

Figure 9.100 The two windows on the front of the train with all the layers unclipped.

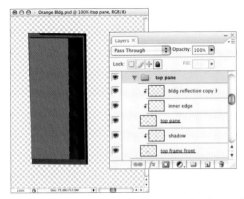

Figure 9.101 One of the windows on the front of the orange building with all the layers clipped.

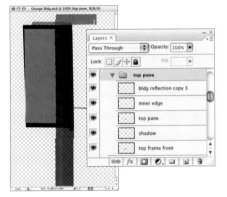

Figure 9.102 The window of the orange building with all the layers unclipped.

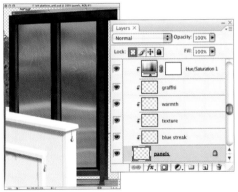

Figure 9.103 The shelter on the platform with all the layers clipped.

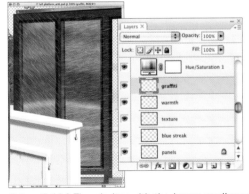

Figure 9.104 The shelter with the layers unclipped.

The Vanishing Point

One of the coolest features introduced to the CS product line was the Vanishing Point filter (**Figure 9.105**). With its introduction, the third dimension came to life. Not that Photoshop became a 3D application. In fact, the inclusion of a 3D Layer in CS3 does not mean you can create 3D objects. It means you can import 3D objects from 3D applications and move them around in 3D space, but the rest of Photoshop is still two dimensional.

Vanishing Point lets you establish the vanishing point of an image and then move objects within that 3D space. It does not add sides to an object, but it will distort that object to conform to the angles of the vanishing lines. In Chapter 1, I provided an explanation of the concepts behind 3D space and vanishing lines. Now I'll show you how I used Vanishing Point in the creation of the platform.

> I provide more detail on the Vanishing Point filter in the Filters PDF file, which you can download at www.peachpit.com/digitalpainting.
>
> **PDF**

Figure 9.106 shows the platform on which the viewer is standing in the painting "Damen." Before I get into using Vanishing Point, let's review part of the creation of the texture that will

Figure 9.105 The Vanishing Point filter.

Figure 9.106 The platform on the left of the painting "Damen."

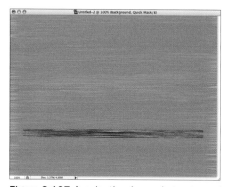

Figure 9.107 A selection is made to generate a single plank of wood.

eventually be distorted in 3D space. The texture consisted of the wooden planks that form the platform. (I cover creating wood in Chapter 7.) Just like the planks that made up the façade of the "Oyster Bar," the individual planks for the platform were selected from a layer that contained the overall wooden texture (**Figure 9.107**). You see the selected area as a Quick Mask.

Selecting from different areas each time a plank was created made each plank look different from its neighbor, as shown in **Figure 9.108**.

Once I had the wood I could make the platform. **Figure 9.109** shows the array of final wooden planks that made up the platform.

In **Figure 9.110** you can see the perspective guides for where the platform was eventually placed in the scene.

In **Figure 9.111** black lines have been drawn to outline the actual platform area.

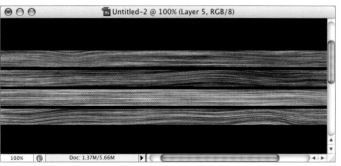

Figure 9.108 Three planks of wood that appear to be cut from different sources.

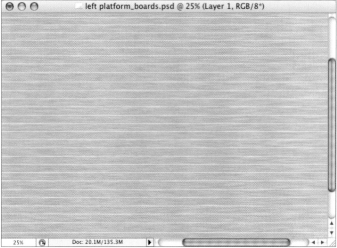

Figure 9.109 The planks of wood for the platform in "Damen."

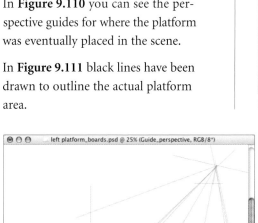

Figure 9.110 The perspective guides for the platform.

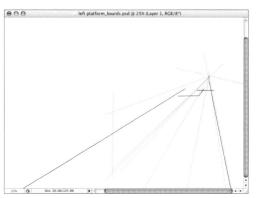

Figure 9.111 The guide for the actual platform generated over the perspective guides.

The layer with the planks was made active, and I then chose Edit > Transform > Distort (**Figure 9.112**).

The layer with the wooden planks was distorted to fit the shape of the platform, as shown in **Figure 9.113**.

It would have been easy to simply select the area of the wood, copy it, reduce the size, and place it farther back in space. However, by doing it this way, the detail of the grain started to blur as it got smaller and smaller with each distortion and copy. The beauty of Vanishing Point is that it gave me the ability to copy the planks as far back as I wanted without losing detail.

I called up the Vanishing Point filter. The first tool available, besides the view tools, is the Create Plane Tool. With this tool you can trace an existing perspective plane in your image. In "Damen" I traced the black, lined guide that denoted the shape of the platform. **Figure 9.114** shows the tool being dragged along the right side of the guide. A blue line displays the grid that is created, and the cursor becomes a target box.

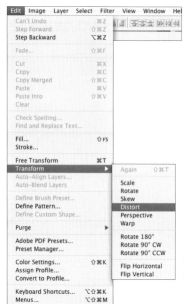

Figure 9.112 The Distort feature (Edit > Transform > Distort).

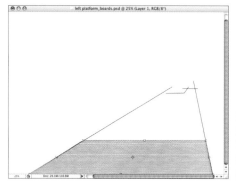

Figure 9.113 The planks for the platform were distorted to fit the contour of the platform shape.

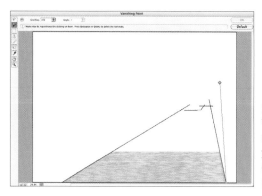

Figure 9.114 The Vanishing Point dialog box where you can see one of the sides of the plane being created.

Each time you click at a specific point, a new line pulls out to follow the next edge, as shown in **Figure 9.115**.

When you have completely surrounded a shape, a blue grid appears, like the one shown in **Figure 9.116**. If you see a red outline, like the one in **Figure 9.117**, you have created a shape that defies the laws of perspective. Remember the lesson in Chapter 1: Perspective is part of nature, and you shouldn't fool with nature.

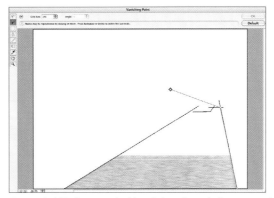

Figure 9.115 A second side of the plane being created.

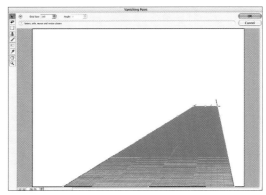

Figure 9.116 The Vanishing Point grid that denotes a perspective plane.

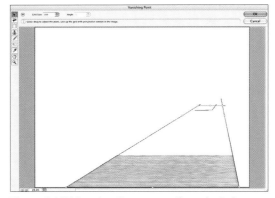

Figure 9.117 A red outline means the selected area defies true perspective.

Switching to the Marquee Tool in the Vanishing Point filter's dialog box, I was ready to select the planks to duplicate them in 3D space. Note in **Figure 9.118** that since I was selecting within a perspective plane the marquee was conforming to the shape of that plane.

Pressing the Option (Alt) key to make a copy, the platform was duplicated and shifted back along the expanse of the platform (**Figure 9.119**).

To save time, when I had gotten about halfway to the rear, I reselected the entire area (**Figure 9.120**) and duplicated it. When the job was complete, I clicked OK. The completed platform is shown in **Figure 9.121**.

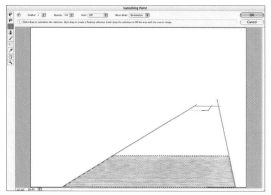

Figure 9.118 The area of the wooden planks was selected within the perspective plane.

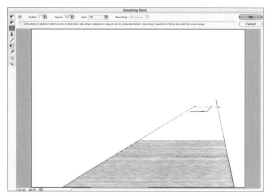

Figure 9.119 The selected area was duplicated within the perspective plane.

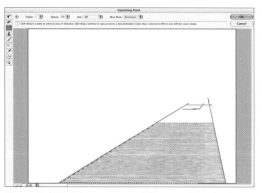

Figure 9.120 A larger area of the wooden planks is selected within the perspective plane.

Eleven months worth of hard work! The end result became an international hit that was written up in many magazine articles around the world. Would I do it again? Will I ever take on a challenge like this in the future? I guess I must be a glutton for punishment because upon completion of this book I plan to embark on the journey of a lifetime. I've been planning a painting that will make "Damen" seem like child's play.

I estimate that the next painting will take over two years to create. Let's see if I make it. In the meantime, take all that I have taught you in these pages and put it to use. To make sure you understand all the techniques I have passed on to you, the next and final chapter turns the tables and asks you to do the work.

Have fun and remember, don't think of it as work, think of it as play. The best way to learn Photoshop is to sit there and play!

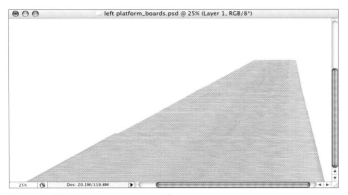

Figure 9.121 The completed platform.

Figure 10.0 "Your Art Goes Here"

Tutorials

Your Turn

So now that you have read the book, where do you go from here?

Throughout the book I have outlined many different techniques. In many cases I demonstrated the same technique but used it in different situations. I also stated a few times that it is not the end result that counts but learning how to get there. Once techniques are mastered, applying a slight alteration to a step will have a dramatically different effect. For example, just by using a different color, the same technique will solve a different problem.

In this last chapter I provide you with some hands-on experience, so you'll not only read about how I did something but you will do something.

This chapter contains a series of tutorials that you can follow. Some of the tutorials are complex, others very simple. A couple of them are provided by request. People have repeatedly asked me to put these particular tutorials in print. All of the tutorials are designed to let you explore many of the techniques I have outlined in this book.

I encourage you to use your own images wherever possible. But if you do use the images I have supplied, redo the exercise and give it a twist here and there to see what happens. Happy accidents are waiting to be found.

Fun with Layers

To make sure you have a good understanding of what layers can do, let's do a short exercise that demonstrates the many uses of layers that were outlined in this book.

You can open an image of your own. Any image will do. You might want to get very creative here, so before you choose your image, let me explain what you'll be doing. You'll create a headline with some special effects and a picture inside the text.

I'll use the image PSBM_damen.jpg (**Figure 10.1**) and work within the current size of the document. All the settings provided in the tutorial work within these dimensions. You can resize the image to the size you want by choosing Image > Image Size. If you resize it, you must adjust all the other settings accordingly.

Figure 10.1 The painting "Damen" in the file PSBM_damen.jpg.

1. Create a new document. If you are using the PSBM_damen.jpg file, set your parameters to match those in **Figure 10.2** (800 pixels wide by 266 high at 72 ppi will match the size of the PSBM_damen.jpg file). You can also select the image (Select > Select All) and copy it (Edit > Copy). This automatically sets the parameters of the file in the New dialog box.

If you are using a file of your own, you can set whatever parameters you want. Keep in mind that this is just an exercise, so don't create massive files that are ready to go on press. You don't want to sit there and watch progress bars crawling across your screen.

2. In the new document, type in the text you want for your headline. Choose a heavyweight font. A heavyweight font makes it easy to see the image that will be clipped into it. My example uses Helvetica Black at 80 points (**Figure 10.3**).

3. Using the Scale tool (Edit > Transform > Scale), as shown in **Figure 10.4**, resize the headline to fill up the space (**Figure 10.5**).

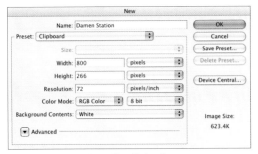

Figure 10.2 The New file dialog box.

Figure 10.3 The text in a layer.

Figure 10.4 The Scale command.

Figure 10.5 The text being scaled.

4. To colorize the text, double-click the text icon in the Layers panel (**Figure 10.6**).

With the text selected, change the color by clicking on the color box in the text options bar (**Figure 10.7**). Pick a blue that is suitable to you (**Figure 10.8**). The color of the text should now be blue like the sample in **Figure 10.9**.

5. Using the Move Tool, drag the image of "Damen" or your own file into the file with the text. Press the Shift key to center the image in the document window. It will automatically fall into its own layer (**Figure 10.10**).

Figure **10.6** Double-click the text icon in the Layers panel.

Figure **10.7** The text color box in the options bar.

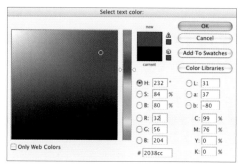

Figure **10.8** The Select text color dialog box.

Figure **10.9** The text color changed to blue.

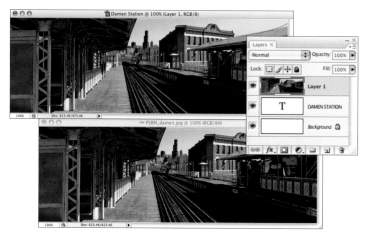

Figure **10.10** The image is dragged into the text document.

6. Create a Clipping Group with the text by Option-clicking (Alt-clicking) between the two layers in the Layers panel. Note that as you pass the cursor over the layers in the Layers panel with the Option (Alt) key pressed, the cursor changes shape as it crosses over the line between the two layers. Without pressing the Option (Alt) key, the cursor remains the same—a pointing-hand icon. **Figure 10.11** shows the picture being clipped by the text.

Figure 10.11 The image is clipped by the text layer.

You want the blue of the text to fade in from the bottom of the text. To get this effect, you'll create a layer mask for the layer with the image. Applying the proper mask to the image allows the blue text underneath to show through precisely where you want it.

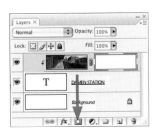

Figure 10.12 The image layer is given a layer mask by clicking on the Add layer mask icon in the Layers panel.

7. Select the layer of the image and either click the Add layer mask icon at the bottom of the panel (**Figure 10.12**) or choose the option from the menu (**Figure 10.13**).

Figure 10.13 The layer mask can also be added from the menu.

8. With the Gradient Tool set to a Linear Gradient and using black as the Foreground color and white for the Background color, draw a gradient from about a quarter inch from the bottom to about a quarter inch from the top of the image, as shown in **Figure 10.14**. In the figure you can see the gradient in the mask icon for the layer in the Layers panel.

9. Double-click on the text layer to bring up the Layer Style dialog box. Make sure you are targeting the text layer, not the image layer.

10. Add a Drop Shadow. Play with the settings as I have in **Figure 10.15**. Your settings may vary depending on how you want the image to look and the shape of your text.

11. Add a Bevel and Emboss. In **Figure 10.16** you can see that I have set the Technique to Chisel Hard. This makes the bevels on the edges very sharp. I also pushed the Depth a bit to make the tones stronger, and I increased the Opacity for the Highlight to 100%. I reduced the Size to 3.

Figure 10.14 A gradient is applied to the image layer, exposing the blue text underneath.

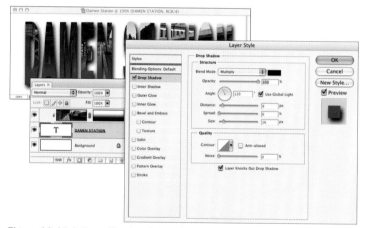

Figure 10.15 A Drop Shadow is applied to the text layer.

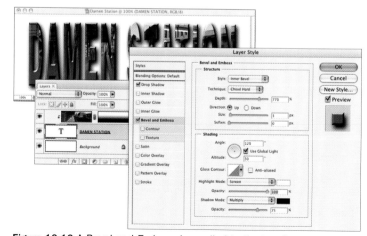

Figure 10.16 A Bevel and Emboss is applied to the text layer.

12. Finally, add a Stroke (**Figure 10.17**). Choose a color and thickness that satisfies your taste and works best with your particular image. **Figure 10.18** shows the final image.

In this exercise, I've shown you some very important features of layers. You used layer masks, clipping groups, and layer styles to create the final image. Use them. Play with the different settings and see what happens. Many more features are available to you—Adjustment layers, for example—that you can experiment with to expand your Photoshop wizardry. Play with layers. Learn them.

Creating Shadows

In Chapter 2 you learned about lights and shadows. In the subsequent chapters you saw how shadows played a key role in creating drama and dimension to the images. Taking into account what has been discussed so far, in the next exercise you'll use layers and create a shadow—not just any shadow but a complex shadow. A shadow that travels over opposing surfaces.

Figure 10.19 shows a tree standing a few yards away from a wall. You will create the shadow that this tree will cast. You can create your own tree and wall or download the image for this exercise.

Download the image TreeShadow.psd at www.peachpit.com/digitalpainting in the Ch10_Tutorials folder. **PSD**

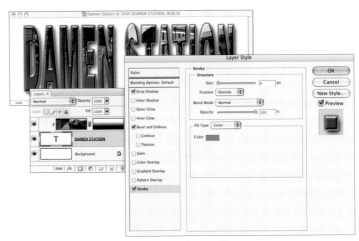

Figure 10.17 A Stroke is applied to the text layer.

Figure 10.18 The final image.

Figure 10.19 The image of a tree and a wall in the background.

If working with the TreeShadow.psd file, the tree is in its own layer. If you are working with your own image, create the tree in a separate layer. If you are working on a photograph, you must separate the tree or object that will be casting the shadow into its own layer. How you select it depends on the complexity of the object.

The Channels PDF file available at www.peachpit.com/digitalpainting, will give you some insight into selecting complex objects. **PDF**

Since the tree is casting the shadow, the layer with the tree is used to create the shadow.

1. Duplicate the layer containing the tree by dragging it over the Make new layer icon at the bottom of the Layers panel. The duplicate layer will appear on top of the original (**Figure 10.20**).

2. Make the original tree layer active (bottom tree layer in the panel) and turn on Preserve Transparency for the layer (**Figure 10.21**).

NOTE: Preserve Transparency allows you to modify only the pixels in the layer that are active. The transparent area of the layer will maintain its transparency.

Figure 10.20 The duplicate layer of the tree appears at the top of the layer stack.

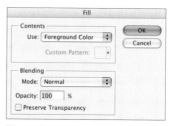

Figure 10.21 The original layer is made active and Preserve Transparency is turned on for the layer.

Figure 10.23 The Fill dialog box with Foreground color chosen for Use.

Figure 10.22 The Fill command in the Edit menu.

3. Set the Foreground color to black in the tools panel. Fill the layer by choosing Edit > Fill (**Figure 10.22**).

In the Fill dialog box (**Figure 10.23**) the Foreground color is chosen for Use.

> **NOTE:** Shortcuts are available for filling a layer or selected area. To use the Foreground color, press Option-Delete (Alt-Backspace). Command-Delete (Ctrl-Backspace) fills with the Background color. Shift-Delete (Shift-Backspace) brings up the same dialog box as when you choose Fill from the Edit menu.

4. Duplicate the layer with the black tree (**Figure 10.24**).

5. Make sure Resize Window To Fit is turned off for the Zoom Tool in the options bar (**Figure 10.25**).

6. Zoom out with the Zoom Tool to expose some of the work area (**Figure 10.26**).

Figure 10.24 The layer with the black tree is duplicated.

Figure 10.25 The Resize Windows To Fit is turned off in the options bar.

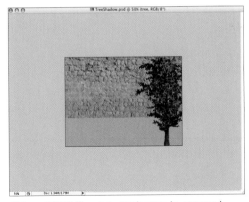

Figure 10.26 The gray work area is exposed.

7. Select Edit > Transform > Skew (**Figure 10.27**).

8. Skew the shadow so it appears to travel across the ground, as shown in **Figure 10.28**.

As a shadow gets farther from the object that is casting it, the shadow starts to blur. To create this effect, it's necessary to apply a blur filter, but it must be applied gradually across the shadow. The only way to apply a filter gradually is to apply it through an Alpha channel.

A more detailed explanation of the Alpha channel can be found in the Channels PDF file, which you can download at www.peachpit.com/ digitalpainting.

PDF

9. Open the Channels panel. An Alpha channel is created by clicking the Create new channel icon at the bottom of the Channels panel. The new channel appears at the bottom of the stack in the Channels panel (**Figure 10.29**).

The channel appears black since nothing was selected.

Figure 10.27 The Skew command in the Transform menu.

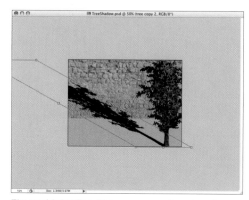

Figure 10.28 The Skew command makes the shadow appear to travel across the ground.

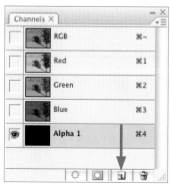

Figure 10.29 An Alpha channel is created by clicking the Create new channel icon.

10. In the Alpha channel, using the Gradient Tool, create a gradient similar to the one in **Figure 10.30**. The trick is to expose the area of the shadow that is farthest from the tree but end it before the edge of the wall.

> **NOTE:** To make it easier to see the exact area where the gradient is being created, you might want to turn the eye on for the color channels. Make sure only the Alpha channel is targeted.

11. In the Channels panel, click on the RGB channel to return to the image. Make sure the layer with the skewed tree is selected, as shown in **Figure 10.31**. Unlock the Transparency.

> **NOTE:** The blur filters create their effect inward and outward from the edge of the object being blurred. A Gaussian Blur of 10 softens the edge 5 pixels inward and 5 outward. Thus, if Preserve Transparency is turned on, the effect will not work properly.

12. Load the Alpha channel as a selection by choosing Select > Load Selection (**Figure 10.32**).

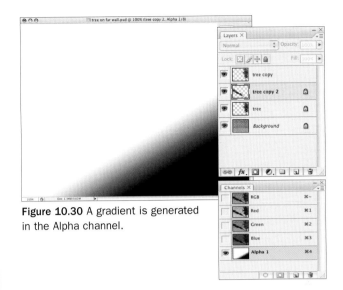

Figure 10.30 A gradient is generated in the Alpha channel.

Figure 10.31 The layer with the skewed tree is targeted and the Transparency lock is turned off.

Figure 10.32 The Alpha channel is loaded.

When Load Selection is chosen, a dialog box pops up (**Figure 10.33**). In this dialog box you can choose the channel you want to load. The figure shows that Alpha 1 has been chosen.

> **NOTE:** A shortcut to loading channels is to Command-click (Ctrl-click) on the channel you want to load in the Channels panel.

13. Choose the Gaussian Blur filter (**Figure 10.34**).

14. Choose an amount for the Gaussian Blur filter to soften the far edges of the shadow (**Figure 10.35**).

> **NOTE:** Keep in mind that the Amount is set to pixels. The amount of 2 shown in the figure will work if you are using the TreeShadow.psd file. If you are using your own image, the amount is determined by the resolution of the file you are working on.

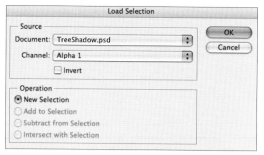

Figure 10.33 The Alpha channel is selected in the Load Selection dialog box.

Figure 10.34 The Gaussian Blur filter is chosen.

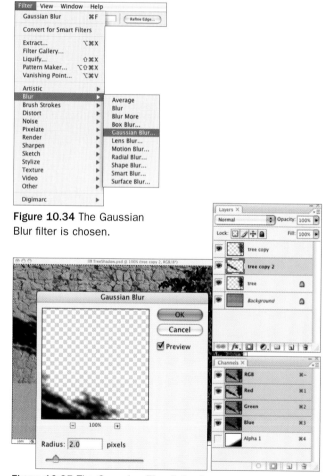

Figure 10.35 The Gaussian Blur dialog box.

15. Apply a layer mask to the layer with the skewed tree by choosing Layer > Layer Mask > Reveal All (**Figure 10.36**).

16. In the layer mask, apply a relatively tight gradient with black in the area where the shadow needs to be hidden (**Figure 10.37**). By tight I mean an area that just covers the bottom edge of the wall where it meets the ground.

When you created the layer mask, the mask became the targeted item. In Figure 10.37 note that the frame is around the mask in the panel.

17. To make the layer the target, click the preview icon for the layer. Lower the Opacity for the layer to about 80% (**Figure 10.38**).

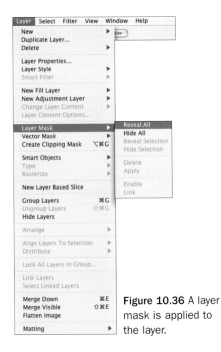

Figure **10.36** A layer mask is applied to the layer.

Figure **10.37** A gradient is applied to the layer mask.

Figure **10.38** The layer is made active and Opacity is reduced.

18. Select the tree layer that contains the unskewed shadow. Using the Move Tool, move the shadow over to match the shadow that is skewed across the ground (**Figure 10.39**).

19. Press Command-F (Ctrl-F) to apply the last filter used, and then reduce the Opacity for the layer to the same amount as in the first shadow— about 80% (**Figure 10.40**).

20. The second tree shadow falls on the wall. Looking at the scene, you can see that the wall is farther back than the tree. Since it is farther away, it should appear smaller. To make the shadow smaller, choose Edit > Transform > Scale (**Figure 10.41**).

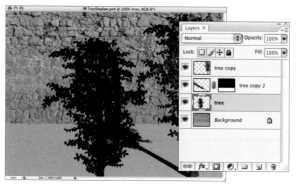

Figure 10.39 The second shadow is repositioned.

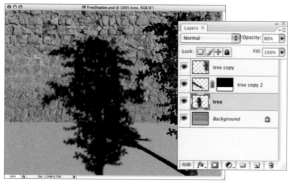

Figure 10.40 The Opacity for the second shadow is lowered.

Figure 10.41 Scale is chosen.

The layer with the second tree shadow is scaled down (**Figure 10.42**).

> **NOTE:** Shadows cast onto rough or textured backdrops must be distorted by that texture to look believable. The effect is achieved by using a specific filter called Displace. This is a very important consideration when adding a shadow to a scene.

21. As in steps 15 and 16 where the first shadow is partially hidden, apply a layer mask to hide the bottom portion of this shadow.

Figure 10.43 shows the final image where the shadow appears to be a single shadow traveling across the ground and then up the wall.

> I go into greater detail about shadows, textures, and filters in the Filters PDF file. Find it at www.peachpit. com/digitalpainting.
> **PDF**

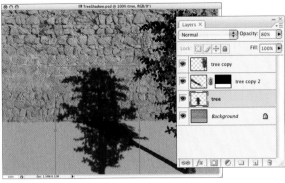
Figure **10.42** The second shadow is scaled down.

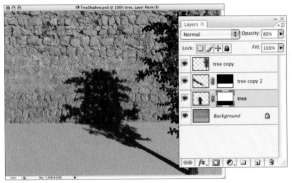
Figure **10.43** The final scene.

Working with Alpha Channels

Throughout the book I used Alpha channels quite a few times. You used an Alpha channel in the previous tutorial. I also used a feature called Calculations in conjunction with the Alpha channels a few times in the book. So let's do an exercise together to see how Alpha channels and Calculations work.

Photoshop offers many ways of doing the same thing. What you are about to do can also be done with layers. In this exercise you'll use the simplest example to help you understand Alpha channels and Calculations. You'll create a planet with a dark side and a corona.

1. Create a new file, as shown in **Figure 10.44**.

2. Invert the image to black by pressing Command-I (Ctrl-I).

3. Create a new layer and make a circular selection. Fill it with whatever color you want your planet to have (**Figure 10.45**).

4. With the circle still selected, choose Save Selection from the Select menu (**Figure 10.46**). In the dialog box that pops up you can name it or just click OK and Photoshop will name it "Alpha 1" (**Figure 10.46a**)

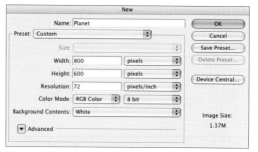

Figure 10.44 The New file dialog box.

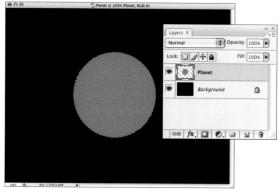

Figure 10.45 A circular selection is filled with red in a layer.

Figure 10.46 The selection is saved to an Alpha channel.

Figure 10.46a The Save Selection dialog box.

5. Go to the Alpha channel that was just created by clicking on it in the Channels panel (**Figure 10.47**).

6. Duplicate the Alpha channel by dragging it over the Create new channel icon (**Figure 10.48**).

7. Blur the Alpha 1 copy with the Gaussian Blur filter (Filter > Blur > Gaussian Blur), as shown in **Figure 10.49**.

8. Turn on the eye for the original Alpha channel (Alpha 1) to make it visible over the blurred channel.

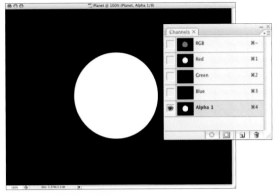

Figure **10.47** The Alpha channel.

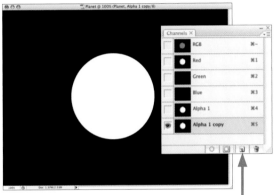

Figure **10.48** The duplicate Alpha channel.

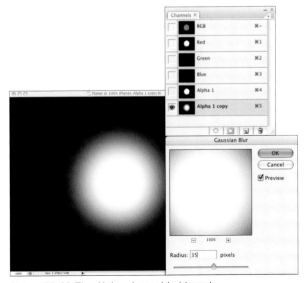

Figure **10.49** The Alpha channel is blurred.

9. Using the Move Tool, move the blurred channel up and to the right, as shown in **Figure 10.50**.

10. Choose Calculations from the Image menu (**Figure 10.51**).

11. Place Alpha 1 for the Channel in Source 1 and Alpha 1 copy for the Channel in Source 2. Set the Blending to Subtract. This will give you the mask to create the corona shown in **Figure 10.52**. The result is sent to a New Channel. If the sources were reversed, you would expose the bottom edge of the planet, as shown in **Figure 10.52a**.

12. Reposition the blurred channel to the bottom left of the planet. Go to the Calculations, and as before, place Alpha 1 for the Channel in Source 1 and Alpha 1 copy for the Channel in Source 2. This time choose Invert for Source 1. This will give you the mask to create the shadow on the dark side of the planet (**Figure 10.53**). The result is once again sent to a New Channel.

13. Return to the RGB composite channel by clicking on it in the Channels panel.

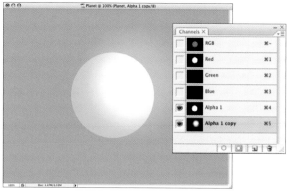

Figure 10.50 The blurred Alpha channel is repositioned.

Figure 10.51 Calculations is chosen from the Image menu.

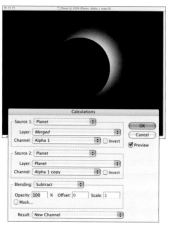

Figure 10.52 The result of the Calculation between the two Alpha channels.

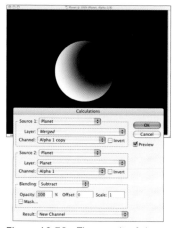

Figure 10.52a The result of the Calculation if the sources are reversed.

14. Make Alpha 3 (dark side) a selection by Command-clicking (Ctrl-clicking) on it in the panel. In a new layer or in the layer with the planet, fill the selection with black to create the dark side of the planet (**Figure 10.54**).

15. Make Alpha 2 (corona) a selection, and then fill the corona with a yellow in the Background layer or in a new layer behind the layer of the planet (**Figure 10.55**).

You now have a planet that has a dark side and a corona above it. It is the process that I hope you learned from this tutorial. It was a simple project that could have been done in other ways, but it is the concept behind channels and Calculations that I want you to understand. I strongly urge you to experiment with Calculations and Alpha channels. Using Alpha channels and Calculations to learn how to control selections for areas to be altered will save you time and effort, not to mention the amount of fun you can have.

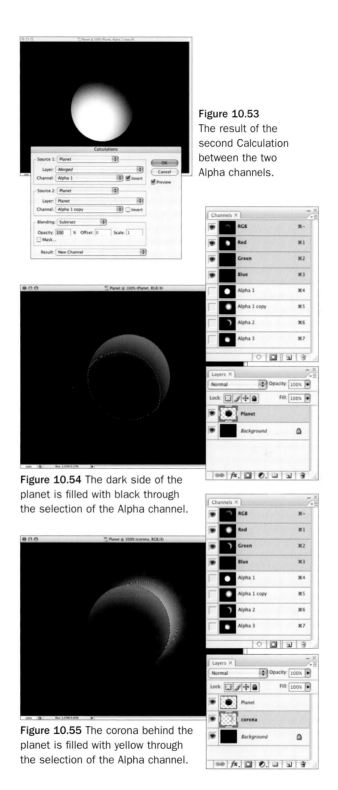

Figure 10.53
The result of the second Calculation between the two Alpha channels.

Figure 10.54 The dark side of the planet is filled with black through the selection of the Alpha channel.

Figure 10.55 The corona behind the planet is filled with yellow through the selection of the Alpha channel.

Using the Brushes Panel: Creating a Tree

To best get a handle on the creation of brush tips, I'll walk you through creating one, and then you'll construct, as Bob Ross would say, a happy little tree. While you're at it, you can brush up on your Pen Tool skills and experiment with a layer style.

A detailed description of all the functions of the Brushes panel are provided in the Brushes PDF file. Download it at www.peachpit.com/digitalpainting.

PDF

1. Create a file using the parameters in **Figure 10.56**.

2. Using the Pen Tool, create a curved line similar to the one in **Figure 10.57**.

Note that I have pulled the first handle at the top out to the left. The second handle has been pulled downward and to the left. I closed the window size to make the figure for the book smaller. The proportion of the path to the size of the canvas is smaller. This is apparent by looking at the scroll bars in Figure 10.57.

Figure 10.56 Create a New document.

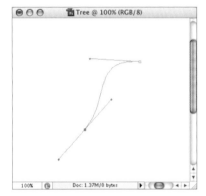

Figure 10.57 Create a path for the left side of a leaf.

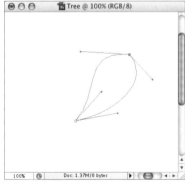

Figure 10.58 A path is created for the right side of the leaf.

3. Press the Option (Alt) key and click and drag on the anchor point to pull a new handle upward and to the right, and then close the top by clicking on the first point with the Option (Alt) key pressed.

The reason for pressing the Option key when ending the path is to make the closing anchor point a corner point rather than a smooth point. A smooth point would not give you the sharp tip that you see in **Figure 10.58**.

4. Fill the path with solid black (**Figure 10.59**). Deselect the path by clicking in the open space below it in the Path panel.

5. Select the leaf shape with the Rectangular Marquee Tool (**Figure 10.60**).

6. Define it as a Brush Preset (**Figure 10.61**).

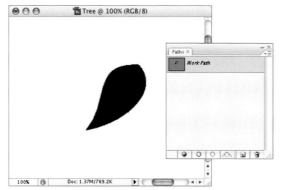

Figure 10.59 The path is filled with black.

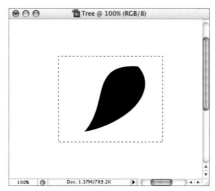

Figure 10.60 The leaf shape is selected.

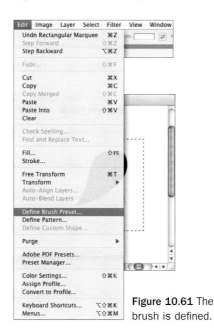

Figure 10.61 The brush is defined.

7. In the Brush Name dialog box that pops up, name the brush "leaf" (**Figure 10.62**). Once the brush is created, the shape that was used to make it can be deleted.

8. Choose the Paintbrush Tool.

9. Then open the Brushes panel (Window > Brushes) and select the leaf. It should appear at the bottom of the list (**Figure 10.63**).

10. In the Brush Tip Shape section, adjust the size of your brush to something that is manageable and will look good on the screen. Also, adjust the Spacing to separate the leaves, as shown in **Figure 10.64**.

Figure 10.62 The brush is named.

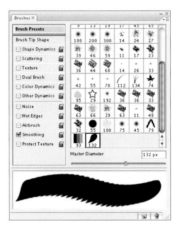

Figure 10.63 The brush is selected.

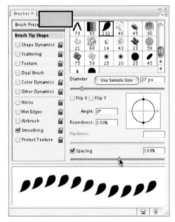

Figure 10.64 The Spacing is adjusted for the brush.

11. Click on the words Shape Dynamics to go to its settings. Set the Size Jitter to 100%, the Minimum Diameter to 25%, the Angle Jitter to 100%, the Roundness Jitter to 65%, and the Minimum Roundness to 25% (**Figure 10.65**).

> **NOTE:** Clicking the check box for any of the features in the Brushes panel will apply that feature but not take you to the controls. Clicking on the name of the feature will apply it as well as give you access to all of the options for that feature.

12. In the Scattering section, set your parameters as in **Figure 10.66**. Keep in mind that these settings are my choice and do not mean you are locked into them. Feel free to experiment with your own settings.

13. Set the Color Dynamics to closely match those in **Figure 10.67**.

Figure 10.65 The Shape Dynamics are set.

Figure 10.66 The Scattering is set for the brush.

Figure 10.67 The Color Dynamics are set.

14. Choose two contrasting shades of green for the Foreground and Background colors (**Figure 10.68**). If you want to create a tree with fall foliage, you might want to use yellow and orange for your colors.

15. Create a layer in your document and call it "leaves." With the brush tip, paint away and create a happy tree! In **Figure 10.69** you can see a cluster of leaves.

16. Add a second layer with another stroke of leaves as in **Figure 10.70**. To add dimension to the tree, add a layer style of Drop Shadow to this second layer to make the leaves pop out over the bottom leaves.

As witnessed throughout the book, the possibilities are endless when you think about this brush engine. I encourage you to play with it. Make different brushes and use them in conjunction with mode settings, layer styles, and the rest of the vast capabilities within Photoshop.

Figure **10.68** Colors are chosen for the brush tips.

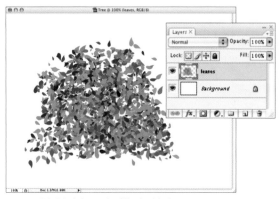

Figure **10.69** A layer is filled with leaves.

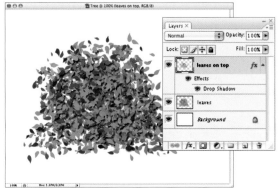

Figure **10.70** A second layer is filled with leaves and a Drop Shadow layer style is applied.

Creating Textures with Patterns

The perfect tutorial to help you to understand complex, interlocking patterns is this one. People always ask me for the recipe. I have done it on podcasts, TV shows, and seminars around the world. So here it is in written form so you can follow and learn.

You'll create the front grill of the Mac Pro Tower. Remember that it is the technique that is important. A change in shape and color will create an entirely different scene.

Creating a pattern of holes is very simple. Draw a circle, select it, and then select Edit > Define Pattern. The pattern will be made of many circles that will be straight up and down and across. For the Mac Pro Tower, the holes are diagonally across. This requires the creation of an interlocking pattern.

You first need to consider what the face of the object being created is made of. The front of the Mac Pro Tower is a thick slab of metal with diagonally cut holes across the surface. Creating a thick slab of metal, well that alone requires some pre-thought into how the pattern for the diagonal holes must be created.

When you start creating the pattern, you'll learn how to create the illusion of the thick metal.

1. Start a New file with the parameters set in **Figure 10.71**.

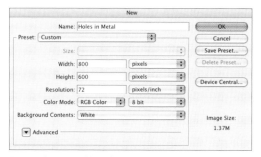

Figure 10.71 A New file is created.

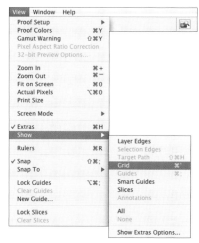

Figure 10.72 The grid is made visible.

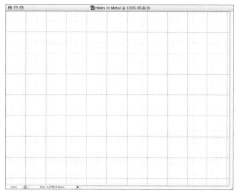

Figure 10.73 A new layer is created and the grid is made visible.

2. Interlocking patterns must be perfectly symmetrical. To make your pattern repeat correctly, turn on the grid (View > Show > Grid) to guarantee perfect alignment (**Figure 10.72**).

3. Create a new layer with the grid visible as in **Figure 10.73**.

4. In the new layer, create a perfect circle with the Elliptical Marquee Tool that takes up a section of the grid (**Figure 10.74**). It should snap to the grid. Do not deselect the circle until you are told to. (In the figure note that the area where the circle is selected has been zoomed in.) You should also zoom in.

5. Fill the selected area with a gray tone (**Figure 10.75**).

6. Using the Paintbrush Tool with a soft-edged tip and black for the color, add shadows to the edges of the circle (**Figure 10.76**).

7. Using the Paintbrush Tool with a soft-edged tip and white for the color, add a highlight to the center of the circle (**Figure 10.77**).

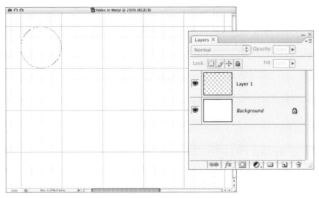

Figure **10.74** A circle is selected in the layer.

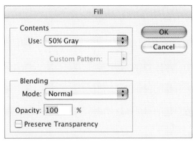

Figure **10.75** The selection is filled with a 50% Gray.

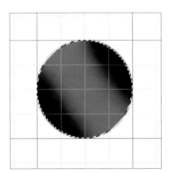

Figure **10.76** The edges of the circle get a black shadow applied.

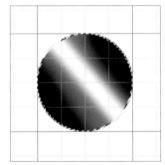

Figure **10.77** A white highlight is applied to the center of the circle.

8. To make a duplicate of the circle, switch to the Selection tool and press the Option-Command (Ctrl-Alt) keys. Click and drag the duplicate to the right.

This additional circle snaps to the grid and is placed directly across from the original with two subdivisions separating them, as shown in **Figure 10.78**.

9. Create a third circle and place it below the other two by snapping it to the grid. It needs to be centered under the two subdivisions that separate the two circles at the top, as shown in **Figure 10.79**.

10. Duplicate two more circles, place them in the third row directly below the top two (**Figure 10.80**). Now you can deselect.

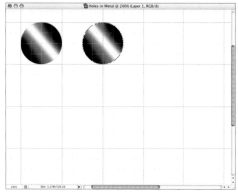

Figure 10.78 A second circle is copied to the right of the original.

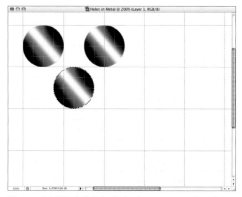

Figure 10.79 A third circle is generated and centered below the top two.

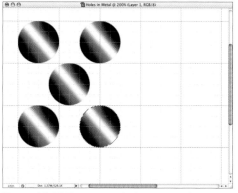

Figure 10.80 Two more circles are duplicated and placed at the bottom.

You are now ready to create the pattern.

11. Make a selection with the Rectangular Marquee Tool that starts from the center of the circle on the upper left to the center of the circle on the lower right (**Figure 10.81**). The selection marquee should snap to the grid.

This sets up the step-and-repeat placement of the elements to create a perfectly symmetrical pattern.

12. Turn off the eye icon for the Background layer to make it not visible.

This allows for transparency between the circles (**Figure 10.82**).

13. To create the actual pattern, choose the Define Pattern option from the Edit menu (Edit > Define Pattern), as shown in **Figure 10.83**.

The Pattern Name dialog box that pops up (**Figure 10.84**) lets you assign a name to the pattern you have just defined. Name the pattern "Holes."

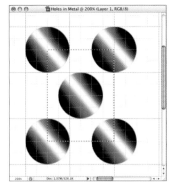

Figure 10.81 The area to be the pattern is selected.

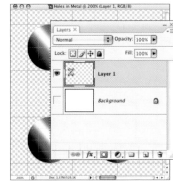

Figure 10.82 The Background layer is turned off.

Figure 10.83 Define Pattern is chosen from the Edit menu.

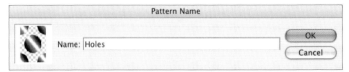

Figure 10.84 The pattern is named.

14. Discard the layer where the pattern was created and turn off the grid (View > Show > Grid). Zoom back out to full screen.

15. Target the Background layer by clicking on it in the Layers panel. Choose a gray color for the Foreground color and a darker gray for the Background, and then use Reflected Gradient (**Figure 10.85**) to diagonally fill the Background (**Figure 10.86**).

16. Create a new layer.

This layer will contain some items that will be seen through the holes.

17. Select a rectangular shape, and using the same colors and Reflected Gradient as the Background, fill the selection with a horizontal gradient as in **Figure 10.87**.

Figure 10.85 The Reflected Gradient is chosen.

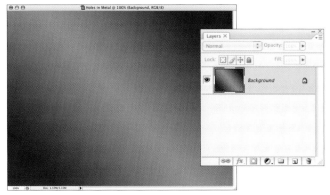

Figure 10.86 The gradient is applied diagonally to the Background layer.

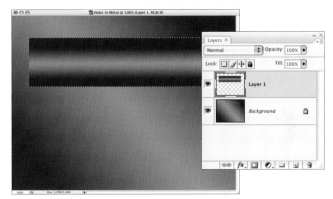

Figure 10.87 A shape is generated and filled with the same gradient as the one used for the Background, this time horizontally.

18. Duplicate the shape. To make the duplicate, switch to the Selection Tool and press the Option-Command (Ctrl-Alt) keys. Click and drag the duplicate down below the original (**Figure 10.88**).

19. Create another new layer and name it "Pattern."

20. Fill this new layer with the pattern (Edit > Fill). The Fill dialog pops up. Choose Pattern for Use and the pattern of the circles as the Custom Pattern to be used as in **Figure 10.89**.

The layer is filled with the pattern (**Figure 10.90**).

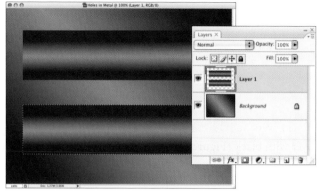

Figure 10.88 A duplicate is made of the rectangular shape.

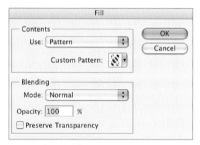

Figure 10.89 The pattern is selected in the Fill dialog box.

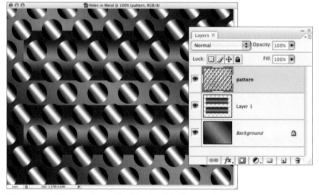

Figure 10.90 The layer is filled with the pattern.

21. Duplicate the layer with the pattern of circles by dragging it over the Make new layer icon at the bottom of the Layers panel and name it "holes" (**Figure 10.91**).

22. Lock the Preserve Transparency option in the Layers panel and fill the "holes" layer with black (**Figure 10.92**).

23. Place the layer with the two rectangular shapes above the layer with the black filled circles in the Layers panel. Press the Option (Alt) key and click between the two layers in the Layers panel to turn the layer with the two rectangular shapes into a Clipping Group with the layer of the holes (black filled circles), as shown in **Figure 10.93**.

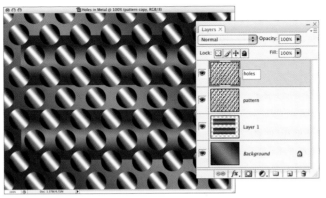
Figure 10.91 The layer with the pattern is duplicated and named "holes."

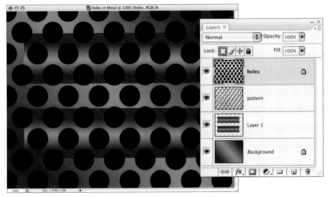
Figure 10.92 Preserve Transparency is locked and the layer is filled with black.

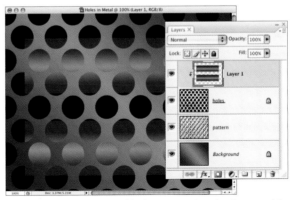
Figure 10.93 The layer with the two rectangles is moved to the top of the stack and clipped with the layer containing the black circles.

24. Choose Merge Down from the panel drop-down menu to merge the two layers into a single layer (**Figure 10.94**).

25. Turn the result of the newly merged layer into a Clipping Group with the original layer named "Pattern" (**Figure 10.95**).

26. Select the Move Tool. Using the left and up arrow keys, slightly offset the layer of the holes with the shapes visible through them to show an edge made by the original holes. This gives the metal the appearance of thickness or depth when seen through the holes.

Figure 10.96 shows the thick slab of metal full of holes.

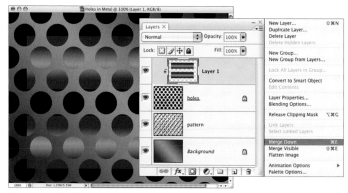

Figure 10.94 The layer with the two rectangles is merged down into the layer with the black circles.

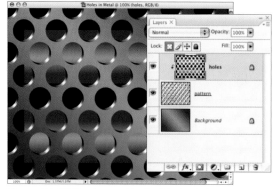

Figure 10.95 The layer with the black circles is merged down into the layer with the original pattern.

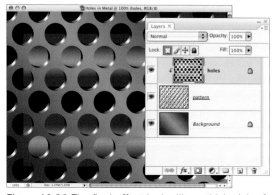

Figure 10.96 The final effect looks like a thick slab of metal with holes cut into it.

Experimenting with Filters

Because of the number of filters available in Photoshop, not to mention the hundreds available from third-party vendors, the next three exercises concentrate on filters.

The first exercise creates a texture and uses a filter for the finishing touch in a way that most people would not consider. The second lets you create the rain mentioned earlier in the book. The third and final exercise is being done by request. It is a technique that I have shown many times at conferences and on TV but has never been offered in any of my books. A short version is available on my Web site, but people wanted more visuals, so here it is.

Rusty Old Sign

In this exercise you'll create a sign that is made of metal and has been damaged by time and the elements. Rust has eaten away at the once shiny metal, leaving behind a sign that is crumbling away to nothing. As with everything else in this book, it is the steps that are important here.

Applying these steps with slight modifications will give you dramatically different results.

1. Create a new file with the parameters shown in **Figure 10.97**.

2. Click the Text Tool and choose a deep brown for the text color that is in the options bar for the Text Tool (**Figure 10.98**).

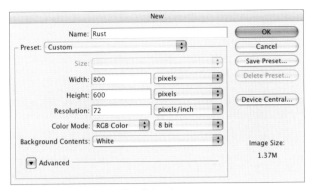

Figure 10.97 The New file dialog box.

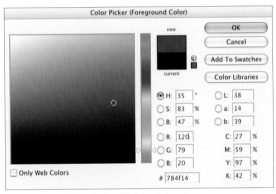

Figure 10.98 The Color Picker dialog box.

Figure 10.99 The text.

3. Type in the word RUST or choose a name or other text. (**Figure 10.99**). It doesn't have to be type. It can be a logo design you've created. Text automatically creates its own layer. If you are using something other than text, make sure it is in a layer.

4. Choose the Scale command by selecting Edit > Transform > Scale (**Figure 10.100**). Resize the text to fit the shape you want (**Figure 10.101**).

5. Choose Layer > Rasterize > Type to rasterize the text (**Figure 10.102**). From this point on the text is just pixels and is no longer editable as text.

Figure 10.100 The scale command.

Figure 10.101 The text scaled.

Figure 10.102 The Rasterize command.

6. To create the basic rust texture, apply the Texturizer filter (Filter > Texture > Texturizer), as shown in **Figure 10.103**.

Set a low Scale and a high Relief, and set the Light to Top Left (**Figure 10.104**).

7. Go into the Layer Style for the layer with the text by double-clicking the layer in the Layers panel. Give the text a Drop Shadow. Increase the Opacity. Adjust Distance to make the drop shadow more prominent. Make sure the light source is from above left (**Figure 10.105**).

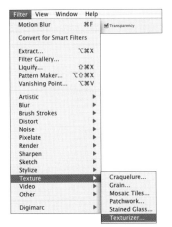

Figure 10.103 The Texturizer filter.

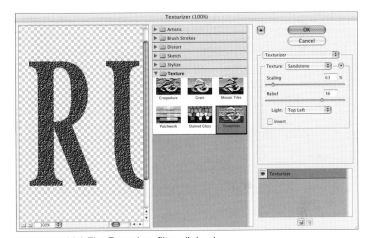

Figure 10.104 The Texturizer filter dialog box.

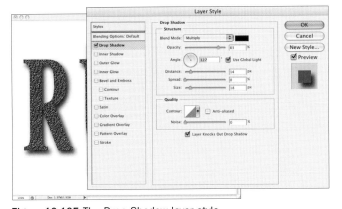

Figure 10.105 The Drop Shadow layer style.

8. Choose Bevel and Emboss. Set the Technique to Chisel Hard. Push the Depth up to increase the intensity of the lights and darks (**Figure 10.106**). Change the Highlight color to a warm yellow (**Figure 10.107**).

The result will be a hard-edged chisel cut with yellow highlights (**Figure 10.108**).

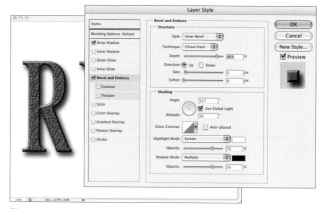

Figure 10.106 The Bevel and Emboss layer style.

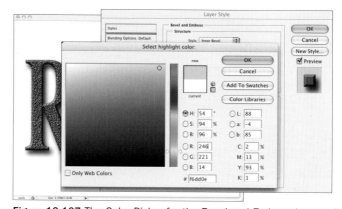

Figure 10.107 The Color Picker for the Bevel and Emboss layer style.

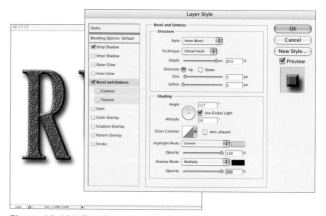

Figure 10.108 The Bevel and Emboss layer style with the Highlight color modified.

9. Choose the Satin layer style. Select the Ring - Double contour under the Contour box, as shown in **Figure 10.109**. Play with the Distance and Size until you get some deep patterns within the letters.

Your results will be of your own choosing but should look something like Figure 10.109.

Click OK to exit the Layer Style dialog box.

The rust looks pretty good at this point. Next, you'll add the corrosion that will complete the look. To achieve this, you'll use a filter in a place most people would not consider using one.

10. Create a layer mask by selecting Layer > Add Layer Mask > Hide All (**Figure 10.110**).

11. Make the letters a selection by Command-clicking (Ctrl-clicking) on the preview icon for the layer in the Layers panel (**Figure 10.111**).

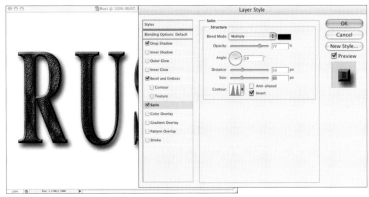

Figure 10.109 The Satin layer style.

Figure 10.110 Layer Mask > Hide All.

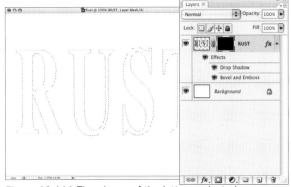

Figure 10.111 The shape of the letters selected.

12. Make sure the mask is still selected as the target. (It should have the frame around the mask in the panel.) Since the shape of the letters are selected, in the layer mask, fill that selection with white (**Figure 10.112**).

The letters are once again visible. Deselect.

13. Make sure the mask is still targeted (**Figure 10.113**).

14. Choose the Spatter filter by selecting Filter > Brush Strokes > Spatter (**Figure 10.114**).

Note that you are applying the filter to the mask of the layer rather than the layer itself. Applying the filter to the mask is what makes this technique a bit more unusual. You can experiment on your own and see the difference when you apply the filter to the layer as opposed to applying it to the mask for the layer, as you are doing here.

Figure 10.112 The letters visible through the layer mask.

Figure 10.113 The layer mask selected as the target.

Figure 10.114 The Spatter filter.

15. Apply settings similar to those in **Figure 10.115**.

Your final image should look worn and corroded, as the one shown in **Figure 10.116**.

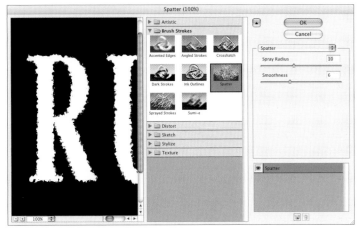

Figure 10.115 The Spatter filter dialog box.

Figure 10.116 The final image.

It's Raining!

As mentioned earlier in the book, creating rain is simply a matter of applying a few filters. In this tutorial you will change a sunny street scene into a stormy one.

You can use the image called Street.jpg that you see in **Figure 10.117**, or you can use your own.

1. Create an Adjustment layer of Hue/Saturation by clicking on the Adjustment layer icon at the bottom of the Layers panel.

2. Choose the Colorize Option and set the sliders as shown in **Figure 10.118** to convert the image to a single color and darken it.

3. Create a second Adjustment layer of Levels.

4. Darken the overall image, as shown in **Figure 10.119**.

Figure **10.117** The street image.

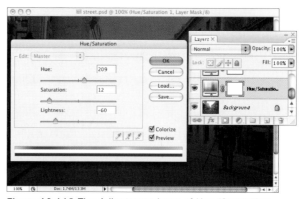

Figure **10.118** The Adjustment layer of Hue/Saturation.

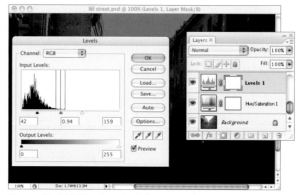

Figure **10.119** The Levels Adjustment layer.

5. With the Magic Wand tool select the sky area and send it to its own layer by choosing Layer > New > Layer via Copy (**Figure 10.120**).

6. Select black for the Foreground color and a light, muted blue color for the Background color.

7. Create a new layer. Choose the Clouds filter by selecting Filter > Render > Clouds (**Figure 10.121**).

Clouds based on the two chosen colors will fill the layer, as shown in **Figure 10.122**.

8. Clip the clouds layer using the layer containing the sky by clicking between the two layers in the panel with the Option (Alt) key pressed (**Figure 10.123**).

Figure 10.120 The sky area in its own layer.

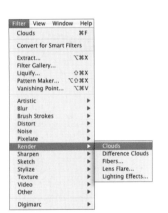
Figure 10.121 The sky area in its own layer.

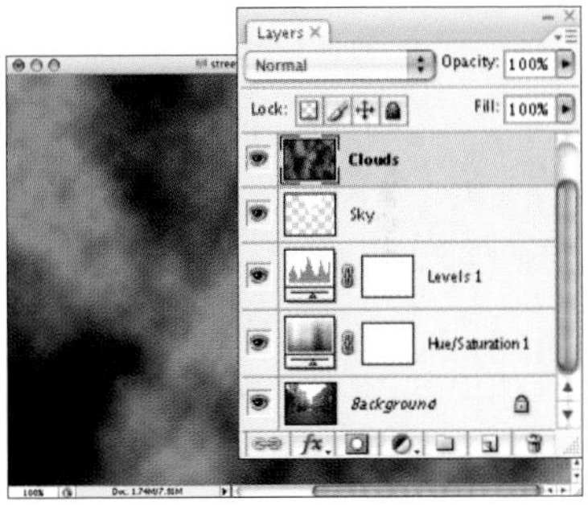

Figure 10.122 The layer filled with clouds.

Figure 10.123 The sky area in its own layer.

9. Create a new layer above all the others.

10. Return the Foreground and Background colors to the default of black and white.

11. Apply the Clouds filter again (**Figure 10.124**).

12. Put this layer in Screen mode and apply a layer mask to hide the top portion of the layer (**Figure 10.125**). This creates a fog mist along the ground.

Now you'll create the rain.

13. Create a new layer and fill it with black.

14. Apply the Add Noise filter (Filter > Noise > Add Noise) to this layer (**Figure 10.126**). Give the noise a large amount, as shown in **Figure 10.127**.

15. Apply the Blur More filter to the layer (**Figure 10.128**).

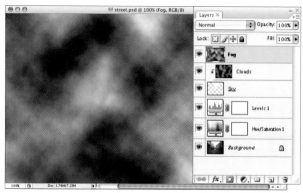

Figure 10.124 The layer filled with black and white clouds.

Figure 10.125 The fog on the ground.

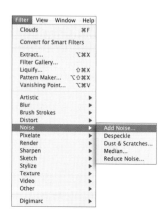

Figure 10.126 The sky area in its own layer.

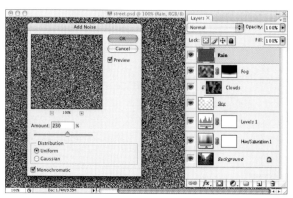

Figure 10.127 The Add Noise dialog box.

Figure 10.128 The Blur More filter.

16. Apply a Levels command (Image > Adjustments > Levels) to the layer with the noise. Move the sliders to lessen the amount of noise, as shown in **Figure 10.129**.

17. Apply the Motion Blur filter (**Figure 10.130**) to streak the noise as shown in **Figure 10.131**.

18. Put the layer with the streaked noise in Screen mode to allow the image below to show through (**Figure 10.132**).

Now you'll add a bolt of lightning.

19. Create a new layer above the layer with the clouds and clip it with the sky layer, just as the clouds layer is clipped.

20. Fill the layer with white, and using a soft-edged black paintbrush, create a shape like the one in **Figure 10.133**. The edge where the black and white meet will become the bolt of lightning, so make sure your shape follows the shape you want your lightning to be.

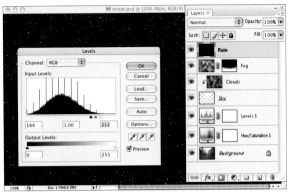

Figure 10.129 The Levels command lessens the amount of noise.

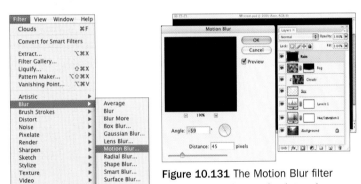

Figure 10.130 The Motion Blur filter.

Figure 10.131 The Motion Blur filter streaks the noise to simulate rain.

Figure 10.132 The image shows through, making the noise look like rain.

Figure 10.133 A black shape is created in a layer filled with white that is clipped by the sky layer.

21. Choose the Difference Clouds filter (**Figure 10.134**) to create a black line like the one shown in **Figure 10.135**.

22. Invert the layer (Image > Adjustments > Invert).

23. With the Levels command (Image > Adjustments > Levels), move the sliders as shown in **Figure 10.136** to lessen the amount of clouds.

24. Set the layer to Screen mode and your image is complete (**Figure 10.137**).

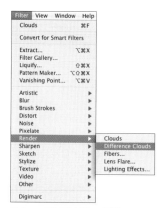

Figure 10.134 The Difference Clouds filter.

Figure 10.135 The sky with a black line through it.

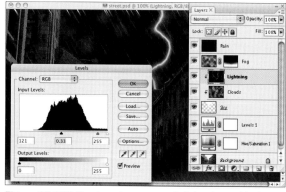

Figure 10.136 The Levels command dialog box with the clouds being darkened.

Figure 10.137 The final, stormy street scene.

Lightning Strikes Again!

As mentioned earlier, this last exercise is added by request. You just created lightning in the previous tutorial. This tutorial takes it to a new level. Back when I was a monthly regular on the TechTV show *The Screen Savers*, lightning was one of the most requested effects. Though I have done this demo many times all over the world for some of my classes, I have never actually published it as a step-by-step exercise in a book. So now I'm making it available to all who need to create lightning.

Let me emphasize one more time that you might never have to create lightning, but the steps to create the end result are important. Remember that a slight adjustment to a particular step can change the entire effect and might be the answer to a totally different situation.

In this exercise you will not be creating a boring single bolt of lightning. No! You'll create a bunch of bolts emanating from the end of the wizard's staff in **Figure 10.138**.

The wizard image was created by my son, Sean. He created it so that I could do this demo on *The Screen Savers*. The one you see here is an updated version.

Figure 10.138 The original wizard image created by Sean Monroy.

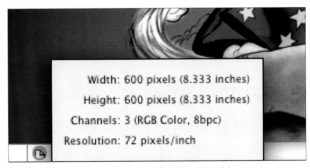

Figure 10.139 The dimensions for the wizard image.

If you want to use the wizard image, download the Wizard.jpg file at www.peachpit.com/digitalpainting in the Ch10_Tutorials folder.

JPG

If you use your own image, keep in mind that the settings shown in this exercise are for an image that is 600 pixels square at 72 ppi (**Figure 10.139**).

1. You'll need some room to play with to make the lightning fall precisely where you want it. To this end, you need to create the lightning in a file that is larger than the one containing the wizard. Create a white Photoshop canvas that measures 1000 x 1000 pixels at 72 ppi (**Figure 10.140**).

2. Draw a vertical, black rectangle like the one in **Figure 10.141**. Draw more vertical rectangles that vary in thickness and spacing like those in **Figure 10.142**. This technique will create the lightning bolts at the edge of contrast.

Each rectangle will produce two lightning bolts (two black sides against white). The more rectangles, the more bolts you will have.

Do not fill the entire canvas with stripes. You want to leave an area of white as in Figure 10.142 so that the wizard will not be hidden behind a bolt of lightning.

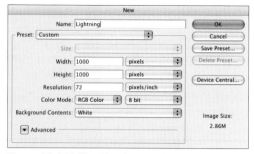

Figure **10.140** The New Image dialog box.

Figure **10.141** A thin rectangle is created from top to bottom of the canvas.

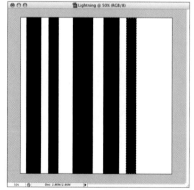

Figure **10.142** Multiple rectangles of varying thickness are created, leaving some white space at the far right edge.

3. Select the Gaussian Blur filter (Filter > Blur > Gaussian Blur), as shown in **Figure 10.143**.

4. Enter a Radius of 20 (**Figure 10.144**). Remember that this setting may vary based on the resolution of your image if you are not using the wizard.

5. Choose the Polar Coordinates filter (Filter > Distort > Polar Coordinates), as shown in **Figure 10.145**.

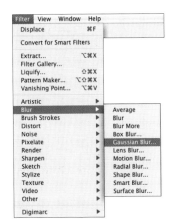

Figure 10.143 Select the Gaussian Blur filter.

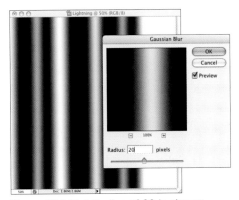

Figure 10.144 A Radius of 20 is chosen for the Gaussian Blur filter.

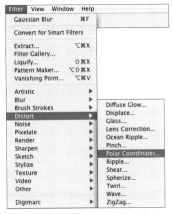

Figure 10.145 Select the Polar Coordinates filter.

6. Set the Rectangular to Polar option (**Figure 10.146**).

The result will be a spinning of the black, blurred bars (**Figure 10.147**).

7. Now the lightning will start to appear. Choose the Difference Clouds filter (Filter > Render > Difference Clouds), as shown in **Figure 10.148**.

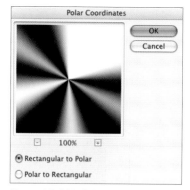

Figure 10.146 Select the Rectangular to Polar option.

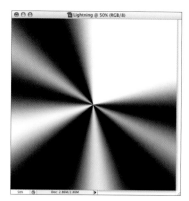

Figure 10.147 The result of the Polar Coordinates filter.

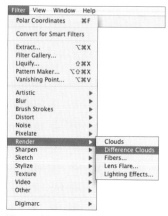

Figure 10.148 Select the Difference Clouds filter.

The result should look like **Figure 10.149**.

8. Select Invert (Image > Adjustments > Invert) as in **Figure 10.150**.

You should start to see the lightning taking shape (**Figure 10.151**).

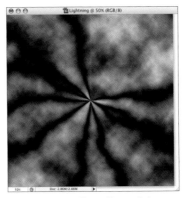

Figure 10.149 The effect of the Difference Clouds filter.

Figure 10.150 Select Invert.

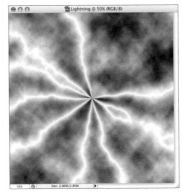

Figure 10.151 The result of inverting the Difference Clouds.

9. Select Levels (Image Adjustments > Levels), as shown in **Figure 10.152**.

Here you will reduce the amount of clouds, making the lightning more pronounced.

Move the Dark and Mid-Tone sliders inward to eliminate most of the clouds (**Figure 10.153**). If there are clouds inside the negative space where the wizard will stand, paint them out with a black paintbrush

10. To add color to the bolts, use the Hue/Saturation control (Image > Adjustments > Hue/Saturation) set to Colorize (**Figure 10.154**).

Figure 10.152 Select the Levels command.

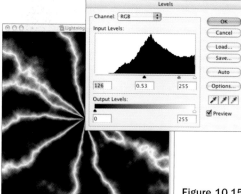

Figure 10.153 The Levels dialog box.

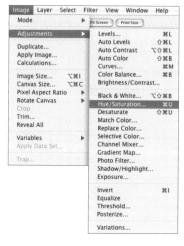

Figure 10.154 Select the Hue/Saturation command.

Play with the Hue and Saturation sliders until you get the desired effect (**Figure 10.155**).

11. Drag the lightning bolt file over to the file with the wizard (**Figure 10.156**).

12. Change the mode for the layer containing the lightning to Screen (**Figure 10.157**). This allows the wizard underneath to show through, as shown in **Figure 10.158**.

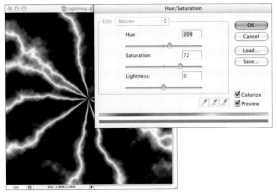

Figure 10.155 The Hue/Saturation dialog box.

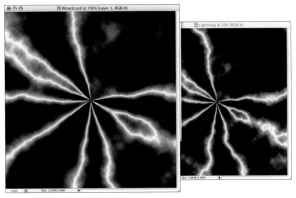

Figure 10.156 The file with the blue lightning is dragged over to the file with the wizard.

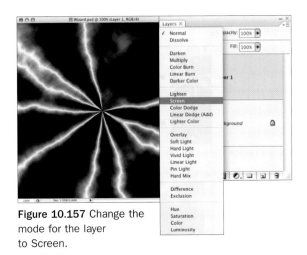

Figure 10.157 Change the mode for the layer to Screen.

13. Using the Move Tool, reposition the center of the lightning bolts to the end of the wizard's staff (**Figure 10.159**).

14. Zoom out to see the work area and choose Rotate (Edit > Transform > Rotate), as shown in **Figure 10.160**.

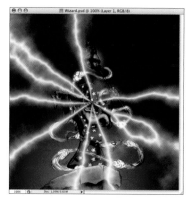

Figure 10.158 The wizard shows through.

Figure 10.159 The lightning is repositioned so that the center of the lightning is centered on the end of the staff.

Figure 10.160 Choose the Rotate command.

15. Rotate the lightning until the wizard is not covered by lightning (**Figure 10.161**).

That's it! You're done! The final image is shown in **Figure 10.162**.

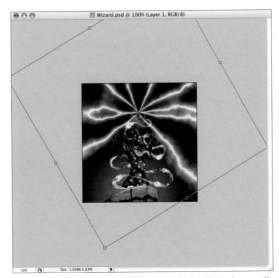

Figure 10.161 Rotate the layer with the lightning until the blank area lies over the wizard.

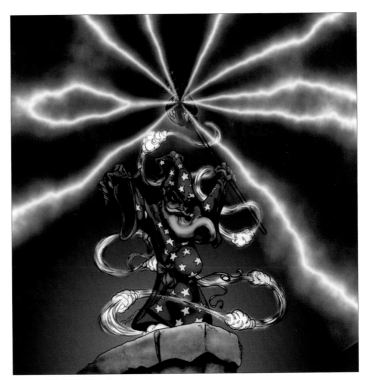

Figure 10.162 The final image.

Farewell…

This brings us to the end of the book. I sincerely hope that the journey we have taken together has taught you many things along the way. My greatest hope is that it has served as an inspiration for you to take the tools available to you and let your imagination soar!

Remember that it is important to understand what a particular filter or feature can do. Combinations of filters and how they are set can solve many of the problems you will find yourself faced with. Slight modifications to various functions can have dramatic effects on final outcomes of their use. Think of the experimentation with Photoshop as a game. Have fun and play to your heart's content!

We have entered an age in which we have all the information we need at our fingertips when and wherever we need it. The tools to be productive and creative are in our hands! Take the ride of your life and may it bring joy and laughter to you all the way down the road!

Later,

Bert

Index